CREATIVE RESISTANCE

Cindy Horst

CREATIVE RESISTANCE

The social justice practices
of Monirah, Halleh, and Diala

The Forced Migration Studies Collection

Collection editors
T. Alexander Aleinikoff & Laura Hammond

First published in 2023 by Lived Places Publishing

The authors and editors have made every effort to ensure the accuracy of information contained in this publication but assume no responsibility for any errors, inaccuracies, inconsistencies and omissions. Likewise, every effort has been made to contact copyright holders. If any copyright material has been reproduced unwittingly and without permission the Publisher will gladly receive information enabling them to rectify any error or omission in subsequent editions.

British Library Cataloguing in Publication Data
A CIP record for this book is available from the British Library.

ISBN: 9781915734389 (pbk)
ISBN: 9781915734402 (ePDF)
ISBN: 9781915734396 (ePUB)

The right of Cindy Horst to be identified as the Author of this work has been asserted by them in accordance with the Copyright, Design and Patents Act 1988.

Cover design by Fiachra McCarthy
Book design by Rachel Trolove of Twin Trail Design
Typeset by Newgen Publishing UK

Lived Places Publishing
Long Island
New York 11789

www.livedplacespublishing.com

Abstract

How can hope and political action flourish from the devastation of war, oppression, and forced migration? For Monirah, Halleh, and Diala, this is not a philosophical question—it is a lived reality. Drawn from firsthand experience of violent conflict and displacement, the stories in this book belong to three extraordinary women who found a path to hope through their social justice practices in the face of violence, oppression, and exile. This book highlights the extraordinary actions of ordinary people in dark times, and draws particular attention to the transformative mobilizing power of narratives.

Keywords

Hope; conflict; refugee; displacement; gender; anthropology; social justice; activism; lived experience; war

Acknowledgments

This book, as all academic writing, is the product of the work and love of so many people. There is no way I can do justice to that reality and express my gratitude to each and every one of you in words, even less so in a single page. Here's me trying:

Monirah, Halleh, and Diala: Thank you so much for sharing your stories with me and allowing me to transform them to text that others can read and be inspired by. Monirah, your story evolved in the months that we worked together. I thank you for your trust in me. Halleh, you have been in my life from the time I was writing my PhD—way back—and I continue to be inspired by you. To many more collaborations! Diala, we are just at the start of our friendship and I want to thank you for making an artist of me. Thanks for the same, to all those who took part in the PRAKSIS Residency 22 in Oslo (Praksis Oslo: transnational arts and culture catalyst. https://www.praksisoslo.org/organisation).

I also want to thank Maja Korac, whose chapter left the book for all the right reasons, and then led its own life by developing into a beautiful special issue titled "Stories of violence, war and displacement."

The TRANSFORM research project team: Ben Dix, Tamar Groves, Marte Nilsen, Kjetil Selvik, Trude Stapnes, and Ebba Tellander. What an amazing group of people, with such depth and breadth of knowledge and humanity. Thanks for our collective learning, your incredible generosity, respect, and humor. A special thanks to Trude, who coordinated the 2019 seminar series for the Centre on Culture and Violent Conflict (CCC) and conducted two of the interviews. And to Ebba, whose PhD on the civil–political actions of a group of teachers and doctors in Somaliland during the dictatorship in the early 1980s shaped so much of my understanding of the extraordinary actions of ordinary people in dark times. Thanks also to Sara Christophersen, who created the TRANSFORM virtual exhibition and from whose work on hip-hop artists in Palestine I learned the importance of embodied knowing. I hope we will all find new ways to continue to work together.

TRANSFORM was preceded by the ACT research project and followed by the INSPIRE research project. I am grateful to the Research Council of Norway for putting its faith and money in us by funding all these exciting projects. Thank you also to the ACT and INSPIRE research teams, and in particular to Noor Jdid and Kasia Grabska. I have learned so much from you, both professionally and personally.

The PRIO community, for being such a wonderful intellectual home with so many smart but equally generous, inspiring, and fun people. Odin Lysaker, for helping me read Arendt. Rebecca Lowen, for her brilliant editing. You enable me to express my thoughts so eloquently, helping me to get to the core in such a professional way. Thank you.

The team at LPP, for loving this book when I started to lose hope. Thank you all for helping me complete the final part of a long journey. Laura Hammond, Alex Aleinikoff and Ebba Tellander for such excellent and constructive feedback on an earlier version of the book.

Miriam Latif Sandbæk, for somehow managing to be my friend and coach at the same time. I cannot even begin to express how much of my sanity, joy, and gratitude for life I owe to you. My parents and brother—the stories in this book make me understand even deeper what it means to have a home. Mine was full of love and safety, and I am immensely grateful for that privilege. My urban family (you know who you are) for making Oslo home.

And finally, Ndirangu, Nina, and Tim. My passion for my work—including this book—has led me to be less present than I would have wanted to be. Nina and Tim, thanks for your patience, but even more so for being such amazing human beings. Ndirangu, you are a rock. There is no way I could have done this without you.

Contents

Learning objectives

This book explores the transformative potential of experiences of war, oppression, and forced migration for those who work artistically or academically with these themes from firsthand experience as well as the role of storytelling in this process. Focusing on the central theme of the transformative mobilizing power of narratives, it has the following aims:

1. To nuance stories of lived experience of forced migration, creating awareness of intersectionality and positioned agency.
2. To show the interlinkages of interests and insights from peace and conflict studies with those within forced migration studies, recognizing continuities in the human consequences of war and exile.
3. To foreground experiential knowledge and to make a case for the need to develop new ways of researching embodied knowing—in particular about violence and oppression.
4. To provide insight into the interdependent roles of storytelling and witnessing, and their relationship to individual and collective healing.

1
The role of storytelling and narrative in transformation

Introduction

> I am a teller; a storyteller. Telling is a kind of breathing. I can't stop myself. I can't stop breathing. I am a storyteller who would like to light stars in dark spaces, to attach stars to a dark sky, a dark roof. Still there are endless black spaces that need endless stories
>
> Monirah Hashemi, *Who lights the stars?*

This book arose from my curiosity about what motivates individuals to try to advance social justice in contexts in which doing so involves great risk and uncertainty. The women whose stories are presented in this book, as well as the individuals I have interviewed in the course of my broader research, speak of the **responsibility** they feel to take political action (Horst and Lysaker, 2021; Horst, 2022; Stapnes, Carlquist and Horst, 2020). In line with Arendt (1958), I understand political action in the broad sense of individuals critically inserting themselves into the human world through speech and action. When do individuals feel called to speak up or act in the face of suffering and abuse? Why do some people act for the benefit of others even in situations in which doing so poses great risks to themselves or their families? What are the defining moments in a person's life story that trigger their political agency?

This book explores the transformative potential of experiences of violent conflict, oppression, and exile for those who have firsthand knowledge, and who currently work artistically or academically with these themes. It is based on a narrative research approach and focuses on three remarkable women: Monirah Hashemi, an Afghan actress and theater producer whose mother fostered in her the urge to speak out about injustices and who does so now through her art; Halleh Ghorashi, who became politically conscious as a teenager during the 1979 revolution in Iran and is currently an engaged academic in the Netherlands; and Diala Brisly, a visual artist from Syria whose collection of paintings and drawings reflect both the everyday horrors of war, oppression, and exile as well as her visions of an alternative future.

Each of these women experienced and witnessed traumatic events and incurred immense losses as a consequence of violent conflict, oppression, and exile. One could argue that it is unsurprising that people would fight for justice in such contexts considering the sheer magnitude of the atrocities being committed. However, there are many mechanisms in place that aim to silence criticism and prevent resistance and that make speaking up and acting against the status quo downright dangerous. Even after escaping war and oppression, it is often difficult to speak up and act against social injustices. In this book, I choose to focus on the narratives of three women who despite the risks and challenges continue to work for social justice, as academics or artists, building on their own experiences.

I have listened to the life stories of refugees and others affected by war and authoritarianism over several decades. The dissonance between, on the one hand, these human encounters and stories, and on the other hand, the public narratives about refugees and others affected by war—widespread in media, policymaking, everyday life, and academia—has troubled me, and left me frustrated by my inability to "make a difference". In public discourse, only rarely are the experiences of individuals who have lived through violent conflict, oppression, and exile shared in sufficient complexity, and ordinary people and policymakers alike spend too little time really listening, witnessing, and caring about those affected by violence and oppression. While the 2022 Russian invasion of Ukraine brought the reality of war into sharpened focus for Western audiences, unnuanced knowledge and limited understanding of lived experiences of war and exile remain a challenge—not least against a backdrop of the many other conflicts around the world that continue to devastate the lives of individuals and communities.

We need to listen to the stories of those with lived experience of war, oppression, and exile not just to ensure that all human beings, including refugees and others affected by violent conflict and authoritarianism, are treated with respect. Listening closely to and caring about the tellers of these stories is, in fact, vital if a society seeks to guarantee human dignity, freedom, and peaceful coexistence to all. These stories—set in contexts of violence and oppression—offer powerful evidence of the value of individual freedom and collective responsibility. They are also necessary reminders that those public goods must not be taken for granted, and that, potentially, any society at any time can exclude and limit freedoms. These stories furthermore enable societies and individuals to gain access to their own trauma and explore tools for individual and collective healing.

The current civic and political engagements of Monirah, Halleh and Diala are shaped by memories of the past and hopes for the future. These women enact their visions of a desired future in a range of creative and inspiring ways. In this book, I zoom in on three aspects of their stories and work: the forces and inspirations that drove them to act; the kinds of actions they have engaged in; and the impact of their actions—as they understand them. In studying their inspirations, actions, and impacts, I seek to understand how experiences of violence and oppression can inspire individuals to engage in political action and how their actions might inspire wider societal transformations. The ripple effects of smaller actions and the narratives about them sustain individual and collective political action, but they remain largely unexplored by social scientists. This reality inspired me to write this book.

Why this book?

For several decades, I have conducted research on the human consequences of violent conflict, oppression, and displacement. Since 1995, I have been engaged in ethnographic research with refugees in a wide range of contexts, including refugee camps, regional urban centers, resettlement contexts, and in the home country to which they have, in some cases, returned. While a student of anthropology, I volunteered in a center in the Netherlands for asylum seekers, which enabled me to develop an understanding of the first phase of refugee life in a Western host country. Between 1995 and 2007, I conducted two years' worth of ethnographic research in the Dadaab refugee camps of Kenya, where most of the inhabitants were from a neighboring country and had spent most of their lives in exile (Horst, 2006a, 2006b, 2008a). I have also conducted research on those internally displaced (Horst and Nur, 2016), on those who return to their country of origin (Horst, 2018; Horst and Sagmo, 2015), and on those resettled in the United States (Horst, 2007) and Norway (Al-Sharmani and Horst, 2016; Horst, 2008b). Additionally, I have supervised students working on the human consequences of violent conflict and authoritarianism (Christophersen, 2020, 2022; Stapnes, 2018; Stapnes, Carlquist and Horst, 2020; Tellander, 2022).

One of the most striking findings of my combined work has been that experiences of war, oppression, and exile can trigger civic and political participation by creating a political awareness and a strong sense of responsibility to act in the face of injustice. Throughout my research career, I met refugees and other conflict-affected individuals who were powerful citizen–activists, occupied with and working toward justice and civic virtue. Through these inspiring encounters, I also learned that there is great power and often poetry in the stories people tell about their lives, their inspirations, their actions, and the waves they make. Unfortunately, the full potential of personal narratives cannot be explored in academic articles and book chapters. I have so often felt that the publications that I (co-) wrote in recent years did not quite do justice to the rich narrative research behind the work and the uniqueness and power of people's stories.[1]

Presenting more extended personal narratives, as I do in this book, can achieve several things. Such extended narratives allow the reader to relate to the story being told, which often consists of recognizable everyday human relations and objects, and creates a connection between individuals who might otherwise feel they have little in common. Often, the stories create understanding on an emotional, embodied, and, not just, cognitive level. Furthermore, a personal narrative can be both unique as well as reflective of the experiences of many people. Stories of violence and oppression, as well as of people's resistance to these realities, have many common traits. And finally, in-depth, holistic representations of life stories make possible more accurate theorization. We are only able to create sound theories and concepts that reflect people's everyday realities in different contexts if we listen attentively to their full stories, rather than asking them only to answer our (academically) positioned questions.

The aim of the book, then, is to explore—through in-depth personal narratives—the key insight that experiences of violent conflict and oppression can impel civic and political participation and create a strong sense of responsibility to act in the face of injustice. In the pages that follow, I explain why this is the case, how it manifests itself in political action, and what the potential societal impact may be. I provide a detailed presentation of the life stories of three of the many extraordinary people I have met over the years, to show just how inspirations, actions, and impacts are intertwined in their narratives. I also illustrate how both personal and collective narratives have real-life implications as they influence what individuals do and how they may inspire and shape other people's narrative identities and actions. This belief in the real-life implications of narratives extends to the narrative of this book.

I wrote this monograph to inspire an audience of academics, artists, and activists who work on and for issues of social justice. I see it as an important supplement to my earlier work because it enables me to present personal narratives in detail, connecting stories in situations of violent conflict and authoritarianism with those that take place afterward, in exile. Thus, I connect findings from peace and conflict studies with those from forced migration studies. The monograph also allows me to present a variety of different but related findings within one book. Further, the articles I have published so far have mainly focused on people's motivations to challenge social injustice in contexts of violent conflict and authoritarianism, and to some extent, on their concrete actions. Prior to this book, I have not published on the impacts or—perhaps more accurately put—ripple effects of these actions.

I have chosen to focus specifically on individuals who contribute to our intellectual and embodied knowledge on violent conflict and displacement through scholarship and the arts. In recent years, I have found it particularly inspiring to explore the human consequences of violent conflict with academics and artists with lived experience from war and exile. Collaborating with these two groups allows me to understand how experiential, embodied knowledge influences work on peace and conflict, civic resistance, trauma and healing, forced migration, and a range of other topics. Academics and artists play key roles in creating public narratives. While mainstream academic and arts institutions may be central in supporting dominant, imperial narratives, many academics and artists—working within and independent from these institutions—are also crucial in contesting such dominant definitions of reality.

In academia, contributions are mainly verbal and numerical and largely ignore more sensuous and grounded ways of knowing that draw on a more fully embodied exploration. Many artists, on the other hand, work nonverbally and engage a range of senses in their art, producing alternative forms of knowledge (Grabska and Horst, 2022). Focusing on artists and academics also allows me to move beyond the public political action, including large-scale mobilizations and political protest, that is so commonly the focus of peace and conflict studies. Many of the individuals whose life stories provide the basis of my work have also participated in various social movements and protests, despite the risks involved. But in this book, I focus on their artistic and academic contributions to societal narratives during and after violent conflict and authoritarianism, with the aim of contributing to studies on everyday resistance to power and domination. In studying the moral inspirations of people's acts of resistance, I seek to develop new ways of theorizing political agency in the context of violence and oppression[2].

Narrative research

In 2000, encouraged by my supervisor, anthropologist Joke Schrijvers, I first started asking refugees from Somalia living in the refugee camps of Dadaab in Kenya to tell me their life stories. During my studies in anthropology, I learned about oral history research and the use of life histories by anthropologists. In a methods course, I used a life history approach to explore a period in my grandmother's life during the Second World War, when she lived in the Netherlands, close to the German border, in an area accidentally bombed by American planes. Throughout my academic career, I have employed the life history method in a range of research projects, and I used it as the key methodology in a study of the civil–political role of women in Somalia since the 1960s. I have also trained others in life history research, which, over time, has become a central research method in much of my work. Over the years, I have collected over one hundred life stories, the vast majority of which were told by individuals who had experienced and fled violent conflict or oppression. In this work, I have often collaborated with (prospective) academics from communities that experienced violent conflict.

Storytelling is an intersubjective practice whereby individual real-life experiences acquire meaning through being heard as well as through being told. Telling one's story to others can be a transformative practice that changes the narrator as well as those who are listening (Maggio, 2014). Storytelling bridges private, individualized passions and collective, shared views (Jackson, 2002). Individual experience is given public meaning through the intersubjective relation created by the storytelling situation (Arendt, 1958). The political philosopher Hannah Arendt's political thought rests on the idea that humans have the capacity to act narratively, and potentially transformatively, and in so doing, to insert themselves in the world by sharing their personal and collective narratives—in short, by storytelling

(Horst and Lysaker, 2021). The listener as well as the storyteller is central in creating this potential transformation. For the narrator, telling one's story can contribute to sense-making and to regaining a sense of agency in relation to one's own life. For the listener, the storytelling process provides access not only to new ways of narrating the past but also to alternative visions of the future.

Narrative research has been used in a wide range of disciplines within the social sciences since the 1980s (Goodson et al., 2016; Pinnegar and Daynes, 2007; Polletta et al., 2011). It incorporates a variety of practices and includes narrative inquiry as a research methodology as well as narratives as objects of study. Some researchers are interested in personal narratives and storytelling—often using a life history research approach—whereas others study the mobilizing potential of collective narratives. The narrative approach is grounded in critical traditions that question the epistemological foundations of positivist social science, recognize the historical and social specificity of all viewpoints and subjectivities, and emphasize the perspectivity intrinsic to knowledge production (Maynes, Pierce and Laslett, 2008). Narrative research is furthermore concerned with understanding individual agency, and as such, with challenging structural determinism. At the same time, narrative research often focuses on individuals and communities facing high levels of structural inequality and exclusion, and thus illustrates how the extent of an individual's power and choice is always positioned in unique ways within larger societal structures.

Narrative research, then, includes both research on narratives, where narratives are the object of study, and research with narratives, where data on human experience are collected through recording and analyzing personal or collective narratives (Bamberg, 2012). Research practices involving the narrative as study object or as research methodology are closely interwoven. Although in the following two sections, I discuss the two separately, my interest in collecting and analyzing personal narratives is closely connected to my interest in the transformative potential of narrative ways of thinking about events and experiences. In line with the professor of education and lifelong learning Torill Moen (2006, p. 57), I use the narrative approach as "a frame of reference, a way of reflecting during the entire inquiry process, a research method, and a mode for representing the research study". I seek to uncover the thematic meanings, acts, motivations, and normative understandings of those sharing their stories, to explore these themes across individuals, and to consider how stories function socially to create possibilities for political action.

The personal narrative or life story

> I didn't give up telling the stories and emphasizing the importance of stories even though I heard enough times that people would say "that is **her** story". Or people would say...people would actually say, "That is too little to consider or too limited to consider. It doesn't give a generalized picture. It is not about refugees, it is about a small group, highly educated..." People who want to disregard these kinds of narratives always find a way to do it. (Ghorashi, 2020)

Halleh Ghorashi is an anthropologist who works with the life stories of refugees as I do. The criticisms that she describes here are familiar to me. Fully aware of the charge that personal narratives are anecdotal or nonrepresentative, I offer here a discussion of some of the epistemological principles behind this approach. In the process, I also situate myself within the wide range of disciplines and perspectives in the social sciences that work with storytelling and (personal) narratives.[3] In my work, I have largely made use of the personal narrative or life story as "a retrospective first-person account of the evolution of an individual life over time and social context" (Maynes, Pierce and Laslett, 2008). The psychology professor Dan McAdams (2008) highlights principles with respect to personal narratives that have guided my work throughout the last decades: that the self is storied; that stories function to integrate lives; that life stories are told within social relationships; and that the focus and content of stories change over time as they are told in the context of lived culture, affected by norms, rules, and traditions at a particular time in a particular place.

Narrative identity

The aim of narrative research is to study how people experience the world, given that individuals construct narratives to create coherence, situate themselves in the past, and move toward an anticipated or imagined future (Bathmaker and Harnett, 2010; Lieblich, Tuval-Mashiach and Zilber, 1998; Moen, 2006; Riessman, 2008).

> Central in narrative research is a focus on the role of narratives as sensemaking tools with the capacity

to produce, challenge and change the identities of individuals as well as collectives. Through narrative and narrativity (the principles and structures of storytelling) we constitute our social identity. (Andersen, Ravn and Thomson, 2020)

The construction of narratives involves connecting individuals with individual others and larger collectives as well as connecting events that have occurred with how they are understood. As the psychology professor Lieblich and her colleagues (1998, p. 7) comment: "We know or discover ourselves, and reveal ourselves to others, by the stories we tell." These stories are always reconstructions, conveying experience by reconstituting it. This is an ongoing process, whereby the intersubjective telling of the story contributes to this meaning-making process (Squire, 2008).

The relationship between life story and self can be explored through the concept of narrative identity, which refers to "a person's internalized, evolving and integrative story of self" (McAdams, 2008, p. 242). The life story has the important function of integrating disparate elements of life, giving order to, and making sense of, what happened, and thereby attempting to explain and normalize what has occurred (Bamberg, 2012). According to McAdams (2008), this process of integration functions in two ways. First, personal narratives aim to bring together various aspects of the self in a way that expresses the individual as a whole despite the many complex and contradictory parts of which an individual consists. Second, people tell their stories to provide causal accounts that explain personal transformations. Doing so requires a retrospective and self-reflective singling out and sequencing of events that shows transformation from past to present self (Bamberg, 2006).

For the narrator, storytelling can be a "vital human strategy for sustaining a sense of agency in the face of disempowering circumstances. To reconstitute events in a story is no longer to live those events in passivity, but to actively rework them, both in dialogue with others and within one's own imagination" (Jackson, 2002, p. 15). The anthropologist Michael Jackson makes this point based on an ethnographic exploration of Hannah Arendt's view on storytelling as a bridge between private and public realms within the context of interviewing refugees and others about violence and displacement. "Storytelling is a coping strategy that involves making words stand for the world, and then, by manipulating them, changing one's experiences of the world" (Jackson, 2002, p. 16). These processes never happen in isolation but take place in a particular societal context.

> The stories we construct to make sense of our lives are fundamentally about our struggles to reconcile who we imagined we were, are and might be in our heads and bodies, with who we were, are and might be in the social contexts of family, community, workplace, ethnicity, gender, social class and culture writ large. The self comes to terms with society through narrative identity. (McAdams, 2008, p. 242)

Given the importance of personal narratives in creating an integrated sense of self that can inspire action, the common anthropological approach to "examine the connections between people and the larger forces that shape their lives" (Waterston, 2020, p. 119) becomes meaningful. Employing a life history approach makes possible the exploration of motivation, personal transformation, and the interlinkages between the personal and the collective. Historian Mary Jo Maynes and her colleagues (2008, p. 23) translate the key components of motivation into the following questions: "How do individuals come to understand their options, what do they bring in from their past experiences, what is the impact of emotions or values on their choices, and how do they themselves understand their capacity to act?" Answering these questions within the historical and social context of the meaning-making individual will afford new insights into individual agency.

> Agency is embodied in persons who evolve in context; people's stories build upon their lived experiences over time and in particular interpersonal, social, cultural and historical settings that they in turn continue to work through and transform in their present. (Maynes, Pierce and Laslett, 2008, p. 33)

Research based on life stories facilitates an understanding of human agency as simultaneously individual and social. Life stories have the potential to promote social action that may lead not just to personal but ultimately also to societal transformation. By working with life stories of individuals with experiential knowledge of "dark times" (Arendt, 1968) of oppression and violent conflict, I recognize both the unique nature of the stories, and simultaneously, their fundamentally collective nature.

The impact of time and place on narrative

Classical anthropologists have often been accused of working in a timeless reality, capturing a life world in a particular community in the here and now in ways that imply this reality to be fixed and unchanging. Collecting personal narratives makes it possible instead to understand the historical dimensions of a person's story as well as societal developments in modern history. Doing research among refugees in the Dadaab camps in Kenya, for example, focusing on refugee life in the here and now, was important for exposing the many injustices that individuals in the camps faced. But to get a sense of life in the camps without reducing individuals to their particular social positions in that moment—refugees living in marginal conditions in a semidesert location—I needed to understand their lives before Dadaab. Listening to their life stories was essential to this.

For the Somali refugees whom I interviewed, experiences of violent conflict and flight were only part of their full stories, which, for most, included living peacefully in a city or rural area in the south of Somalia. The stories of some started in Ethiopia or Somaliland and included several cycles of war and displacement. All of these stories provided insights not just into historical dimensions of the refugees' lives but also into different geographical realities without which their circumstances and experiences in the here and now were not fully comprehensible. For example, neglecting the full life story, with its temporal and geographical transformations, of Ayaan Moxamed—whom I spent considerable time with during my one-year stay in the camps in 2000—would have reduced her to a suffering refugee in a camp in a semidesert border area. This would have rendered invisible her life before the war, which involved being a diplomat for the Somali government, traveling the world, and speaking several languages.

The "indivisibility of past-present-future" (McLeod and Thomson, 2009, p. 8) or what sociologist Barbara Adam (2005) calls "timescape"is what makes understanding the historical dimension of a life essential. A particular narrative that includes individual meanings, acts, motivations, and normative understandings is always created under conditions where past, present, and future interconnect. Personal narratives document the lifelong consequences of transformative experiences as well as details in everyday life that often prove only in retrospect to have been salient (Maynes, Pierce and Laslett, 2008). What happened in the past influences people's understandings of the world and their own actions. One's narrative identity, while mostly based on a sense of one's core being, is also continually reconstructed in relation to experiences in and narratives of the past as well as imaginings of the future.

A personal narrative does not simply play back past events; it is always mediated by the storyteller. It involves perspective through which past events are tied together and made relevant for the here and now, with an eye to the storyteller's future orientation (Bamberg, 2006). Further, how one understands oneself—the narrative one tells about oneself—influences one's present-day understanding of the extent of one's power and choice as well as how one imagines possible futures. This understanding, in turn, influences one's actions and potentially the course of one's life. Ultimately, "we constantly construct and reconstruct a self to meet the needs of the situations we encounter, and we do so with the guidance of our memories of the past and our hopes and fears of the future" (Bruner, 2003, p. 210). This personal process is also integrated within the larger context in which a story takes place and is told. The stories that people tell about their lives "provide unique insights into the connections between individual life trajectories and collective forces and institutions beyond the individual" (Maynes, Pierce and Laslett, 2008, p. 3). Life stories are never simply individual and fixed; they are told in historically and geographically specific times and places.

Narrative research acknowledges the close interaction between individuals and collectives, within specific sociopolitical and historical contexts. Dominant narratives in specific contexts influence how people create their own narratives, as postmodernists and critical theorists have argued. Any claimed voice consists of a plurality of culturally and historically situated voices (Bakhtin, 1986 in Moen, 2006). People's voices are shaped through dialogue with others throughout their lives, and what people say is also influenced by the audience they envision listening to them. This reality has been described as "the stranglehold of oppressive metanarratives that establish rules of truth, legitimacy and identity" (Bathmaker and Harnett, 2010, p. 4). And yet, I would argue, narratives are both uniquely personal stories shaped by the experiential knowledge, values, and feelings of individuals as developed through interactions with thousands of others, and they are fundamentally collective stories that are shaped by the cultural, historical, and institutional settings in which they are shared. They represent the dialectical reality that individuals are always part of collectives, with the many opportunities and challenges this creates for establishing individual authenticity and autonomy.

Introducing marginalized stories, creating counternarratives

Most narrative research focuses closely on voices and stories that have been silenced or marginalized, often with the aim of refuting universal claims and generalizations. Many of the researchers who collect personal stories seek to expand the narrow empirical base on which the social sciences rest and to show both the range of agency from below and the significance of factors not captured through other modes of inquiry (Maynes, Pierce and Laslett, 2008). This tendency has received renewed impetus from the revitalization of the decades-long call to decolonize research approaches within the social sciences, arts, and humanities. By employing a more holistic, detailed, and inclusive approach, dominant narratives based on the perspectives and experiences of the privileged can be challenged. Rich accounts of the particularities and complexities of the lives of real people can call into question dominant narratives that are at odds with the experiences of individuals whose perspectives and stories were excluded from past research (Bathmaker and Harnett, 2010). Further, personal narrative research can reveal social or historical aspects that have been deliberately silenced or distorted by interested parties (Maynes, Pierce and Laslett, 2008).

Without such efforts to draw on a greater variety of experiences and perspectives, dominant narratives are easily taken for granted. As Ghorashi (2017b, p. 2428) argues, "the particular impact of discursive power—especially of the discourses that are most salient at a given time and in a given space—is that it works through normalization." Those in dominant positions, whose experiences and perspectives are well reflected in prevalent discourse, thus often hold unreflective positionalities that reproduce the status quo. Discourse disciplines action and interaction in largely subconscious ways, not only through its content but also through the language that is used and the manner in which it is uttered (Lakoff, 1987). Members of dominant groups—irrespective of whether their privilege is based on gender, skin color, or class—learn in the course of socialization and through their everyday experiences in private and public settings to use language, posture, and facial expression to convey authority and self-assurance. Members of marginalized groups, on the other hand, more often learn to be accommodating and invisible.

One of the aims of working with personal stories is to make the unreflective elements of the identities of people in majority positions, which are taken for granted, visible and less "normal". By contrasting dominant narratives with the stories of those with other positionalities, experiences, and perspectives, the taken-for-granted is questioned. My own life history research over the years suggests that those in marginalized positions more often hold deeply reflective positionalities simply because they are confronted in their everyday lives with the mismatch between their own perspectives and experiences and the dominant discourses. Social activist "Forough"[4], whose parents were political exiles from Iran, for example, highlights the everyday racism she has encountered throughout her life in Norway, while also describing a number of serious incidents of racism that posed a threat to her family (Horst, 2019). As a consequence, Forough is very occupied with representation, and believes that making people invisible or underrepresented in certain arenas, contributes to racism. She says it contributes to exoticizing and producing stereotypes. In response to a question about what motivates her to be civically engaged, she reflects:

> We take part because we have to. After all I am very privileged, I have a job, I am married, I have a family…I have the money, I am very privileged…When I get how things connect together then I just can't not do something. So it is not necessarily because I think it is fun and it is not necessarily because I feel brave, because I do not…(Horst, 2019, p. 50).

The deep reflectiveness that Forough engages in when discussing social justice issues, including her own position and responsibilities, is not new to me; I have observed this time and again when conducting life history interviews with people who have refugee or immigrant backgrounds. Ghorashi (2017b) describes this deep thoughtfulness as "strong reflexivity". Yet the mismatch between one's own perspectives and those of others is tough for an individual to deal with. It is part of what Bulhan (2015) calls "the occupation of being", and what Fanon (2008 [1951]), following W. E .B. du Bois, terms "double consciousness". Those who have fled violent conflict and authoritarianism and live in exile in addition must cope with the disconnect between past and present dominant narratives. One illustration of this is Iranian women who were labeled "radical communist troublemakers" in Iran and, as refugees in the Netherlands, have become "oppressed Muslim women" (Ghorashi, 2003).

Stories by those in marginalized positions are needed and they need to be listened to. Both telling and listening to these stories to happen on their own terms and not in relation to dominant narratives. Power works subtly in our own normalized practices and beliefs, which are taken for granted; we must therefore exercise critical, independent thinking to deconstruct the invisible biases in our own thinking. We must unlearn the imperialism in which academia has played an integral part, as professor of modern culture and media Ariella Azoulay (2019) reminds us. This necessitates a continuous attempt to present stories in their own right rather than filtering them through the lens of an invisible but ever-present norm, and to reflect critically on audience and voice. My own approach to this has been both to develop narrative in close interaction with those whose stories I share, building on their words and analysis as much as possible as well as working toward leveling the academic playing field for those in marginalized positions.

The transformative mobilizing power of narratives

How do the ways that humans narratively make sense of their lives shape social action? As sociologists Ditte Andersen, Signe Ravn, and Rachel Thomson (2020, p. 367) argue, "if stories actually shape what we do, then not only individual life trajectories but also collective futures depend upon [narrative sense-making]". Work on resistance and mobilization has shown that counternarratives play a central role in mobilizing people to act differently and/ or to start to resist hegemonic forces and narratives (Ewick and Silbey, 2003; Goldfarb, 2006; Polletta, 2006; Scott, 1989). Sociologist Francesca Polletta (2006), for example, analyzes the power of storytelling in African American sit-ins against racial segregation in the 1960s. While the initial actions mattered, the stories that were told about these actions and the way the stories challenged the dominant narrative about mobilizing influenced the political and social movements that followed. If these stories would not have been told, the impacts of the political action would not have been the same.

In this book, I trace the role that narratives can play in the process of personal transformative action that inspires wider societal transformation. How do personal narratives interact with collective ones to lead to societal transformation? To link the individual and collective dimensions of "inspiring transformation", understanding the relevance of personal narratives and life stories to people's perceptions and actions is essential. This understanding then needs to be connected to scholarly work on the power of public transcripts. In doing this, I build on the classic work on resistance from the margins by the political scientist James C. Scott and the sociologist Jeffrey Goldfarb. Despite the clear merits of these works in broadening the understanding of resistance, for the most part, they ignore the individual. In line with more recent work on forms of (everyday) resistance (Selvik, 2021; Selvik and Groves, 2023; Tellander, 2022), in this book, I place individuals front and center, presenting their unique experiences, motivations, and actions. I will first focus on the individual and then describe the collective dimensions of the transformative potential of narratives.

Narratives and trauma: individual transformations

In an overview of personal narratives and life stories in the field of personality psychology, Dan McAdams (2008) argues that negative life events place greater demands on individuals to make narrative sense of their experiences and seem to require individuals to engage in more storytelling work in order to mobilize the resources to cope. In exploring how people process negative experiences, research shows that writing about them and working through them positively affects health and well-being. Commonly, those who have experienced traumatic events try to discount them, at times through extreme measures such as suppression, denial, or dissociation. Sometimes, however, people cannot, or choose not to, discount their trauma, and instead try to work through it and create meaning out of the suffering they experienced. Various studies have found that both exploring negative experiences in depth—seeking to acknowledge what happened and how it felt—and understanding the experiences and what they may lead to—extracting some positive meaning from them—are associated with life satisfaction and emotional well-being (McAdams, 2008).

In fact, medical anthropologists, such as Arthur Kleinman, have criticized a focus on trauma in relation to adverse events, arguing that doing so medicalizes powerful human experiences and assumes individuals are passive and helpless in their wake (Scheper-Hughes, 2008). A reframing of these experiences in terms of morality and political responsibility may be part of a process of meaning-making that helps individuals regain and develop resilience (Kleinman, 2007). This process simultaneously connects the individual effort to find meaning with collective action, since meaning-making, if combined with the moral recognition that "I am, so I ought to", often impels individuals to act politically. If, additionally, the narratives about the ensuing political action are shared with others, the potential of personal narrative to affect social action is heightened (Ewick and Silbey, 2003, p. 60).

Storytelling is vital to processing harrowing experiences, but it is extremely difficult to share such stories if no one wants to hear them. Halleh Ghorashi describes how crucial storytelling has been for her, and how her privileged position as an academic created the space she needed to explore and tell her story. In an article on the importance of life stories to research on refugees, she discusses the value of the life story work she did for other women who had to flee Iran, and how this work also contributed to the reworking of her own narrative identity:

> By telling their life story, some women were not only confronted with a past they would rather forget, but finally, they were offered an opportunity to give this past a place in the present. They also discovered that their experiences are shared by others. Their pain is a common pain, the pain of an entire generation. This did not take it away, but it did help the person who had experienced this pain to feel stronger by realizing that her story was a collective story. The stories of other women made my own past revive. I started having recurrent nightmares, because the past, despite my efforts to forget it, had come to life again. Yet, my confrontation with the past gave me the chance to build up a new relationship with the memories. (Ghorashi, 2008, p. 121)

Personal narratives about experiencing "dark times" can be demanding both to tell and to hear. It is arduous to make narrative sense of such experiences, and the work of extracting meaning means reliving the parts of the past that are painful, and that one may have repressed or tried to forget. Furthermore, those in exile rarely have space for telling such stories, except in official, sterile settings in which their stories are transformed into asylum cases and treated with utmost suspicion. This occurs, for example, when questions posed by a bureaucrat focus on exact dates, times, places, and other technical details—things that those who have been traumatized often have difficulty recollecting—to probe for inconsistencies and reasons to deny asylum. Outside of this context, the stories of refugees are of little interest. Hannah Arendt realized this during the Second World War, as a refugee in France: "Apparently nobody wants to know that contemporary history has created a new kind of human beings [sic]—the kind that are put in concentration camps by their foes and in internment camps by their friends" (Arendt, 2017 [1943], p. 265). Thus, for personal narratives to have transformative mobilizing power, several conditions need to be met—not least being listened to with respect and with the sensitivity not to push the storyteller where they do not want to go.

Narrative power and collective resistance

Two classic works on everyday resistance—James Scott's *Domination and the arts of resistance: hidden transcripts* (1990) and Jeffrey Goldfarb's *The politics of small things* (2006)—stress the powerful role that narrative plays in collective resistance. Scott contrasts the "public transcript" with the hidden transcripts of resistance, drawing on a wide range of historical cases of oppression, such as slavery, feudalism, and the caste system.

Public transcript refers to the open interaction between subordinates and those who dominate; the latter seek to affirm and naturalize their power and to create perceptions among subordinates that contribute to maintaining their power over them (Scott, 1990). Hidden transcripts are created beyond the direct observations of power holders, because they are uttered only to trusted others or only in an indirect way. They undermine the dominant narrative and provide subordinates with a form of everyday resistance. In his book on resistance movements in Eastern Europe in the 1980s, Goldfarb argues that "the power of the definition of the situation is the engine of the politics of small things" (Goldfarb, 2006, p. 8). According to Goldfarb, before structural conditions can lead to change, the definition of the situation must first be changed. This changed understanding of reality must then become public and be acted upon—bringing what Scott defined as "hidden transcripts" out in the open.

It is important to study the crucial shift from private to public, to zoom in on the moment when the hidden breaks out into the open, when what is said at kitchen tables is chanted on the streets, when the everyday actions of professionals begin to affect the institutions they inhabit. Once everyday resistance that was previously limited to private spaces appears in the open, struggle arises. That which was hidden is what belonged in the public sphere in the first place but had been pushed out or repressed. This breaking out occurs when the two faces common to totalitarian regimes—the private persona and the public one—are rejected, and when individuals express previously hidden perspectives and ways of being in public. Once resistance has become customary, it generates its own expectations about what is permissible. It also raises the political and administrative costs for any regime that subsequently decides it will commit itself to enforcing the rules (Scott, 1990). For everyday resisters, there is safety in numbers, and successful resistance builds its own momentum, not least through the stories that are told about its success.

Polletta (2006, 2008) studies the role of storytelling in protest and politics, drawing on cases ranging from the sixteenth-century tax revolts to post-9/11 debates over the best use of the World Trade Center site. She stresses the interconnections between culture—understood as institutionalized schemas—and social mobilization. She probes how people come to interpret their grievances as political and collective rather than as private and individual, how culture sets the terms of strategic action, and when movements succeed in changing the rules of the institutional game. Polletta's work illustrates how familiar, routinized practices become problematic when people's commonsensical ideas about the world are challenged and become arenas of contention with new actors and interests. While prevailing beliefs often reproduce the status quo, at times culture becomes a counter-hegemonic force. This is more likely to happen during "unsettled" historical periods and crises, when different ways of doing things become conceivable because increasing numbers of people understand that the old ways no longer hold. We see this for example at the start of revolutions, as the stories of Halleh and Diala will show. In Syria—as Diala explains—the growing civic unrest in the wake of the 2011 Syrian uprising led increasing numbers of artists to courageously create and share work critical of the government, making visible just how many critical artists had been there all along. As Diala reflects "This is exactly what scares the government…".

A life history approach

The data on which this book is based consist of transcribed life history interviews, transcriptions of public events, publicly available digital material of relevance (presentations, interviews, etc.), and a selection of individuals' academic and/or artistic works.[5]. I used purposeful sampling to identify artists and academics whose work has focused on the human consequences of violence and oppression and who themselves have experiential knowledge of these topics. Each of the women whose life stories I explore in this book engage in social justice practices, which Professor of Critical Education Studies Lee Anne Bell (2007, p. 2) defines as practices that aim to:

> enable people to develop the critical analytical tools necessary to understand oppression and their own socialization within oppressive systems, and to develop a sense of agency and capacity to interrupt and change oppressive patterns and behaviours in themselves and in the institutions and communities of which they are a part.

Due to the global lockdown in response to the COVID-19 pandemic, interviews conducted in 2020 were virtual. However, prior to the lockdown, I met with all those featured in the book in person and established a personal connection with each. Diala and Monirah took part in a series of Conversations with Artists that I initiated in 2019 as part of the Centre on Culture and Violent Conflict (CCC) at the Peace Research Institute Oslo

(PRIO) where I work. Diala also took part in a month-long artist residency I initiated in Oslo, which took place in the summer of 2022. Halleh is a close colleague and friend who I have known for more than two decades. My interviews with each of them ranged from a total of two hours of transcribed interview material in the case of Halleh—whose academic work is based on her life story—to ten hours in the case of Monirah—whose life story evolved in the process of a series of conversations. Interviews were supplemented by shorter conversations of various lengths via email and phone as well as audiovisual and written material representing their academic or artistic work.

Positioned agency

> The dominant theories and methods of the social sciences have tended to view individuals and actions primarily through categories (e.g., race, gender, sexual orientation, social class or occupation, citizenship) that locate them in the "outside" or social world. Motivations, predispositions, and actions are typically explained largely through reference to these categorical affiliations. Individuals are thus reduced to clusters of social variables that serve as proxies for persons. Consequently, within such frameworks, human agency is reduced to social position…Social actors are treated as if they had little or no individual history, no feelings or ambivalences, no self-knowledge—in short, no individuality (Maynes, Pierce, and Laslett, 2008, p. 16).

Instead of analyzing the impact of one or more fixed characteristics in isolation, I take a holistic, life history approach. Personal narrative offers insights from the point of view of the narrator whose story emerges from lived experiences within particular sociocultural and historical contexts. To analyze such narratives, I use the conceptual perspective of "positioned agency". Building on feminist classics (Harding, 1987, Haraway, 1988), the concept of positionality refers to the social and political context that creates one's identity in terms of race, class, sexuality, and ability, and the way in which this identity influences one's understanding of the world. I define "positioned agency" as the degree of power and choice individuals have given their position—through both material realities and personal and collective narratives—in a particular time and place and given their gendered, classed, racialized, embodied, and other identities. Positioned material realities determine how a narrative can be shaped. Yet narrative also shapes realities, enabling or constraining particular forms of action by influencing both someone's own sense of power and choice and how others judge one's level of agency.

Agency is embodied in people who evolve in context; the stories people tell about themselves build upon their lived experiences over time, and in particular, their interpersonal, social, cultural, and historical settings. They in turn continue to work through and transform these situated lived experiences in their present (Maynes, Pierce, and Laslett, 2008, p. 33). Following this understanding of agency as positioned, within a particular temporal and geographical context, I ask how individuals come to understand their options and how their (narratives about) past experiences affect this understanding. Further, I explore how individuals understand their capacity to act and how their values shape their choices. Answering these questions contextually, within the historical and social context of the meaning-making individual, will afford new insights into individual agency.

The women whose stories I share in this book have articulated, crafted, and processed (parts of) their personal narratives, often from their positions as artists or academics and over many years. This means that, although they are or have been marginalized in a range of ways, when it comes to their narrative strength Monirah, Halleh, and Diala are in privileged positions. Yet their unique stories highlight themes that have emerged from my 20 years of life history research on the human consequences of violent conflict, oppression, and exile as well as from my more recent work on the political agency of refugees—also with individuals who had not yet processed their life stories to such an extent. In addition, by choosing individuals who have worked in public ways with their experiential knowledge of, and their personal and collective stories about, violence and oppression, I am able to introduce not just what they said to me, in one-on-one conversations, but also what they do, in their actual public performances and artistic or academic contributions. I am thus able to go beyond just studying their motivations and to analyze as well their political actions and even, at times, their impact.

Research methods

The research behind this book builds on transcribed life story interviews, audiovisual, and textual materials. Those who conduct life history research, myself included, aim to create an atmosphere that will allow the person interviewed to set the direction of the conversation, and to offer sufficient space and time to do so. Several narrative researchers have indicated the importance of this unstructured approach especially when working with marginalized groups whose experiences are far removed from dominant discourse and knowledge. Halleh Ghorashi describes the difference between a life story conversation and a more structured, typical research interview "in which the researcher struggles to find answers to a list of questions, sometimes in a somewhat artificial way". She also contrasts life story interviews with the interviews that refugees undergo when they claim asylum.

> My personal experiences as an asylum-seeker have given me a certain loathing of the type of interviews that are too fast, too purposive, or much too short. During these years I often felt I was being treated like a number or a file. I was blamed for any sentence I did not formulate correctly, or for my "inappropriate" attitude. All of a sudden, I could be facing a suspicious official who just wants to finish this case and an interpreter who is staring at me inscrutably, translating my passionate story in an indifferent voice. I was certain that both I and the other women who had gone through these procedures, had become thoroughly disturbed by officials reducing our stories to one among others, not doing justice to their "reality". (Ghorashi, 2008, p. 118)

The kind of interview described by Ghorashi is the opposite of what the life story interview strives to be. Life story interviews should be unhurried and open-ended in order to provide enough time for individuals to tell the stories that matter to them and to offer space and time for silence, for reflection, and for emotions that could come up in the interview. As a result, the interview may be lengthy and may need to take place over several sessions.

To conduct a life story interview, I begin by asking the individual to tell me "the story of their lives", aiming for them to talk freely, without interruptions, for at least 45–60 minutes. I inform them beforehand that the interview will focus on their life story, and explain what a life story interview entails, so that they know what to expect. My role in this first phase is to support the narrative flow and encourage the individual to talk freely and openly (Bamberg, 2006). I listen attentively, conveying care, and I mostly freely express my emotions in response to what is said. I laugh along at something funny and let my tears flow freely in response to a painful story. At this stage I may occasionally pose a factual question, such as asking for the year something happened, to make it easier for me to follow the story. I try to do this in the least disruptive way possible, waiting, for example, for a natural break in the narrative.

Although I tape life story interviews, unless the person I interview does not want the conversation to be taped, I also take extensive notes and write down questions that arise for me as I listen. Then, once the life story has been told, I go back through my notes and ask my questions one by one, in the order in which they have arisen. The post-narrative questions can be ones that encourage the person to elaborate on a particular aspect of the story. They can ask them to reflect more deeply about something. They may challenge the way the story was told, saying, for example, "You talked about [a particular event] in an almost lighthearted way but it sounds like a really tough experience to have had at such a young age. Could you say more about how you felt at the time?", or "You suggested [a particular decision] was easy to make, but it sounds like a real dilemma to me. How did you manage?" My questions can also seek to test my understanding of a particular situation to ensure that I do not draw incorrect conclusions.

By asking questions in this phase of the interview, my aim is to do justice to what was actually said and not put words in someone's mouth. My extensive notes come in handy, often allowing me to quote something someone said word for word. I strive to ask questions that respect the individual's storytelling, to present their perceived sense of agency accurately, and to highlight the parts of the story that I believe reflect remarkable choices made or exceptional difficulties faced. If I detect inconsistencies or silences, I approach these gently. I may wait for a later opportunity—when trust has increased—to address them. Sometimes, I notice them only when reading through the transcript of the interview or revising the text I have written based on the interview, in which case I will address them in a next interview.

During the part of the interview that follows the storytelling and involves an interactive conversation, I share my reactions to what is being said. I also ask follow-up questions, with the aim of prompting further reflection as well as to bring forward aspects of the story that are particularly relevant to my research. Finally, I ask questions about predetermined topics (if they have not been addressed yet) that specifically relate to my research. Conducting a life history interview over two, three, or even more sessions is often helpful because people commonly return to something they said in a previous session or offer additional thoughts in response to one of my questions. This also happens when I ask them to read through a transcript. Multi-session interviews thus allow me to explore themes of importance to those whose life story I create. They also let me come back to a previous interview to identify questions and topics that only become clear to me after a close reading of the transcript.

In addition to the transcribed life story interviews, I collected audiovisual and textual materials that showed what the three participants interviewed for this book actually did and not just what they said to me in our conversations. Working with artists and academics, I had rich material at my disposal. While much of it consisted of words, either written or spoken, these words were meant for an audience and not just for the privacy of a one-to-one exchange. Additionally, they were spoken (or published) as part of their professional lives. Within that context, they constituted acts and not just speech, I would argue.

For the chapter focused on Monirah, I watched a number of online clips and other materials she sent me. These included videos of her work in Afghanistan with the community theater, a short excerpt of the film she made in Italy, short video clips of her theater work in Sweden, and a video of a full-length play that she had performed in Swedish in a studio (due to COVID-19 restrictions). I also listened to a few of her (mostly radio) interviews that I found online. In addition, I listened to and read the transcript of Monirah's presentation within the Conversations with Artists series. At the event, Monirah performed a portion of her theater play and talked about her work. I also read the scripts of Monirah's two major plays in Sweden, one in English and one in Swedish and English. These materials allowed me to appreciate the creative work that Monirah has done over the years; the plays—especially the second one—also provided further insights into her life story.

Halleh, an anthropologist by training, has drawn on her own life story throughout her academic career. Among the written materials that were useful in crafting her life history were her monograph, which is based on her PhD (Ghorashi, 2003), her MA thesis (Ghorashi, 1994), and several more recently published articles. Halleh has talked about her own experiences extensively and weaves them into her teaching and public lecturing. Some of her lectures, public talks, and interviews—both in English and Dutch—are available online. In particular, I found her TEDx talk from April 2017 about critical thinking, which I transcribed, a valuable resource. She is the one person I knew well before I interviewed her. She is also the only one with whom I conducted a single interview, since her written and oral descriptions and analyses of her own life story provide such a wealth of material to draw on.

For Diala, I also had access to extensive audiovisual and textual materials. I watched or listened to the interviews she has given to a host of media channels across Europe. She also participated in an event in the Conversations with Artists series at PRIO, where she interwove a simplified telling of her own life story with a visual presentation of her art from different periods of her life. I studied the transcript and audio recording of this event as well as the visuals. Many of her paintings, animations, and drawings are available on her social media accounts, although she is so productive that it is hard to get a complete overview of her work at any one time. I explored Diala's artwork mostly in relation to what she said about her work during interviews, which was crucial to helping me grasp some of the nonverbal aspects of her story. However, I did not do a systematic analysis of audiovisuals for this book.

Writing process and co-creation

In narrative research, stories of lived experience are shaped through discussions, through a "collaborative dialogic relationship" (Moen, 2006, p. 61). Moen's understanding of the life history approach describes well how I have worked with Monirah, Halleh, and Diala as well as how this book came about. The collaborative relationship is maybe most strongly evident in the process of writing the chapters. I sent transcripts of our interviews and, later, one or two draft versions of their life stories to the women themselves in order to solicit their feedback and ensure that my description of their stories was in line with their own telling and understanding of their stories. The ultimate aim at this stage for me was to arrive at a shared understanding of the narrative, before I added my own analysis and again sent the full draft chapters to each individual for feedback.

My research for this book benefited tremendously from Monirah, Halleh, and Diala's own labor. Their academic or artistic work provided me with additional source material. They had already spent time and effort remembering, finding words for things that are challenging, and sharing their stories. Diala has presented her work regularly across Europe and publicly shares bits and pieces about her life and her experiences as they relate to her artwork. Halleh had spent years of her academic life—while working on her MA and then her PhD—processing and conveying her life story within the context of political realities and the experiences of other Iranians after the revolution. Monirah had recently begun the work of sharing one of the darkest parts of her story, first with a few trusted friends in privacy and then through a theater piece she originally performed with no audience in front of a camera after which she shared it with a small group of close friends.

How much input I solicited from each woman varied depending on how well developed the life story narrative already was before our interview, on how much time I felt I could ask each to expend, and on how confident I was about how my chapter drafts would be received. If I suspected extensive revisions would be needed, I asked for input more frequently. After receiving feedback from the women on the interview transcripts, I wrote drafts of their life stories. Writing a first version of each story was very straightforward in some cases and more complicated in others; the more years the women themselves had worked on their stories and processed them, the easier the writing was for me. After receiving their feedback, I then wrote full chapters that included not just the life stories but also my analyses, and then shared them once more for input. In the case of Monirah, reading the draft chapter became a step in her own processing and shaping her stories, and thus, we labored extensively together on her chapter as her story evolved.

In addition to my own data analysis, collaborating at length with Monirah, Halleh, and Diala in the writing phase of my project and letting each of them decide how much rewriting was required was crucial to the process. Narrating someone else's story and situating it in a larger context is a huge responsibility and I do not see how this could be done properly in the absence of a collaboration that yields greater insight for both parties. Sometimes, the feedback I received was written and in other cases, another conversation was needed. There were also occasions on which I received both written and oral input. In a few instances, the explanations and requests for changes were so substantial that an additional taped conversation was needed. This was then transcribed and drawn on in writing this book. Over the 18 months from my first request for an interview to my completion of the chapter drafts, Monirah, Halleh, Diala and I worked with dedication to get the story "right". This involved hard work because the conversations and the processes of recollection and reflection that they generated for some stories, meant that our understandings of the stories changed during the time we worked on them.

Narrative truth and ethics

The general notion of validity concerns the believability of a statement or knowledge claim, or the extent to which it is well founded and corresponds to the real world. In narrative research, two levels of validity must be taken into account: the validity of the life story told by the research participant and the validity of the analysis provided by the researcher (Riessman, 2008). The validity of the life story may become an issue when the storyteller experienced meaning differs from the story they tell about their experiences (Polkinghorne, 2007). Thus, it is important to underscore that, although a reported meaning obviously corresponds to an actual life event, the "truthfulness" of a narrative work relates to its narrative truth rather than a historical truth. "Storied evidence is gathered not to determine if events actually happened but about the meaning experienced by people whether or not the events are accurately described" (Polkinghorne, 2007, p. 479).

Narrative "untruth" may arise because the storyteller struggles to find language to describe an experience and the meaning they have attached to the experience. Or it may be that they have not reflected sufficiently to be able to access the meaning. Or it may be that social norms discourage the storyteller from sharing the meaning. Monirah, Halleh, and Diala all express themselves verbally and nonverbally as academics and artists. This reduces the likelihood of narrative "untruth" resulting from difficulties with expression. To minimize the possibility of a lack of reflectiveness, the women were asked questions and given ample time to reflect before answering. Furthermore, they had mostly already reflected deeply on their own experiences and had also themselves shared their stories with others in their professional engagements or in private settings.

Like the anthropologist Michael Jackson, I am suspicious of any efforts to identify a "real meaning" that lies beneath what people say and do. I believe that any such effort is, in fact, patronizing and often shaped by unreflective class, gender, and/or race biases. Discussing academic research with indigenous communities, Jackson argues:

> Methodologically [...] I consider it imperative that we break a long-standing academic habit of reducing human actions to some unconscious meaning, ulterior motive, or hidden cause. For what the hermeneutics of suspicion all too often means in practice is not only an academic subversion of nonacademic perspectives but an interpretive license that avails itself of indigenous

exegesis to justify its own excessive claims. (Jackson, 2016, p. 31)

Those who are in some way marginalized are actually more likely to have reflected thoroughly on their own realities because they face the strongest discrepancy between their self-perceived reality and dominant societal narratives. I aim to reflect the perspectives, interpretations, and representations that were communicated to me in a way that does justice to the meaning conveyed. I do, of course, add my own perspectives, interpretations, and representations to the mix but I seek to be as explicit as possible in doing so to make clear whose views I am putting forth. Although this book is mine, the life stories on which it is based were cocreated. I aim to reflect the co-creative, conversational way in which these life histories were constructed and thus to do justice to each storyteller.

I worked to mitigate the possibility that social norms would lead the women to tell narrative "untruths" by striving to build trust throughout the research process. From the first contact, I sought to be transparent about the process and my aims, and shared and discussed my own interpretations and writing to allow opportunities for dialogue about my interpretations. Monirah's story is one example where vital information was added that had not been provided originally, and then, information from earlier conversations was changed. Shortly before I shared the draft life story I had written based on the first two interviews, Monirah had begun working with a part of her life story that social norms discouraged her from sharing. In one of our later conversations, she indicated that the story she had first told, at the beginning of our collaboration, had perhaps been true for her at that time but it was not accurate. It was simply the story that she could tell at that time. She indicated that she was comfortable with me and trusted me; this trust, I believe, developed and grew over the course of working together. My hope is that the transparency of the process that produced this book, including my seeking input from Monirah, Halleh, and Diala at every stage, not only allowed me to validate my own analyses but also increased trust between us and thus reduced any potential distortions.

The validity of the analysis—the story told by the researcher—relates to how well the storied text corresponds with the interpretations of that text. Validity is not inherent in a claim but is an intersubjective judgment that involves presenting good arguments that convince an audience. The interpretations will always be situated truths, dependent on the time and place in which the analysis is made and the particular audience that engages with it. If the analysis by the researcher results in a published text, it will be available unchanged for decades. But over time, the audience for the text will change, and this has implications for validity claims. As Riessman (2008, p. 185) argues, research projects are situated "within the parameters and debates of the particular social science discipline, and by the epistemologies and theories that ground the empirical work". The arguments required to convince will be different for an audience versed in the realist tradition compared, say, to one committed to a feminist one.

Issues of validity strike at the heart of some of the key ethical concerns in narrative research (Smythe and Murray, 2000). A dilemma can occur if the researcher and the person whose life story is told interpret specific events in different ways or if those interviewed question the interpretive authority of the researcher (Moen, 2006). In such a case, narrative ownership becomes an issue. Narrative accounts are told from multiple perspectives and encourage multiple layers of interpretation. Yet in this book, possibly because of the collaborative analysis and writing, my perspectives and interpretations are not necessarily at odds with those of the women whose stories are told within these pages. When Halleh provided her feedback on her chapter, she thanked me for writing her story, commenting "it is an honor to read this text as created through your eyes and beautiful pen. You have connected the different parts in a convincing way" [my translation] (Ghorashi, 2021). Diala thanked me "for this deep analysis and writing. It was very emotional and helpful for me to read it and read myself" (Brisly, 2021c). And after she read her chapter, Monirah told me:

> It was the first time seeing and reading myself in a whole 25 pages and thinking "my God, it's like the first time I am seeing myself as a little bit more whole". Because here and there I was talking and I never had the time to go back and reflect, and now reading this, I realized that this is also part of the healing. Talking is very important. And we do it for ourselves. The first step is to do it for ourselves. And then when you pass [the first phase in this process]—you stop shivering, you stop shaking, you stop crying—then you can share it with others. And that is where the collective healing comes in. Your work has been part of my personal healing and our conversation has been part of my personal healing. (Hashemi, 2021b)

These comments, and the intersubjective engagements I have had with them throughout the process of creating this book, give me the confidence that my presentation of their stories stays closely to their own experiences and intentions, as narrated to me.

Inspiring transformation with stories of hope

> To be hopeful in bad times is not just foolishly romantic. It is based on the fact that human history is a history not only of cruelty, but also of compassion, sacrifice, courage, kindness. What we choose to emphasize in this complex history will determine our lives. If we see only the worst, it destroys our capacity to do something. If we remember those times and places—and there are so many—where people have behaved magnificently, this gives us energy to act, and at least the possibility of sending this spinning top of a world in a different direction. And if we do act, in however small a way, we don't have to wait for some grand utopian future. (Zinn, 2009, p. 14)

I understand historian and political scientist Howard Zinn to be saying that the stories we present about the world as it was and is can influence that world and the future. This points to a crucial motivation of this book. What we choose to focus on analytically and methodologically ultimately may influence ontological reality. As academics we can and do study reality in various ways, asking different questions from a range of angles. Violent conflict and oppression have been studied extensively to understand and delineate their destructive effects, providing important knowledge about the terrible consequences for individuals and communities. Less attention has been paid to how the experience of violence or oppression can trigger political action, both in the midst of and after "dark times", and both in the places where it takes place as well as in exile. The potential of such "new beginnings" (Arendt, 1958; Horst and Lysaker, 2021)—counteractions with potential ripple effects—is always unleashed by individuals. As such, the central contribution this book makes is to offer a closer look, through the detailed presentation of the stories of three remarkable women, at the motivations, actions, and transformative influence of individuals, as part of larger collectives.

Political action cannot thrive without hope: individuals need to believe it is possible to make a difference (Horst and Lysaker, 2021). In my own work on political action, I have often asked people how they manage to persist despite the many challenges and, at times, threats they face. I asked Bashar, a Palestinian filmmaker based in Norway, whether he feels he exercises any influence through his art projects. His response was, "I have to. If I do not have influence I need to find something else. There has been a lot of change because of the films I have made." (Horst, 2019) Forough also explains that seeing that one has effected change is essential, even if the transformation is difficult to spot and takes place on a small scale. When I ask her how she manages to persist, Forough reflects:

> I think it is because…we do see some changes, we do, otherwise I would not have…it is not so easy to find the changes, it is not always so easy to catch, but

it happens. And that's surely without me knowing how I would have managed if there would not have been any. But that is probably one of the reasons that we continue, yes. We see the small steps, we see that our voice—even if we become angry, then maybe event organizers will think next time before they do something, or maybe researchers think more carefully next time they do a project for example. (Horst and Lysaker, 2021)

Forough in our conversation explicitly argues that the ripple effects of smaller actions enable her to continue fighting racism and other ills in Norwegian society. For her and others to persist, the ripple effects of individual acts must be visible, which necessitates storytelling that highlights the injustices, the critical political action, and its ripple effects. Telling such stories is vital since, as Zinn reminds us, what we choose to emphasize will determine our lives. This book, then, focuses deliberately, perhaps naively, on courageous individual action in dark times, in order to share, support, and possibly even encourage vital political action for social justice at all times. This chapter started with a quote from one of Monirah's plays, where she says that "there are endless black spaces that need endless stories". My wish is that sharing how Monirah, Halleh, and Diala light stars in dark spaces provides new wisdom for those reading this book, strengthening their response-ability in the face of social injustice.

2
Monirah Hashemi: Who lights the stars?

The echo of the mountain answered me.

One day we were told "run, run everybody! Save your lives, save your children, save the girls! And the women." The time was so short. Shorter than a breath. "What should I take with me? Oh my God, I can't think, I can't make a decision. Money? Clothes? Food? How long will we be running? Do I need to take warm clothes?"

I don't know how long it took to gather myself. To find out what was important to take. My life, my children…"Where are my children? [louder] Where are my children? Mariam! Basir! Where are you? It's not a good time for hiding. No more hiding, we should run away this time, we should leave. Now!" (Hashemi, 2019c).

Monirah Hashemi is an actor, playwright, and director. In her work, first in Afghanistan and then in Sweden, she has used theater and film as tools to address a range of social justice issues, particularly as they relate to women's rights. I invited Monirah to Oslo in December 2019 to take part in a seminar series run by PRIO's Centre on Culture and Violent Conflict. She performed a fragment from her solo theater show *Sitaraha* (The Stars) for an audience of around 40 students, academics, artists, and civil society members, among others. The play explores women's experiences during different wars over the decades in Afghanistan and exposes some of the atrocities committed against women and children. Monirah takes on the characters of both the men committing the atrocities and the women affected by them.

Her powerfully chanted *"Allahu akbar"* rings through the seminar room, both pushing against conventions and limits and challenging me, as a member of the audience, to reflect on those boundaries. Later in the play, Monirah starts singing in a strong, clear voice, while striking her chest as if it were a drum, beating out a rhythm. She sings in the Dari language in a way that I can only describe as lamenting. It is my first time attending a performance by Monirah, and I am deeply moved. The atrocities she explores are so unfathomable, the justifications offered by perpetrators and the larger structures of which they are a part are so absurd, and the expressions of suffering are so painful to witness that I can only sit and let her performance wash over me. I experience a profound sense of tragedy. The audience and I watch in heavy silence and, after the performance concludes, offer respectful applause.

Monirah then discusses her creative work. She briefly describes her personal background and then discusses some of her professional film and theater engagements. She cofounded the Simorgh Film Association of Culture and Art in Afghanistan, where she led the association's theater department and offered workshops on a range of topics. Initially interested in film, Monirah gradually shifted to theater, producing and performing plays both nationally and internationally. She also engaged in participatory community theater across Afghanistan with the US-based Bond Street Theatre, cocreating performances for a wide range of venues, including schools, prisons, NGOs, and the streets. Much of her work in Afghanistan focused on the human consequences of violence and abuse in society, especially for women.

Today, Monirah lives in Sweden, where she works as an actor and director. Her artistic path was neither direct nor easy. In what follows, I present her story as it unfolds across the geographical contours of Iran, Afghanistan, and, finally, Sweden. I then discuss how Monirah's story powerfully illustrates both the crucial role that marginalized outsiders can play in questioning what is taken for granted and the space that creative practice can generate for critical expression in contexts where freedom of expression is quite limited otherwise, both politically and socially.

The complex layers of Monirah's story show the process through which she and other women come to understand violence in much broader terms than her community at large would define it. Violence to her includes behavior that involves force intended to hurt, damage, or kill not only in the public but also in the private sphere. Her story brings forth a wide range of forms of violence and oppression that Afghan women face. Simultaneously, Monirah addresses these issues from a perspective that refuses to see Afghan women as victims. She argues that the essence of resistance exists in every woman, and the Afghan women she has met are fighting all their lives, but in ways that Western audiences do not easily recognize. For Monirah, representing violence and oppression as not purely defined by victimhood is particularly important considering the geopolitical context in which Afghan women are presented as vulnerable victims that need saving from violent Afghan men. Her personal experiences and the experiences of the women whose stories she tells through her creative work, have led to an embodied understanding of the complex nature of victimhood and resistance, and her theater performances balance the two carefully.

Childhood in Iran: growing up as an outsider

Monirah was born in Iran in 1986 to Afghan parents who had fled the war in Afghanistan as children. When Monirah was 19, she, her parents, and five of her six siblings moved to Afghanistan; an older married sister stayed in Iran. Although she had grown up in Iran, speaking fluent Farsi, and her parents had lived there most of their lives, Monirah felt that she could never really belong in Iran. She states that she and her family were told "no" all the time and faced lots of red lines: "You can't do this and you can't do that, can't go here and can't go there." Monirah describes her life in Iran, and that of Afghan refugees, in Iran, in general:

> And for myself there is no future. Because, first, I'm an Afghan. Second, I'm a woman. And both identities prevent me from studying, or working, and having a decent job or doing something that I want to do in Iran. So it's...I mean, sometimes I think about what would have happened if I had been born in Afghanistan and had lived in Afghanistan. Was it different being in Iran?

Because the situation we, as Afghan refugees. had in Iran was...There were places where it was written: "Afghans and dogs are not allowed", and we could not go. We could not travel freely in the country. If we wanted to visit someone who was living somewhere else, we had to get a kind of certificate or a letter, permission, to be able to travel without being stopped by the police or being sent to jail or deported back to Afghanistan. [...] Afghans in the eyes of some Iranians, probably I can't say everyone, but some nationalists and racists, Afghans were the lowest class. [...]

When you were being harassed by a gang of boys just for being an Afghan girl, you could not find a single person coming to interfere and say: "Let her be, she's human", or "he's human". Everybody closed their eyes, just passed by. "Ok, he or she is an Afghan, so it's ok to do that to him or her."[6] (Hashemi, 2019a)

Monirah learned English in an Afghan-run school. She did not have access to consistent, formal education in Iranian schools, having been rejected by the regular schooling system many times. She describes an incident in which her younger sister, a top student, was permanently expelled, along with all other Afghan students, by the principal.

And then one day my younger sister, [...] she came home one day from school, and she was very intelligent [...] She is very intelligent. She was so good in school, and she got...a few weeks before she won a scholarship to join a school for [gifted students]. So she won, actually, in a competition, that scholarship, but they didn't give it to her because she was a refugee and she was an Afghan. So they gave it to another person who had Iranian nationality and citizenship.

But one day she came home, and she was crying like hell, and I was home and asked what had happened. She said: "The principal of the school, she just sent me home and said" 'don't come back to this school, you cannot study here anymore', and I was shocked. I called her at the school, and I was so angry. She was not listening and didn't want to give any answers. "What is the reason that you are sending a kid out? You should have a reason. Is she not good in her lessons or is she behaving bad? What is the reason?" She said nothing. (Hashemi, 2019a)

Monirah describes this incident in great detail, explaining how her father became very angry and went to the school to demand an explanation. He learned that his daughter had been sent home, as had 400 other Afghan girls, because the rector of the school had come to distrust all Afghans. Allegedly, one of the rector's Afghan servants had told her that, if Iranians ever sought refuge in Afghanistan, they would be killed.

"Return" to Afghanistan: discovering film and theater

In 2004, shortly after this incident, Monirah's father's parents were deported from Iran and Monirah's parents then also decided to return to Afghanistan with their children. Monirah was struck by the difference between being a refugee with no rights and being an Afghan in Afghanistan.

I think that living that life, under those circumstances, probably taught me to try to change things when I had the opportunity to. Because I remember in Iran there were, there were no questions. You could not ask someone "Why do you treat me like this?" because we were told "You are Afghan refugees and this is not your place." That's what this teacher, when we called her and said, "Why did you send my daughter out of school?", she said: "If you're not satisfied, if you are unhappy, go back to your own country."

So it means that this place, when you live here as a refugee, you do not even have the right to ask a question. And this is what we grew up with. We thought that we could not ask any question. When we meet injustice in society as a refugee, we have no right to ask the question, "Why?" But when I went back to Afghanistan, I noticed…. The first thing I was really happy about was that now I could ask that question. Now I could ask "Why?" Now I could try for change. (Hashemi, 2019a)

A main priority for Monirah's family, now that they were in Afghanistan, was education, and so the school-age children were sent to school. Because Monirah was behind compared to children her age, she studied from home initially; once she passed her tests and exams, she too began attending school. Although the family enjoyed greater freedom in Afghanistan than they had in Iran, being ethnically Hazara, they faced a challenge as they settled in Herat, in the west of Afghanistan, where the Hazara are in the minority. Monirah explains that the ethnic conflict that caused war and violence for decades was still a problem at that time.

In her first year in Afghanistan, Monirah heard about a TV channel that had started in Herat. Occasionally, the channel ran movies that were dubbed in Dari, with one actor voicing all the parts, which Monirah found particularly amusing. She wanted to work there. During her pursuit of a job, she heard about a group that was producing films and she joined it. She was initially afraid to tell her family, and so she told her mother only that she really wanted to join this film group. Her mother advised her to try the group for a bit without telling her father, since she might not like the group, and in that case, there was no need to upset her father. If, on the other hand, she did like it, they would discuss how best to share this information with the family.

After Monirah told her father, he came to her workplace at times, to check to see that she was not behaving indecently and that the colleagues she worked with were respectful and good people (even though Monirah said that, in reality, they were not, and she faced substantial harassment at work). She worked very hard to convince her father, as he was an essential ally to whom she could turn in the face of pressure from her extended family. There was worry that the reputation of her grandfather, the head of the extended family, could be damaged if people knew that his granddaughter had "started acting and appearing on TV screens and working with strange men". Thus, her uncles, grandmother, and grandfather pressured her to leave the job.

When she first began, Monirah provided all kinds of behind-the-camera support. Although there were female actresses in the company, she was the only Hazara woman, which meant that she was working with colleagues with different ethnic identities. This created a range of problems for her, one being that she was initially not allowed to appear on the screen because she looked different from the majority ethnic groups in this part of the country. Yet she finally got the opportunity to prove herself as an actress when one of the lead actresses was stopped by her family from working there. With no one else available to take the role, Monirah was asked to play the part. The group changed the script somewhat and applied makeup to try to make Monirah "blend in", and from then on, Monirah was also an actress.

When Monirah sums up the environment for self-expression in Afghanistan, she says, "People always think that they have the right to interfere, to comment on people's lives, on what they do, and on what they should not do." She explains that they felt especially free to do so in the case of a (young) woman. Persisting in her attempt to work in film was not easy, and Monirah faced challenges from many directions. She experienced sexual harassment by her colleagues, and she ascribes this to her being a Hazara woman. She coped by just trying to do her work, sticking with it, and refusing to be intimidated by male colleagues or by the men in her neighborhood who followed her to and from her workplace to find out what she was doing and with whom she was meeting. The general view was that Monirah's movements, particularly her returning home alone after sunset, were highly inappropriate for a woman.

Despite her efforts to continue quietly doing what she wanted to do, ignoring intimidation efforts, Monirah was one day stopped in her tracks. Someone had started distributing letters to her home and to the neighbors that contained malicious gossip about her. Her mother woke her up one morning to say that she had found letters in the yard.

> Someone had written text. And it's not like one or two or ten letters, it's like, I don't know, probably 30, 40, or 50 letters that someone just threw in our yard. So my mother wanted me to read them. I opened the letters. One, then two, then three, and finally, I had to open all of them, and they were about me. They said things like I am a very bad girl. I mean, "She is in a relationship with lots of men. She is going to be pregnant soon. She's the shame of, not only the family, my family, but also the shame of all the neighborhood." So my mom and I decided that we were going to destroy these letters, and not show them to anyone, and I would just go and do my work. (Hashemi, 2019a)

Yet Monirah's grandmother and the neighbors also read the letters, so Monirah could not avoid the shame they brought upon her. In the end, she broke down and did not leave the house for three months, doing very little. Her father bought her a recorder so that she could play some music, but after three months, her mother came into her room and talked to her.

> One day she came and said to me that this girl that I am now, this is exactly what these people want, "and you are giving this person to them. You are becoming that scared, frightened woman that cannot do anything, and is just stuck in the corner of the house and doesn't go out…". And then she told me, "Every second that you go out until you come back, I die. But I want you to go out. I want you to go for your dreams." She told me

something that really stayed with me, and it is going to stay with me all my life. She said, "I feared once in my life and I never experienced happiness and freedom ever again. I never want the fear to find its way to your heart. Go and do whatever you want to do."

So for me, it was like, I knew…. I grew up and I have always been aware of my mom's feeling. I was always seeing how my father's family, his brothers, father or mother, sisters, were treating my mom, as a woman who came from another family and married into a family which she will never be part of. You will always be this enemy to the family. And then you are the subject of violence which is mostly applied by women. I always could see that. And then I noticed that fear, that…that trembling moment when she said "I die every second when you go out until you come back. Every second for me is death. But I want you to go out and don't let the fear find its way to your heart."

I was thinking, how can it be possible that a woman who has gone through so much in her life still wants to stand up and wants to be that solid ground for her child so her child will not fear? To stand up and rise again. Though I didn't know how to go out again. I was scared. I didn't know if these people still remembered, if my neighbors remembered the letters. But I decided to go out. (Hashemi, 2019a)

Monirah's struggle in this key period of her life was, as her mother's words show, a struggle bigger than just her own, and it had profound effects. The conflict between individual freedom of expression and societal pressures to conform to expectations about how to live one's life generally, and specifically, as a young woman, extended beyond this specific incident. In these years, her father also had to deal with considerable pressure. For example, he was stopped on the streets and asked why he allowed his daughter(s) to engage in theater. In the end, it became too much for him, and in late 2005/early 2006, he left the family and moved back to Iran, and did not return until five or six years later. People's "right to interfere", as Monirah terms it, had profound effects both for those who adjusted their actions and speech accordingly and for those who did not.

Art as political creative practice

> When you cook...you always should have...yeah, salt. You can avoid pepper, you can avoid all the other spices, but you always should have salt. And I think, in bringing political issues, or…somehow involving politics in my plays, I think it's like that salt into that dish, or into that food or cooking. I can't…I don't remember that I've done something which has not been political. (Hashemi, 2019a)

The malicious-letters incident fundamentally changed Monirah's commitment to her art. When she reflects on how her interest in art developed, she points out that she came from a religious, traditional background, and thus her interest had no precedent in her family. Yet, she says "she was always interested in art". Monirah describes how, as a child, she loved listening to stories and then imagining those stories. Although she insists that she is not a poet, as a child she tried to make sense of her feelings, writing them down "in a very poetic way". Monirah recalls that when her family returned to Afghanistan and she became involved in film and theater, she initially was drawn to what she imagined was the glamour of an actress's life. But when she returned to film and theater after her three-month seclusion, she decided to set up her own company, Simorgh Film Association of Culture and Art, with a few friends. Her creative work was no longer going to be just entertainment; she wanted to do something more, something meaningful.

> I remember that at the end of 2004, after this experience that I had, when we had received lots of letters—exactly there, I was already changed. Because when I started my own company in 2005, I had a clear picture of what I wanted to do. I wanted to create a space for women, for young girls, where they could come and practice art, do whatever they want, express themselves in any way they want, without being harassed by any man. Without thinking that coming here will damage their family honor, will violate…I don't know, their values. So I was trying in the beginning to make that space for these women, because I never had it myself.
>
> Then I was thinking that, for me, art is never going to be for entertainment. Theater and film are never going to be for entertainment. For me, it would be the most important tool. For me, art would be the torch, a kind of guiding torch, a light that I can take to make the path clear for myself. But also in that way, of going that direction, many other women can also use that torch. So it was quite clear to me what I wanted in the beginning. (Hashemi, 2019a)

Thus, her relationship to creative practice changed when she started exploring it both as a way to express herself and stir debate in society and as a creative space for others to express themselves. She now saw art as a tool for exploration—for herself, her sisters, and other young women.

> When I was doing theater for the first time, that was when I realized that I can…I can be happy. Because being famous did not make me happy. But I could make myself happy in another way, by reaching other women. By helping other women to find out. I could see how theater has changed my life, how art has changed my life, how art gave voice, gave solid ground to me, helped build my worldview, to change that kind of hard childhood into a more clear future where I had some more hope. Then I was thinking that I could use art to reach women who are closed into themselves and cannot get out of those red lines and boundaries, and everything that the society and the family and the culture and religious institutions has created for them. (Hashemi, 2019a)

Monirah's insistence on telling her own and other women's stories, on creating debate in communities, and on encouraging young women to use their voices may have come from her mother's commitment to allowing and encouraging Monirah to express herself, to "keep her own stories alive".

> My mom always said, "As long as you are silent, you allow the people who are abusing you, who are using violence on you, the perpetrators, to live on, to go on with their actions." She taught me to never keep silent. Never shut down. Never…yeah, always tell. Always talk. Always tell what's happening. If the people who

engage in bad actions are not ashamed of their actions, you should not be ashamed of what is happening to you, what has happened on you, what you have experienced and gone through. (Hashemi, 2019a)

And indeed, storytelling that focuses on the stories that are not being told, approaching them from an angle that is not commonly taken, is central to Monirah's work. To create these stories, she conducted what she calls field research, talking to elderly men and women who, like Monirah, called themselves storytellers. In her creative work in Afghanistan, she wove together present-day experiences with what she learned about the past, and engaged in a variety of creative practices that, at their core, were all geared toward transforming societal practices, perspectives, and thus, experiences.

A variety of creative practices: performances, community theater, and training youth

Besides appearing in films, throughout the years Monirah has written and performed in plays that address taboo subjects, such as violence against women and children, early and forced marriage, social participation, and democracy. She has also produced community theater, where her aim was to engage with these themes locally, within a particular community. And she has trained children and youth, mostly girls, to express themselves through theater performance. In 2006, Monirah became increasingly focused on theater. She was invited to take part in the first educational theater festival in Herat after the fall of the Taliban. At that time, she was largely working as a film actress, but since she was one of few women in Afghanistan in the performing arts, one of the festival directors invited her to produce a play together with a school.

Despite her lack of experience or education as a playwright and producer, Monirah accepted the challenge. She wrote a play, selected a girls' school, selected the cast, and spent a month rehearsing with them. The school she selected was one for Hazara girls. The festival attracted 21 schools, of which 10 were boys' schools and 11 were girls' schools. The performance venue was quite large; Monirah estimates that the audience comprised more than 2,000 people. When the performers realized that the audience was to be mixed—males and females—none of the students from the other girls' schools wanted to perform. Monirah was not dissuaded, however. The Hazara girls' school was the first to act before a mixed audience, along with the ten boys' schools. The girls' school ended up winning the festival, which allowed Monirah's group to perform in the national theater festival in Kabul as well as in international festivals in India, Turkey, and elsewhere. From then on, Monirah began taking theater more seriously and becoming more involved in it.

Winning the festival in Herat was not a problem-free triumph, however. The outcome created a lot of tension. When the results were announced and Monirah went up to the stage to receive the prize, she heard people in the audience shout "death to Hazara" and "go back to where you came from". She tells me that, at that time, there was societal friction in Herat. Many who lived there expressed the belief that the Hazara did not belong, even if they had lived in Herat for centuries and made up a substantial percentage of the population in the Herat district of Herat province. When Monirah was on the stage, men in the audience, still shouting, started throwing chairs. The threatening atmosphere led Monirah to wonder whether the award was worth this kind of trouble. After waiting a couple of hours in the venue to make sure that tempers had cooled and the audience had gone home, Monirah's group was finally able to leave.

Initially, Monirah recognized that the negative reaction was strongly focused on ethnic identity. It was also likely a response to the play having been directed and performed by women. But in hindsight, Monirah believes that the play's content and its message may have further provoked the outbursts or even been the main cause of them.

> I was thinking that the effect of the work that we have done, the issues that we have been talking about, the play, was nothing…. It was just about women's issues, women's stories. And I used lots of religious texts, lots of religious figures and characters. Female characters from the Koran, and also Muslim figures, female icons, characters, that…when it comes to giving examples of what a good woman is, we often talk about them.
>
> But when we look at the current society, the women that we have now or the women that we want or request now, they are nothing like those women. So there is a big contrast. And I was talking about this contrast. What is our good picture, our ideal picture? And what is it that we are applying and making in the society?
>
> And I could see how it has affected women. Because many of them—like I said in the beginning—those women who had been performing didn't want to

perform in front of men. Whereas in the religious texts, in the religious stories and sayings, it says that female characters spoke publicly, they spoke loudly, and they have been part of the society. In Shia, we have Zainab Kobra, Muhammad's granddaughter, and in Sunni versions of Islam, there is Aysha, Muhammad's wife. So I was talking about this contrast, and I could see that it has been received very well by women. (Hashemi, 2019a)

And yet the play was clearly not well received by all in the audience. The various societal issues that Monirah has sought to address through her artistic performances and creative practice have not always been easy to tackle and have created resistance. Participatory community theater has provided her with another means of creating spaces to discuss these difficult social issues. For her, community theater that was interactive and participatory was a platform that enabled direct contact and communication with the audience. As opposed to the formal theater performances she had participated in, which involved writing a script, directing a play, and then performing it for an audience, community theater offered a much more participatory work method and creative process, which enabled the director, actors, and audience to engage both separately and together in new ways. Monirah explains how certain topics were taboo, and describes community theater as one way of creating space for discussing such topics.

When it comes to talking about or addressing social issues, it's hardly possible to do it through a face-to-face dialogue. Because people hate to talk about their family issues, or violence…Domestic violence is very common, kind of a tradition in many families. They have been doing it for centuries or for decades. And to talk about it would be like interfering in someone's affair, in a family's affair.

But if you put it in the form of performing art, theater, visually on stage, then people can relate to those issues and see the negative aspects of using violence in society, in the family. And then we can, we can actually create lots of moments for discussion, for dialogue, where people can talk about it. Whereas just going to someone whom you know for sure is going through a violent experience...they don't talk about it because it's a personal matter.

But if you see it on the stage, then you see how people are reacting, and it becomes a shared problem. [Most] women are going through the same thing. And then they start dialogue. And then the dialogue is not pointing at a specific person. Everybody is more neutral. Nobody tells his or her story, but people talk about another person, about a neighbor's, a friend's, a relative's story. And everybody knows where those stories are coming from, but it gives them the basis for telling those stories. (Hashemi, 2019a)

Monirah started collaborating with the Bond Street Theatre, a theater company founded in New York in 1976 to work on social justice issues, and now mainly working internationally, teaming up with local theater artists. She used community theater, with its interactive, co-creative methods, as a platform or tool to engage with specific controversial topics that are hard to talk about generally and are taboo in Afghanistan. By performing the plays in schools, shelters for abused women, prisons, and a range of other settings, in ways that are accepted by the community, everyone is welcomed into the conversation. As Monirah explains, she has "always tried to address issues that were very controversial in the society and hard to talk about. And use art and this space in a different way, where you invite everyone to be part of the discussion." (Hashemi, 2019a)

Other elements central to her activities have been training young women to work in theater and film and creating a space for these women both to express themselves and to learn how to deal with challenging situations. In 2006, Monirah started the theater department of Simorgh Film Association of Culture and Art, which she describes as very active initially—"always performing in different places, both for men and women" (Hashemi, 2019a). She also sought to spend more time working with women in both film and theater. At a time when the (international) funding for the arts was focused on projects involving women, Monirah worked a lot with young women. She recalls that, in one of their projects, they had "120 girls making films, doing editing, cinematography, screen writing, directing. And they were taking the cameras, going out, finding locations, shooting outside."

Importantly, these girls received training through courses in acting, filmmaking, and theater, but also in English and in computer use. At this time, Monirah also created a space for the young women in which they could freely express themselves, discuss issues they were facing, and even role-play difficult situations. Monirah recalls long meetings,

> discussing topics and issues and books and ideologies and thoughts and how we can apply those ideologies. How we can change the society. For example, if I am

harassed at the office, if I have been abused at the school, if my female teacher is addressing me in a bad way because I am an actress, how am I going to respond? (Hashemi, 2019a)

I remember many times that my students came and said, "you know, today I had this guy on the street, he was harassing me, and I said this and then I did this…". They were talking, sharing, "no more women harassment". Young girl harassment in the society was a taboo, it brought shame on the girl. They were bringing up the conversation and converting, changing, the victim and the perpetrator. These things were actually practiced, through art form, through theater. (Hashemi, 2019b)

She also notes that some of the girls started in theater when they were still children, between the ages of 9 and 12. These were the ages of the girls involved in the first play that Monirah ever cowrote with children. She let them improvise and decide what they wanted to show on stage. Despite their youth, the girls would raise issues that were highly political. When Monirah expressed her surprise, one of the girls told her, "You know, I have seen my mother's life. I have seen my sister's life. And I prefer we quit the doll…playing with the doll, being cheerful kids in the street at this age. But I would like…to work more seriously now, and to be able to have a different future. Not like my mom, not like my sister. I have to start early rather than have a more unhappy life in the future." (Hashemi, 2019a) Monirah is proud to note that some of the women she trained are still active in the fields of art, culture, and media, and a few are now successful artists in their own right, as photographers, filmmakers, theater producers, or providers of workshops for others. While Simorgh is no longer operational, Monirah's legacy from those years lies in training and mentoring these young women.

(Self-) censorship and facing threats

In Afghanistan, Monirah explored free artistic expression, whether through performances, community theater, or training the next generation of young women, but she did so within the limits of what she considered possible at the time. She always had to take her audience into account and the context in which she performed when deciding how the artistic work could take shape. During the public event at PRIO in Oslo, Monirah explained how she had to try constantly to maintain this balance in her work in Afghanistan between what she wanted to express and what was permissible.

> For me, art always has been a tool for reaching society, for changing the society. But the ethical question […] for me was…not manipulating the stories, but…. In storytelling, we used to do different kinds of work: one was educational—social performances—and the other was professional performances, where we could do performances at a Kabul festival or internationally. So […] our work would be different, completely different, from what we performed in Kabul and in India, for example.
>
> In Kabul, we could not do many things because we were forbidden to. Otherwise, we would put the lives of these young girls at risk. So we had to self-censor. I used to censor my text, my writing, myself, when I was in the process of writing. Then I used to censor myself and my students when we were rehearsing. And then

we would say, "OK, this year we cannot perform at the French Institute's center, then we are going to perform in the Bagh-e Babur Gardens which is open-air. Let's, guys, change this scene."

Where you want to go, where you want to perform, what you want to say, always changes [according to] the circumstances. But the ethical question always remains. And it is about the security, how far we can go. If anything puts your family members, anything puts your students…. Your work might put them in danger. But, I mean, that is the only tool we have. (Hashemi, 2019b)

Within the tight space that was available in Afghanistan, the arts and creative practice still provide more opportunity for critical expression and for challenging societal practices than anything else, Monirah believes. Knowing that her art was the only tool available for some form of free expression, Monirah walked a tightrope: She strove to contribute meaningfully with respect to the issues she cared about without stepping onto the territory of unacceptability. It should be clear, however, that her efforts were not without risk. Whether directing and performing theater plays, creating space for discussion with an audience through community theater, or providing a space where young women learned to express themselves in ways that challenged society, Monirah's creative practices were readily understood as potentially threatening as soon as they were publicly expressed.

Over the years, Monirah was increasingly invited to perform internationally, and in 2012, she was asked to come to Sweden. With her group, she performed a play based on women's narratives about the first Afghan Civil War (1989–1992) at the

Women Playwright International Conference at the Södra Teater in Stockholm.

> We had stories from survival of the civil war…[about] women who have been shut down for years because of what happened to them. They were thinking that what has happened to them is kind of… They didn't actually want to talk about their experience during the civil war, because talking about it would bring shame on their own family. They were thinking, it's not going to solve any issue, it's not going to bring any change, so it's better to keep it inside. But then, I did a series of plays where we focused on women's narratives of the war. What happened with the war, in the war, what happened with women's bodies in the war, how their bodies have been abused in the war by different groups. (Hashemi, 2019a)

Her Swedish hosts asked whether Monirah would permit them to record the performance and share it online, and Monirah agreed. She had performed quite a lot and the government had never reacted to what she was doing. The government does not watch the actions of women, she reasoned, and she liked the idea of being able to share her performance in Sweden with her friends and colleagues who could not see it live. She did not imagine any consequences. But when she returned to Afghanistan, Monirah discovered that both her brother and father had been threatened. Then she herself began facing lots of threats.

> The threats were not only to me and my family; they were also addressed to my students, my colleagues. And they were young girls, very beautiful, innocent

girls, who only wanted to change the society. To change the atmosphere around themselves. To change the mentality of the people, of the society, to let them go out, study, work, and have freedom in the society. That was the only thing they wanted.

But then I noticed that what I'm doing not only puts my family in trouble and danger, but also them. And I know this is a very common thing: That when you see a woman you cannot control, or you cannot make her obey you, or quit something she is doing by threatening that person directly, then…these people start to threaten the family. Because, of course, the family is more precious than you yourself, your body. Because these women in Afghanistan who are working for change at the front line are not thinking about themselves. They have thought that this path will be dangerous, full of threats of death, so they decided that, yeah, they are ready to die any minute. But they don't want their work to put their family in danger, to put their students or colleagues or loved ones in danger. (Hashemi, 2019a)

Monirah first tried to move to other cities in Afghanistan, attempting to live a less visible life, breaking contact with her family, colleagues, and students. But the threats continued. After a year of deliberation, she concluded that she had to leave Afghanistan.

I was thinking that if they do anything to me, the effect that it can have on other women in my society can be huge. The effect that it can have on my students will be huge. I am sure that their families will not let them work in theater and film anymore. I am sure that their families will not let them be involved in art and culture anymore. And I am thinking, "no, I won't let that happen. I won't let it change, because my death is also going to change many women's lives. Not in a positive way, but in a negative way. Because families will also be scared for their own young girls' lives." So I decided to get out. (Hashemi, 2019a)

Monirah is deeply conscious of the significance of her actions. She envisions her death to pose a threat to the wider community she has fostered, possibly leading to the destruction of everything she has worked for in relation to free creative expression. This is one of the reasons why she decided to leave Afghanistan when she could. She contacted Riksteatern in Sweden and other organizations she had been working with, asking for help. Riksteatern invited her back to Sweden, where her project was to be hosted by Riksteatern Varmland in Karlstad. She has been living there ever since.

Free expression in exile: uncovering, telling, and performing her personal story

Since moving to Sweden, Monirah has worked with theater and film in a range of ways, including writing plays for children and adults, acting in an Italian movie, and providing creative workshops for young people. Her artistically most demanding project so far, though, has been a set of monodramas—*Sitahara* (The Stars), and its sequel, *Who lights the stars?*, both written and performed by Monirah and directed by Leif Persson. Monirah originally performed in English, but she now performs in Swedish locally. In April 2021, I conducted a virtual interview with Monirah to fill some gaps in my understanding of her story, especially about how her art has evolved since moving to Sweden and her reflections on the impact of her art.

The interview was emotionally intense for both of us. Monirah had hinted at some key aspects of her story when we met in Oslo in December 2019, but I felt that there were deeper layers that remained untouched at the time—protected behind the mask of the actress. In our virtual conversation more than a year later, she was willing and able to be vulnerable, sharing openly. This was clearly tough for her to do and our conversation was full of long silences. I assumed Monirah was merely pausing telling her story, and I thus waited for her to continue. However, I had sensed in our earlier interviews that Monirah at times lost the thread of her thoughts. In this interview, she revealed that she suffers from severe PTSD (post-traumatic stress disorder) and often loses track of what she was saying. I thus let her talk at her own pace but intervened when I thought that was needed to move the conversation forward.

Beginning our interview by addressing my question about her life in Sweden and the evolution of her art, Monirah almost immediately named the unnameable:

> I remember that I was 11 or 12 years old when I faced sexual abuse, rape. I was angry and I wanted to reveal the perpetrator's identity. But I was only yelling, threatening these people. I would yell that I will tell. The people threatened me, were scared that I would tell. I was beaten and tortured not to tell, but I did not care.

Then my mother said, "your anger will not get you anywhere. It might get you killed, get all of us killed." She asked me to control my anger. She said, "we don't have any power today, no one will believe us. You are now a victim. But one day, you will have power, you will have voice. Now you can't go against it but one day, if you don't talk then that is your decision." I made a promise not to tell, but all that time I promised myself also that one day there will be that platform and I can tell my story.

When I started acting in 2004, I thought I will tell my story. But then, in Afghanistan, no matter how many projects there were on human rights and such, it was not possible. To tell the story, I would have to talk about my childhood, about incest. But there, the father figure is holy; you cannot question the father. Thus, I shifted my approach to the story, and I did talk about women's issues, but from another angle. It was okay to talk about violence in society. This was a good start, as long as we can talk about violence. People accept that violence is going on. But not domestic violence, nothing too personal, and no naming of the perpetrator.

Coming to Sweden, I asked, "how long will I hide myself?" These stories need to be told, the effects of this patriarchal system. I got into a personal crisis and struggle. I hid my story behind the story of other women. But what about my personal story?

[…] This period after coming to Sweden, I have spent to find myself. I was pretending that I was not going to talk anymore, that I had forgotten. From when I made the promise not to let them kill me for telling my story, I thought I was just pretending, but I was actually losing myself. After a long time, I forgot that it was just pretending. (Hashemi, 2021a)

Feelings of deep sorrow and compassion washed over me while Monirah spoke. The interview was emotionally intense for me as well, in that I felt that I had to create a safe space for Monirah to share these deeply traumatic experiences while engaging with my own feelings as well. It was clear to me that it was demanding but also important for Monirah to share these aspects of her story, and I choose simply to listen and be present, with my emotions, in the virtual space we shared.

During this interview I learned just how central Monirah's two monodramas are to her story. *Sitahara* was written in 2014 and performed during a world tour that ended in 2019. *Who lights the stars?* was written in January 2020 and, due to the global lockdown, has so far only been performed and recorded without an audience. The first play tells the stories of several Afghan women at different points in Afghan history, whereas in the second, Monirah tells her own story. In what follows, I will present selected parts of these plays in order to explore Monirah's story in greater depth.

Sitahara: the personal is deeply political

It doesn't matter what forms of violence is going on, they are of course connected. But one thing that is shared: they all need to be told; they all need to be talked about. All forms of violence need to be talked about. (Hashemi, 2021a)

Sitahara moves between different time periods in Afghanistan. Gul Begum tells the story of losing her family and becoming enslaved in 1892, during the war that followed the second Hazara uprising against Abdul-Rahman Khan, the emir of Afghanistan. The uprising was put down and the inhabitants of Hazarajat were displaced, enslaved, or murdered. Sara's story, which Monirah performed in Oslo (as described at the start of the chapter), takes place in Kabul during the civil war of 1989–1992. This is after Soviet forces withdrew from the country and the mujahideen— who received support from the United States as part of the Cold War dynamics of the time—engaged in plunder and murder. As in the story of Gul Begum, the fighters believe that their victims are heathens, nonbelievers who deserve no mercy; this forms the justification for their rape, abuse, and murder.

The play comprises stories told by different characters, including a narrator, the women themselves, and their male perpetrators. The stories are conveyed verbally and through the expressiveness of Monirah's face and body, dances, and songs. The women's stories are all unique but also similar in many ways despite being set in different periods and contexts. The narrator, in the middle of telling the women's stories, reflects:

> All these untold stories, who is going to tell them? In the current situation, when religion goes into politics, the male interpretation of it, women's world becomes smaller and more violent. Meanwhile men find larger space to parade and more religious interpretations that legitimize their actions. Today, religion is a tool to further the anger of men, to satisfy the lust of men. A

women's world doesn't experience anything but men's anger and lust. (Hashemi, 2014)

The play starts and ends with the story of Halima. Although it is not placed temporally or geographically, the story seems to take place in recent times. It is not about violence during war, but rather about violence committed against women in the domestic sphere. Halima, who has been sentenced to death by stoning because of an extramarital affair, speaks about a wide range of abuses, sexual and otherwise, that she has suffered at the hands of close male relatives, religious men, and strangers. She did not have an extramarital affair. Rather, she was raped by the son of the man she had been married off to by her father, who had also had an incestuous relationship with her. Thrice abused, she was then sentenced to death by a mullah who, she knows, abuses children sexually.

Sitahara raises many questions about the patterns and underlying causes of the severe abuses experienced by the featured women at the hands of different men in various phases of Afghanistan's history. It raises for me the issue of interlinkages and the similarities and the differences between war-related violence and domestic violence. When I ask Monirah to reflect on this, she is silent for a long time, sighing and thinking. Then she says:

> The problem is that when you talk about violence against women, domestic violence, the definition of violence is completely different there. They don't see these kinds of things as violence. I don't know, probably there are many different reasons and elements to how a society can define violence but [silence followed by a sigh] ...but this mentality that...the whole situation

women are living in, with all these rules and all these
things going on, that is not really defined as violence.
(Hashemi, 2021a)

She comes back to this point later, reflecting on her childhood,
during which violent incidents were common in the household
and she learned to recognize them as violence—thanks to her
mother—whereas others did not.

We had to talk quite a lot about violence and what
violence is. On my paternal side, for them, slapping
or kicking a child or sending him or her to work—
these things were not violence. They were part of an
education system or training or letting the kids get a
little bit tough. But my mother, from childhood, she
was talking about what counts as violence. Everything
that makes someone sad, every word that you say that
makes the other person sad, feel bad about himself or
herself, physically have pain, I don't know, mentally, she
was talking quite a lot about everything.
[…] I think the way that Mom brought us up helped
us all in a way to get a clear understanding of this, and
how we can decide or choose to not be part of that.
[Sighs] And I think it is, it is [silence] Making different
kind of violence visible, I think, that was part of my
work since I was in Afghanistan. Yeah, different forms
of violence. But I think it is also very important to make
[sighs, silence]…to make these discussions a little bit
wider in the society. Of course, we, the whole country,
are talking about violence now. But it doesn't mean
that in a country like Afghanistan, where we have a kind

of war going on, the Taliban sitting at the negotiation table and [trails off]. When it comes to violence, we cannot prioritize. We cannot say only this part of violence concerns the whole society or, I don't know, the well-being of society or country. We cannot ignore the violence against women that is going on.

[…] We cannot silence half of the society. And it is like we are silencing women, we are silencing children. When it comes to the government, we do not have any plan to develop a better society, we have no tolerance. But at the same time, we want to be…we want to attain peace in our society. But peace is not going to happen when we silence half of the society, when we have no tolerance towards their stories. So for me nothing makes sense as long as women's narratives are not included. (Hashemi, 2021a)

Sitahara also includes men's narratives, as told by the characters of the mullah and a mujahideen fighter, both of whom justify their abuse of women and their use of extreme violence. But the absurd form of the narratives—both are voiced by Monirah— keeps the focus on the implications for women of their abuse and invites the audience to condemn their narratives. The reactions to Monirah's performances are mixed, however. Not everyone is willing or able to listen to the stories without experiencing great discomfort or dismissing them as lies. Monirah reflects on how the play challenges conventions and common social practices in Afghanistan.

We have created this kind of cultural structure, system, way, to—from the very beginning—make the victim believe that it is her fault. But I think through telling, through talking about our experience, we can also create a tolerance in the society to just listen. I know it is very weird, it is very uncomfortable for a patriarchal society that has only listened to men. Where religious figures define how a woman should be, what she should wear, what she should eat, to whom she should talk. We are used to hearing all this nonsense from a male figure, all this nonsense we are used to hearing from a man, but we are not used to hearing a story from a woman, especially, in our context, on the stage in an art form.

And I have noticed, I have realized, that when you talk about certain experiences—women's experiences—this feeling of discomfort in men makes them to either make some cow's noise [mooing], or just leave the audience, because it is too much for them. It is too much. And I think if we just hear the women's narratives, the women's stories, hearing [them] is too much. You cannot just sit there and listen or watch how we, by our silence, by defending the way, system of thinking, religion…how we are supporting the society to do these things to women, to children. And I think, for me, storytelling is not only empowering women, but it is also helping the society in developing a tolerance towards women's experiences.

[…] We don't have to share everything, but we need to—in order to find ourselves—we need to make sense of our narrative, we need to make sense of our stories. And that is only happening by telling, by creating tolerance. If the society is tolerant towards the stories, towards women's narratives, then probably I would not feel this obligation to talk at all. But as long as that doesn't exist, I think that's become my obligation, because I have come to this awareness that women are abused and exploited... I see it as a moral duty to talk about it. (Hashemi, 2021a)

Through *Sitahara*, Monirah aims to tell women's stories in theatrical form not just to encourage the telling of these stories, but also to train society to hear them. The extreme abuse that forms part of women's experiences creates strong emotional reactions that also raise questions about the responsibility of those who witness the play and at times, have also seen the original violence. Storytelling through theater allows Monirah to lift these real-life experiences out of their ordinary context so that they can be recognized as less than ordinary and thus less than acceptable.

One way that Monirah achieves this is by mixing temporal events and by combining other people's stories and her own personal experiences. What emerges, she argues, is a meeting of the present and the past, which reveals how events repeat themselves over time, how abuses are repeated. When she performs past women's experiences, Monirah says, she is criticizing the current situation in Afghanistan and allowing people to recognize themselves in performances. To Monirah, there is a kind of game involved in which she asks herself questions and then answers the questions, and then must hide her answers in her performances. The most important aim of *Sitahara*, I assume, is to trigger individuals in the audience to reflect critically and honestly about society and their own roles in it. In a way, Monirah thus takes women's stories out of the private, domestic sphere and puts them squarely in the public sphere, shifting them from being simply the private affairs of individual men (and women) to being the public responsibility of all those "witnessing" the play and the stories it tells.

Who lights the stars?

In *Who lights the stars?*, Monirah tells her own story through various story lines that take the audience back and forth between different periods in her life. Although there is a heaviness to the play due to the dark story it tells, there is also considerable beauty in the different art forms through which the story is told. *Who lights the stars?* starts and ends with a Tai chi-like dance, providing serene bookends for the disturbing material in between. At the most intense parts of the story, music accompanies the acting, and in the course of her performance, Monirah reveals two paintings and uses the shawls that cover them in her acting. She also uses other clothes hanging on the stage, draping them around her body as she assumes different characters. With only these few simple props, in addition to a broad range of facial and bodily expressions and various movements across the whole stage, Monirah tells her story through a variety of characters and perspectives.

The story includes very personal revelations about the extreme abuse Monirah and her family experienced. Monirah is open about the fact that the story is her own and that, by telling it, she no longer "hides behind the stories of other women". When she welcomes the audience, she introduces herself in order to explain why her storytelling evolved as it did in recent years:

> My name is Monirah. Monirah Hashemi. I am a storyteller.
> I tell stories about people that I know or used to know.

Not revealing to whom the stories belong, I give details about the environment, class, social condition, the tension, background, and the history. "How do I know all of these when they are not my stories?", you may ask. "How am I to know them so well, as if I was there when they were happening? How the hell do I know the exact feeling, smell, and taste of fear, blood, hate, revenge, salvation, redemption, or liberation?" I asked myself that too. (Hashemi, 2021c)

Before she unspools her own story, Monirah ends her introduction with reflections on how her own account has been long hidden even from herself:

Memory is so amazing, isn't it? Through manipulation—as a survival technique—it helps us normalize our own feelings, our understanding of ourselves and the people around us. Makes us to accept! To accept "what has happened".

And talking helps. It helps to find the parts which have been suppressed. We talk and talk and each time we come to those flickering blurred pieces, the memory releases a little bit of what has been locked for so long. The more we talk, the more we encourage the memory to unleash the new images. To understand that it's ok now. To understand I am going to be fine.

And now, let's open the door and let you into my story. (Hashemi, 2021c)

After Monirah as storyteller has welcomed the audience, the play starts with a conversation between the woman of the story and a Swedish woman working at a helpline who learns that the caller has remembered something and now plans to throw herself out of a window. Monirah as storyteller moves between this scene and various stories from her childhood living with her family in Iran and, for a short period, in Pakistan. She repeatedly cuts off the story when her memories become too painful. She describes the fight between different "storytellers", or versions of herself, who argue about the value of telling this story. A skeptical version exclaims, "When has talking resolved anything?" As the many dark details of the story are slowly revealed, this skeptical version despairs.

> My heart beats fast. I am certain of my death and I feel the trembling in my bones and veins. If I open my mouth, I will not survive. It's going to kill me. I'll be crushed, ground, shattered like a broken glass that can never be repaired. I won't be able to put myself together, ever again. I am acquainted with faking myself. I have learned how to stand up when my whole body screams in extreme pain. I know how to smile when tears flow inside me. I know nothing about a world, where everyone knows everything about me. Me! That's an unknown world. It's dark, cold, and I know nothing about people there. (Hashemi, 2021c)

As the story continues, memories are revealed one by one, one small piece at a time. In one key scene, Monirah as storyteller describes meeting a fortune-teller in Iran, who identifies her as an outlaw, a rebel, someone who will always fight. In another, the narrator recalls being very young, maybe five, and running from her father in fear; when her mother protects her, her father lashes out with an axe and slashes her mother's watch from her wrist. The story moves back and forth in time, connecting the episodes through associations or memories. Monirah as storyteller is at one point in a Swedish psychiatric hospital with her sister visiting her. Monirah's sister looks at a painting Monirah has made of a large head with the face turned sideways that reminds her sister of a scene of severe abuse from their childhood. Her sister says, "This picture reminds me of that day; you on the floor, in your blood, you were exactly this. You were painless. You were dead." (Hashemi, 2021c). In the hospital, the staff suggest that she use lighter colors in the painting, and the storyteller says "What can one say? Can you share anything other than your own?" (Hashemi, 2021c).

The storyteller then recalls a scene from childhood, when she was 11 and her mother was away, giving birth, and her father raped her. She tells the audience, "The painting is me, numb, crushed, dead. You know the moment of silence. When…you don't see anything. You don't hear anything. You don't feel anything. You are suspended, flying around, hovering at the edges of air and soil." (Hashemi 2021c). When the women in the family go to the police and the mullah, they are ridiculed, berated, and sent away. Monirah develops an intense anger about what has happened. The storyteller learns that her anger is dangerous; it can kill her and her family, and so she needs to forget, for now. Then, the fortune-teller reappears and says:

> You have this anger inside you. So deep. You like to be disobedient. To destroy. To burn all the bridges and all that is sacred. Question. You question and you do all that you are forbidden to do. You will be famous one day. You'll become a writer! One day you will become a famous writer. (Hashemi, 2021c)

And the storyteller remembers her younger self hearing the fortune-teller's prophecies.

> I wanted to yell at him, what do you know about me? I don't want to be a writer. What the hell can a writer do? I want to be a police officer, arrest my father and put him in the prison. I want to be a prosecutor to bring him to justice. I want to be a judge and sentence him to exile, to death, and eternal annihilation. What the hell can a writer do? (Hashemi, 2021c)

What a writer can do is tell the story, and by the end of the play, the storyteller who has become the dominant one is the one who believes in the transformative power of storytelling. This narrator reveals important parts of her story, giving voice as well as bodily expression to key events, allowing the audience to witness not just the storyteller's trauma but also her incredible strength. Monirah as storyteller is able to make this shift from trauma to healing when her mother says to her, "You are completely your own, so live. Live like all women wish they could live their lives." (Hashemi, 2021c).

> I hear Mom, over and over again. Madar! Why do you worry so much my dear? You need to remember that you also fought, and you changed the situation. You brought us all here, safe and sound. No one is dead, or had their nose or ears chopped off. We are not physically injured, and we can always heal our wounded souls. Purify and clean them. From now on, we build our own past! Together with family and friends, we build our own history. (Hashemi, 2021c)

The ingenious ways that Monirah, in this play, uses the tools available to her through theater, moves me profoundly, as does her incredible strength in telling and performing her story. At the same time, seeing Monirah suffer on stage in a way that appears to be authentic rather than performative, causes me deep discomfort. After watching the play, I cry for a long time, both distraught over the reality that human beings hurt each other in terrible and interconnected ways as well as moved by the incredible internal power that telling this story required.

Trauma and storytelling

During our follow-up interview, when Monirah reveals that her father sexually abused her and talks about her new play, which discusses incest, I ask her how she found the courage to share such a dark story.

> It is really awful. Sometimes, I think I just don't have the language, I don't know how to talk about it. I know it's very…it is difficult… But I think it's along all the other ways of surviving, struggling, and finding your way… There is a way also to be able to take control, which is probably new to me but, yeah, it is very difficult. And sometimes it is… [breaks off] When you do it in a very theatrical art form, give this kind of structure to a story which is very dark, very uncomfortable…it is another way….
>
> But I think sometimes it also feels like torturing yourself. But I think…. I think it is time, at least for me personally, that I need to acknowledge that this has happened, and this is happening, and if there is a way that I can contribute anything to at least make this issue visible

a little bit in the society, talk about it, then I will take all this hard time and horror and all these hard moments for me to do it because…. I think that is because I made myself a promise when I was a child, whatever I do…. [trails off] Talking about women's experiences has been something that I came to realize from early childhood that is missing and that is very important to highlight. (Hashemi, 2021a)

Who lights the stars? illuminates the mismatch between women's need to tell their stories and society's ability to listen. As Monirah said when discussing *Sitahara*, "storytelling is not only empowering women but it is also helping the society in developing a tolerance towards women's experiences" (Hashemi, 2021a). These stories, then, help the larger society learn to listen. This combined need—to tell stories and to develop a tolerance to hear them—is central, it seems to me, to both individual and collective healing. However, a scene in *Who lights the stars?*, which shows Monirah's interaction with the Swedish psychiatric system, reveals the professional mental health service as lacking the willingness or capacity to listen. After being diagnosed as a threat to herself, Monirah is hospitalized. Within the formal professional, expert space of the hospital, there was no room for the human interaction that would help Monirah process trauma. The storyteller describes a nightmare she, the patient, had in the hospital about her father. A nurse comes, asking what she wants.

Patient: I had a nightmare, a horrible dream.

Nurse-assistant: What medicine do you need?

Patient: I don't know! I need someone to talk to….

Nurse-assistant: I'll talk to the night shift nurse and come back.

When the nurse-assistant returns with medication, the patient says:

> I don't think I need any pills. I had a nightmare and need to talk to someone. I am scared! I see things. Can't sleep! I can't…
>
> Storyteller: There was no point in saying all of that. He [her father, in her nightmare] was gone. Even if he had remained, she [the nurse] was not going to see, to understand. She has never been equipped with a pair of understanding ears that could listen to the nightmares of the night without judging. (Hashemi, 2021c)

In the hospital, Monirah realized that she must talk if she is to survive. After her release, she called on three close colleagues, all male, to listen to her tell her story. Monirah and her colleagues came together for a series of seven or eight sessions, some taped, during which she unspooled her story, talking directly to them and partly to herself. These storytelling sessions provided the basis for *Who lights the stars?* When I ask Monirah how she developed the strength to do something so incredibly difficult, she first describes one of her last performances of *Sitahara*. Only after having staged the play over one hundred times was she finally able to perform it without suffering.

> Where do I get the power to do it? [Silence] I don't know, but one thing I'm sure of is that I still do believe what my mom said that "if one day you gain a chance for your own voice and the power, that day you should drag the perpetrator down. If you don't do that…."

Because I had this feeling of guilt all my life when I was a kid. She would say, "you are not the guilty party here. But if one day, probably, if you grow up and you get the power and if you stay silent, then you can feel some guilt about yourself because then you have the choice, you have the freedom to…." She always used to say "drag down", drag down the perpetrators. "When you can do it, then do it. Don't hesitate because of who the perpetrator is, don't think about the relationship, think about what is going on in the name of this relationship, in the name of religion. How the society is abusive to women, towards children." So I think all of my mother's words through these years—to keep me alive… [sigh]…. are still with me.

And I do believe in them. I do believe that, no matter the relationship, the biological relationship of this man to me, it doesn't matter. If I am not able to talk about one perpetrator that destroyed my childhood, that destroyed my youth, if I am not able to talk about him, then I am not able to talk about this violence which is going on in the whole country, whole society. Because they are all connected to each other. So I think [long silence]…. Um…. I don't know where this courage comes from, but I think it has something to do with my mom. (Hashemi, 2021a).

Another stage in Monirah's journey relates to the public nature of her storytelling and the audience with whom she shares her story. When she started performing *Sitaraha* in the spring of 2014, first in Sweden and later internationally, Monirah hesitated to perform for Afghan audiences because of the conditions under which she had had to leave the country. She instructed her director to make sure the play was not advertised to Afghans, but one day, the venue had done so against her instructions. Monirah's audience was made up mostly of Afghans.

> So I was stressed. Because they were going to see their histories on the stage. And I was thinking, "Oh God, if one of them thinks I am lying, what will happen?" There were lots of things, and then my director said, "Okay, I can see from your face that we are going to cancel. Either we are going to cancel the performance, or we are not going to let Afghans come in." But I said, "Both of them have consequences, so let's …let's do this" (Hashemi, 2019b).

After the performance, Monirah's director came and told Monirah that there were two elderly women waiting outside to meet her. She decided to go to them, and they were wearing traditional Hazaragi clothes, scarves, and makeup; they were Hazara like Monirah herself. When she approached the women, one of them hugged her, and she said, in the Hazaragi language, "You almost got us killed".

> And [voice trembling] …that was very tough for me. That was actually very tough for me, that day. I had… […] prohibited a group of people who have been… systematically…killed and… [trails off] We went through different genocides, but, then I had contested these people's…right to see their history on the stage. So I…I really hated myself that time. (Hashemi, 2019b)

The realization that she had been refusing to perform stories to those to whom they mattered most pained Monirah. Since then, she has made sure that Afghans are invited to her plays. As she points out, the personal stories she tells are unique, but at the same time they are common stories of violence, abuse, and oppression that are rooted in structures that affect millions of people. Allowing Afghans to engage with these stories supports processes of individual as well as collective healing.

Questioning and challenging the status quo

As I reflect on Monirah's stories, I realize that throughout her life, she has persistently questioned the status quo, particularly with respect to the position of women in society. Doing this publicly can be emotionally challenging and possibly dangerous, as Monirah's story shows. In Afghanistan, Monirah felt she constantly had to make choices about how to tell certain stories so as not to endanger the young women with whom she worked. And yet she also was driven to keep asserting herself through her artistic practice, ultimately aiming to contribute to change. Underlying her desire to express herself freely was often a wish to question realities, openly and publicly, to refuse to be quiet when others were. Monirah's mother had taught her never to stay silent or to be ashamed of what happened to her, but to resist by telling her story. Monirah indicates that her mother was not the only one sharing this message with her children.

> So there are lots of women like this, who are doing the same thing. Whispering in their children's ears: "Go on and be a different person." Whether [their children are boys or girls], they give them other options, other alternatives while they are living a traditional life, while they are practicing that traditional life they

have. Because they know that they cannot go against the tradition, against the system at once. But they are making sure that their children are not going to experience…that exact life. (Hashemi, 2019a)

When I note at one point that her mother is a remarkable woman, Monirah considers how her mother came to be who she is. Later, she cites her grandmother as someone who may have inspired her mother.

> My grandmother, mother's side, she was not afraid of talking the truth. She was telling the truth in different forms. If she could stand and confront the party who was the abuser or liar […] she would do it. If that was harmful or that was dangerous, she would take another approach. She […] had a community of women who could share everything between themselves. And I think that is probably what Mom also had learned. To create a circle of trust, by sharing and also…trying to find…I don't know—[to] somehow empower each other by talking. (Hashemi, 2021a)

Thus, Monirah's tendency to question and challenge can be placed in the context of these strong women in her family, who, under very constrained conditions, still managed to find the space to speak up and thus resist, while also being careful precisely because speaking up was dangerous. Furthermore, these women envision change as something that takes more than one generation; they are fighting for their children to live under better circumstances. Monirah, once in exile, is in a better position to fight for her own generation, for change in the present. Yet doing so requires her to learn to share deeply traumatic private experiences with others, and at the same time to think very carefully about the negative impact her work might have.

Countering narratives and lighting stars in dark spaces

One of the key ways that Monirah questions the status quo is by telling stories not commonly heard in society, either in Afghanistan or in an international context. During our conversations, Monirah provides examples of common forms of storytelling that she believes misrepresent reality or leave unexpressed significant aspects of people's experiences. She clearly sees her artistic practice as contributing to alternative storytelling, whether through performing a one-woman theater piece in a large theater in Stockholm or developing participatory community theater in a school in a small village in Afghanistan.

In the public seminar at PRIO in Oslo, Monirah describes her wish to use her art to tell "different kinds of narrations" (Hashemi, 2019b). She has a keen desire to create a counternarrative to common depictions of Afghanistan, and in particular, of Afghan women. She does not recognize herself in the mainstream narratives, but more importantly, these narratives do not tell the stories of the resistance and the power she observed in women during her life in Afghanistan. As has Monirah, I have been occupied for years with the partiality of dominant narratives. And like her, I find deeply problematic the invisibility of both everyday resistance to structural conditions and the powerful consciousness displayed by people in deeply disadvantaged positions. Monirah describes how she does field research for her art, which involves listening to the stories of (elderly) women and men and using their stories to inspire her artistic practice.

> I call myself storyteller. So I would really like to go and find, see, the differences, the different kind of narrations which exist […]. For me those aspects are very interesting, those aspects that haven't actually been brought up in the media, in the literature, in the history books, that haven't been captured by researchers or academics.
>
> My inspiration is mostly these stories that we have in the society. And there are lots of them. […] It's like…. You will see the violence, as Westerners, but you don't see the resistance, you don't see the struggle. And that's the part when you… In understanding something, we miss some information. I was always seeing all this resistance in the society from our women, in different fields, in different forms, on different levels. But then in the media, we just have these posts without any self-determination. Afghan women under the burka, *chadaree*, always crying and begging for mercy. But that is not actually their story. The essence of the fight and the resistance exists in every woman, and they perform it differently according to the situation. (Hashemi, 2019b)

Through her art, her theater, and public engagements like her seminar at PRIO, Monirah attempts to create alternative images, especially about Afghan women. She wants to change the single narrative that exists about Afghan women and Muslim women, more generally. This, she believes, is a crucial contribution she can make with her artistic practice outside Afghanistan.

> I dedicated myself to change that single narration. I believe that Afghan women are not victims. They refuse to be victims. They are rebels. They are fighting, and they have been fighting, actually, all their lives. But we…we don't see that fight because we have a standard for that. We have…a standard for fighting, struggling, going against norms. And those things which do not fit within our standards, we don't recognize them. And I would like to say that the fight of Afghan women is real, and we have to recognize it. And we have to accept and respect that they don't want us to look at them as victims, because they don't, they don't look at themselves as victims. They don't live like victims, they are fighters. And they've always been fighters.
>
> […] Talking about women's rights, women's issues, is not one thing we can understand. There are different elements that intersect and they form women's lives. This needs to be highlighted, this needs to be mentioned and talked about. After acknowledging and recognizing that Afghan women are not these poor victims, then we can start the real discussion. And then we can negotiate and then we can see how we can change the society. But as long as you put me on the other side of the table saying "you poor thing, I am here to defend you", nothing is going to change in the society. Because we are not equal, at this table. (Hashemi, 2019a)

By telling alternative stories about women in Afghanistan, Monirah aims to show the many nuances of these women's varied experiences and realities. When I write to Monirah for the first time, to ask her if I may share her story in my book, telling her why I want to write the book, she gladly agrees and further explains why she thinks it is important to share nuanced stories:

> It seems that, as artists with refugee and Muslim backgrounds, our work is not valued based on its artistic expression but rather seen as a reference to the "victimization" of certain groups, at the same time strengthening the cultural, regional, and religious misogynistic ideology which exists. What I am tired of is that stories coming from across the water are generalized to the whole community. Rather than viewing these experiences as social behaviors and phenomena, they become politicized and are used as tools against a particular group. This is limiting, restraining an artist who, fearing wrong interpretations, chooses silence. (Hashemi, 2020a)

And yet Monirah does not remain silent, continuing to tell complex stories that offer alternative ways of understanding social realities in Afghanistan and elsewhere. Doing so is important because women's stories are commonly silenced in Afghan society, even in the private sphere of their homes.

> When my mother talked about her childhood, my father would constantly correct her, even though they had not met then and were not even in the same place. The male figures in the family, whether the father or the husband, have the right to tell the story of the

women but also to manipulate the story, fix it. I did not want that to happen to me. I promised myself as a kid that when I will grow up, I will tell it. My experience is unique, growing up in a patriarchal society with an abusive father, both physical and sexual. But there are also collective aspects: religion is a tool to control women and their bodies.

I have felt like this from the beginning, when I came to be an actress. But now I have made a clear decision. This is happening in Afghanistan: sexual abuse happens to children. In Afghanistan, religious thought helps to silence and ignore it. I feel it is upon my shoulders because I do not want this to happen to others. My work becomes a statement: I am a survivor of sexual abuse and trauma, but that is not who I am. I have this experience, but also the will and courage to talk about it. My objective is to start a discussion in the family, breaking the silence. For so long, women's stories have been silenced. If we want to change patriarchal society, but we close the doors to women's stories, how will we change it? If we think it will bring dishonor to the country, the nation, the religion, we are not able to do it. (Hashemi, 2021a)

Monirah talks about a feeling of responsibility that stems from her not wanting others to experience what happened to her. But she also stresses that telling her story is important not just because it draws attention to the abuse and violence that is happening in Afghanistan, but also because by telling it, she is refusing to be defined by her personal trauma. In a follow-up interview to discuss a draft of this chapter, Monirah explains how she realized in the hospital that she had to stop telling a "weaker" version of reality because it meant that she was betraying herself as a child, "that little girl, whose dream was to share, to tell what happened" (Hashemi, 2021b). She asserts that she had become too conservative in hiding essential parts of her personal story, covering up the biggest trauma. She argues how she needs to focus on her own personal healing before she can fully address her sense of duty to prevent the trauma that was inflicted on her from happening to anyone else. And yet, it is this larger purpose that allows her to push herself in the way she does. This is an important and recurring topic in our conversations. Storytelling helps her to process her trauma; the sense of responsibility the storytelling engenders is what gives this processing meaning in the first place.

When I ask Monirah how she has become strong enough to tell her personal story as she does now, through the play, *Who lights the stars?*, Monirah refers again to her mother's teachings.

> And I think she somehow made me understand this from early childhood, that it is our action, it is our words that can create circumstances, can create situations, change situations. So for me, if my words and talking about this silence, this cultural silence within religious Islamic countries, societies, I think …I don't know… But yeah, I think it is my mom's teaching that made me believe that, as a person or as a woman who has access to some platform, to some resources, then I do believe that it is my duty to bring up this discussion. (Hashemi, 2021a)

For Monirah, theater and storytelling can create safe spaces for women to talk about their experiences. This is necessary as long as women lack such spaces in society, and as long as the narratives heard are those that others tell about them, one of the many ways that women's experiences are silenced. This is exactly what *Who lights the stars?* is about. Being a storyteller, Monirah wants to shed light in dark spaces, to illuminate the many hidden, ignored, or silenced stories, from the perspective of women themselves and, more specifically, from her own perspective.

The role of marginalized outsiders

In creating counternarratives to mainstream narratives, marginalized outsiders often play a key role. Monirah's sense of being an outsider arose at a very young age, when she was growing up as an Afghan in Iran. She describes many instances and everyday realities, from the most mundane interactions to clear red lines and restrictions, that drove home to her that she and others like her were outsiders in Iran, tolerated at best.

> I remember once I bought some vegetables, which were a little bit expensive at that time. I don't know the English name, but it's *karafs* (celery), and it's not very expensive, but you can make very good food with it. Very delicious food. And I have the vegetables in my hands and am coming home…and then I see people calling, "Oh, Afghans also eat *karafs*, so funny".
> And I mean, there were lots of stereotypes, clichés, places you could not go. You could not go to any park, because Afghans were not allowed to go to those parks. You could not study. And you could not be the

person you wanted to be. Even though there were a few people who could go to university, they could not study whatever they wanted. (Hashemi, 2019a)

Monirah also explains that, although she and other Afghan refugees had green cards that allowed them to travel freely in the city, the police would sometimes still take them into custody or to a refugee camp. This created a fundamental uncertainty that affected them more deeply than all the explicit restrictions they faced.

> So these issues we talked about a lot within the family, because it was not only issues like, "Okay, I faced this kind of racist behavior and treatment today", or "this person, I heard the child of this family has been kicked out of school". We heard every day that people went missing, like young boys are missing, men of the family, the head person is missing. They depend [trails off] …. [T]hat person is the only one who is going to work and have an income, and when they don't exist and nobody knows where they are, the whole family is… not functioning anymore, because there is no work, there is no money, there is no income. So that was the issue.
>
> […] And I was thinking, I believed, that there is no good person in Iran. There is no one who is not affected by this…. Or simply to say, everybody's racist there. But then when I moved back to Afghanistan, social media became more popular, more accessible, Internet and everything, and I heard different stories about Iranian people…. So yeah, one thing at that time was, of course, the media, the media was controlled by the

government. They were only trying to give a single story. They always wanted the society, the people, the nation, to believe that [the reason] why the society, why the economy is not working, is the refugees. Because we have too many refugees. If they were not here, the employment rate would be less, we would have more opportunities for our own people. (Hashemi, 2019a)

When Monirah talks about her degrading experiences as a refugee in Iran and how they affected her choices later in life, she says:

I mean, there is something when you're living [laughs], when you're living with lots of…limitations, and when you are living…well, you are always at the margins, outside of a group. Like I lived in Iran. I was born in Iran, and I always thought I speak the language as fluently as everybody else there. And I knew the culture, and I knew the history of Iran. But yet I never became part of that. And then when you are under so much oppression and pressure that you struggle every day, for every single thing […]. Then everything that you don't know becomes so precious, becomes so far beyond reach. (Hashemi, 2019a)

When her family returned to Afghanistan, they were hoping to escape these everyday challenges. But in Afghanistan, Monirah was also an outsider. This was partly because her family settled in the west, in Herat, where the Hazara were a minority. Although the second civil war had ended a few years before, ethnic animosities were still common there. Monirah describes the challenges she faced not only as a woman but also, and more specifically, as a young Hazara woman, as she started working as an artist in Herat.

> I was the only Hazara girl in 2004 who was working with a group of people from outside my own community or ethnicity. So that created lots of issues and problems at that time,…threats that were coming from my community—"You cannot work with these people"—and I also became the subject of sexual harassment and such [from my colleagues]. (Hashemi, 2019a)

The issue of her identity became particularly pronounced and even dangerous when her group won the theater festival prize in Herat in 2006. This, according to Monirah, was highly sensitive politically.

> A Hazara girl, or a group from a minority which should not live in a part of the country—they have won the prize…. [T]hat can make a group of people angry. But then, then I decided that I would focus more on theater, so that I can…work directly with the society. With those groups of people that have less, or probably no access to information. And then we can use theater as a platform where we can discuss issues which are…not common to talk about publicly, or in a very traditional way, in Afghanistan. (Hashemi, 2019a)

Here, as she has before, Monirah has both described the challenges she faced as an outsider and also explained that these challenges encouraged her to continue in theater, a new endeavor, which offered her a way to discuss and share information with the community. Thus, being marginalized in several different ways seems to have driven Monirah's work and the direction it has taken over the years. And yet, her marginalized position has also complicated the potential impact of her storytelling, as she must consider how and when to perform her new play and tell her personal story.

> I know it will be really hard for me, especially in this time now. I think you're following the news in Afghanistan on all this peace negotiation with all these kinds of conflicts and this civil war that people are talking about is coming back again. This situation actually makes it really horrible to talk about this experience because women have been—or women's stories, women's bodies have been—kind of filled with the war all these years in Afghanistan.
>
> And now anything…especially when it comes to minorities, any kind of discussion which goes out now about a specific ethnic group, especially women, it's going to be really problematic because unfortunately we still are living in this division, ethnical division of Hazara, Pashtun, Tajik. And if a woman from the Hazara community comes and says, "I had this experience, I am going to talk about incest relations, I am going to talk about child sexual abuse" and all these kinds of things, that would be characteristic, or it would be defined, interpreted as a characteristic, for the minority, for the Hazara, for the Shia group, for I don't know, all these things. My concern now is: Do I as a woman talk about my experience and ignore what other consequences it might have, what other? …. Or just…sacrifice and wait. How long should we wait? (Hashemi, 2021a)

Monirah's reflections suggest that, although people in marginalized positions may more easily see the problematic nature of a dominant narrative, they at the same time face challenges if they try to offer a new narrative. Rather than being seen as reflecting the diversity of perspectives and thus as a counter to single narratives, the "new story" maybe misinterpreted to represent a fixed reality for a whole group or be deliberately misused in an essentializing and reductionist way. Thus, Monirah finds sharing her painful stories to be difficult in part because of the many negative and reductionist responses she expects, based on experiences in the past.

> But I think eventually that they cannot put me in that trap of feeling guilty and making me silent. Because I think that is another way of silencing women. To blame them for whatever is going on. […] Silencing women shows itself in different forms; you always need to make the woman feel guilty. If I talk about my childhood, I Iazara people will be accused of something. If I talk generally about Afghanistan history, I will be accused of dishonoring the national honor of Afghanistan. So many different sorts of accusations, so many different sorts of violence, pressure. But I think, that aside, I look at them as something that makes me learn. Because I would fall into this trap, I was trying to wait and was thinking…one year, two years, three years. I think they were quite successful in making me step into that trap. But realizing it's another form of violence, another form of silencing, then I can make another decision, then I can take another approach. I can choose another way to talk around this topic

without…. creating more sensitivity, especially in this situation in which we are right now. (Hashemi, 2021b)

The transformative potential of art

When I ask Monirah whether she believes that her art has created change for herself or others, she reflects in detail about a range of effects that she thinks her artistic work has had—for herself, her family, and society.

> Through my work I have seen the effects, in Afghanistan. […] I had different strategies, plans, but my first intention was to create a safe space for women, where they are not sexually abused, physically abused. So that they can just come, earn the trust of the family. All these things were my intention. And then, now when I am following my students back in Afghanistan, I can see how patient, how understanding, how careful they are when it comes to women's stories. It doesn't matter whether they are men or women—of course we had lots of students, both men and women— but those who were involved with this art, with theater, they really have been affected. […]
>
> I had a mother who was very wise, who was always giving very useful counsel…. But also, it was after we started doing film and theater, after 2004, that it gave both courage and voice to every member of my family…. We were a family of five girls and two boys and, of course, growing up in a very traditional system, there were many things first of all that I was not aware that I can do. I didn't know that they exist. […] Theater, the

effect for me was that it helped me, maybe not to see myself as a whole, but it helped me to see part of me. And I think it has created or given these feelings, this sense of finding oneself, to many of my students, to many of the people who I performed for. I remember that when I was performing in Sydney, when I was performing *Sitahara*, the stars, there were, as I remember…two men came to me, very emotionally touched, red eyes, can't control crying. And then they said "after so many years, you made us realize, as men, how we, how we behave as men, what we do as men. You take it and you see it as a pattern of very harmful movements or beliefs or set of actions, but we only see one side of the story, that is our story of our understanding of harmless actions, but we don't see the other side". […] So for me, I think it has its effect, all forms of art have their effect, especially when it comes to women's narratives, I think. Even though these stories are really dark, they also help us to see the dark side of ourselves.

… [I]t might have affected people's lives. I know it has affected me. It brought me all the way here to decide that, finally, I am going to talk about this very dark topic. And all is happening just because…not just because…all is happening, today I'm standing here thanks to theater, or today I am standing, or sitting, here and doing this talk and having this plan that I will— hopefully soon—be…standing on my feet again to take this issue, this topic forward. (Hashemi, 2021a)

Monirah has always thought carefully about the potential impact of her work, seeking to anticipate and minimize any negative effects while strategizing how to make the largest positive imprint. As she argues, this depends to a great extent on how she tells a story and how the artist uses the creative tools at hand. When she was working in Afghanistan, Monirah systematically tried to understand the context within which she performed, so that she could use her art creatively to show things that were hidden in plain sight.

> For us, when we do a play, it is important what can be told and how it can be told, how to convey our message. Are we going to exactly put our finger on this and say, "okay, this is the scar, this is where the pain is coming from", or no, we just talk around it and we refer to it somehow?
>
> Because […] for us to get to this point, how we can reach our audience, how we can have the best effect so they don't think that we are accusing them of something, or we are judging them, we use social, anthropological, different kinds of research to understand our society and then choose the best way for how we can talk to them. The language, the literature, how to approach them. For us, the research field is an eye-opener to the places that we are going to and their social, cultural, historical, political background.
>
> Talking about women's lives and stories in Afghanistan is very critical and you need to be very careful with that. For example, when […] I was performing in Afghanistan and I was performing outside, we used to do some movements, use some movements. Kind of choreography. At that time, I asked everyone in my group or my company, when it comes to choreography, movement, to just call this harmony movement. It is

not dance, it is harmony movement [laughs]. No one
is going to oppose that [laughs]. We are not dancing;
we are just doing some harmony movements. We had
to rephrase, change, create different concepts, create
different understandings, and it is not just like "you go
there, you do a performance". (Hashemi, 2019b)

Such an approach requires in-depth knowledge and
understanding of the context and the audience, but at the same
time a deep knowledge of and experience with different creative
tools and words. It requires creativity to come up with alternatives,
dedication to the issue being addressed, and a refusal to censor
oneself. It requires the artist to consider and really understand
one's audience and to test the boundaries of the possible in
order to create the desired impact. Whereas in Afghanistan,
Monirah's concern was to use inventive and creative means to
ensure that the art stayed within acceptable and safe bounds, at
the international level, her concern is to counter the single story
that Western audiences have heard about Afghanistan while
striving not to contribute to such a single narrative.

In conclusion: lighting stars in dark spaces

How have experiences of war and oppression inspired Monirah
to engage in political action aimed at challenging injustice?
Monirah's inspirations, actions, and potential impact do become
clear through her life story, which has shaped her work as an
actor, director, and playwright. Having these creative tools at her
disposal, Monirah has relentlessly questioned taboos in society;
inspired by her own traumatic experiences. The metaphor of

lighting the stars can evoke the visual sense of illuminating an area of darkness but, for me, calls to mind speaking about, and thus bringing to light, dark issues that are customarily hidden by silence. The issues that Monirah has brought to light in performances—whether through participatory community theater in Afghanistan or monodrama performances in Sweden—reveal the dark side of human nature and are very often both unspoken and unspeakable. Monirah suggests that at times she even lacks the language to speak about these things, about the enormity of the evil—perhaps particularly unfathomable in the context of the nuclear family—that people are able and willing to inflict on others. And yet, her own traumatic experiences push her forward in her quest to learn to express the unspeakable and thus pave the way for others to do the same. Thus, her story simultaneously shows the courage and strength that are equally part of human nature.

An important reason that Monirah is able to express the unspeakable, I believe, is because theater provides her with the needed artistic tools. Through theater, Monirah does not need to rely on words alone. She can use silence, facial expressions, bodily movements, and a range of props to express not just what happened but also how it felt and what the consequences were. Monirah can also "hide behind" the formal performativity of theater; she can become Monirah, the actress, telling a story. And this story can be told with the help of particular structures that theater offers. Performing a play multiple times adds repetition to the storytelling process within a very controlled context; as such, it can help Monirah slowly gain mastery over the story she tells on stage and, thus, over her own story.

In her creative contributions, her awareness—as a result of lived experience—of the overlapping and interdependent systems of oppression and violence that are based on social categorizations such as gender, national identity, and ethnicity, plays a central role. Monirah focuses on the structures and systems that construct or allow various forms of "red lines", abuse, and violence against women, and she does so in work that focuses on everyday realities in the domestic sphere, in the public sphere (schools, the streets, the performing arts), and in times of war. She shows women are not the only category of people who are restricted and abused; other groups—Afghans in Iran, Hazaras in Afghanistan, for example—are as well. By explicitly connecting the oppression of these different groups and the way that different identity markers intersect, Monirah's work reveals the systems of oppression and violence underlying the experiences of people who are placed in such categories.

Monirah's personal experiences scarred her deeply and caused her to develop PTSD. Monirah's mother reminded her that she was alive and unscarred physically, telling her that mental scars can be healed. The process of healing, however, can be incredibly difficult. Telling stories about one's experience, with others respectfully listening, seems to be central to a healing process that can last a lifetime, as Monirah also clearly states herself. Learning to tell one's story takes time and can cause enormous psychological stress. It seems clear that sharing one's story with others, and eventually in the public domain, can support the process of healing from trauma. In doing so, light is shed on dark issues—for example, rape and incest—that have afflicted others, and hope emerges that revealing the ugly reality may help spare others from suffering it. Storytelling is thus not just therapeutic for the traumatized person. It is also an act of resistance, a way to challenge societal realities for the sake of others who are subjected to violence and oppression; this act of resistance may itself be therapeutic. Of course, public storytelling that challenges dominant structures may also lead to reaction and the risk that more trauma will be inflicted. The endeavor is thus a very difficult one.

Monirah's story suggests that the process of resistance and change involves and may require many generations. In saying this, I do not mean that there is a linear evolution toward a reduction of oppression and violence. Rather, I mean that resistance and the notion of a duty to resist are taught and remembered across generations; thus, the ripple effects of individual action may require many generations to bring about societal change. In the context of Afghanistan, both Monirah's grandmother and mother resisted when they could, speaking up where and when it was safe to do so and whispering in their children's ears when it was not. It was Monirah's mother who taught her an inclusive definition of violence in a context where violence was so narrowly defined as to be largely invisible. Monirah then managed, through the creative tool of theater and by leaving Afghanistan, to transform her understanding of violence into powerful artistic works that she performs around the world. Her stories about her grandmother and mother tell of incredible patience combined with an adamant unwillingness to accept life "as is". As Monirah was taught, as a victim, she should not feel guilt or responsibility, but if one day, she was in a position to act and she did not, then she too would be guilty. This message is a forceful call to hold victimizers to account, even if doing so takes many generations.

3
Halleh Ghorashi: From revolutionary to engaged academic

I was reading all these books, but I thought, "Okay, these are books, but what I can do now—that is quite a unique situation—is that I can contribute to the future of Iran. I can fight for freedom, for democracy, for all these things." And also discuss the issues, …and say, "Okay, with all these issues, what is needed for humanity to be more fair, to be more equal, to be more free from all these challenges"? (Ghorashi, 2020)

I have known Halleh for more than two decades, from the time we were both PhD students living in the Dutch town of Nijmegen. Halleh was a couple of years ahead of me, and a great mentor at the time. At present, she is a professor at the Vrije Universiteit (VU) Amsterdam and an engaged academic. I have followed her career and we have been in touch occasionally throughout the years. When I asked her whether she would like to take part in my book project, she immediately responded with an enthusiastic "yes". Although I was thrilled that she accepted, it is only when I started to analyze the transcript of my life story interview with her and her written and oral work, that I realized just how well her life story and work exemplifies the commitment to social justice that I wanted to explore in this book, and how our interests and perspectives overlap.

Throughout the interview, Halleh puts into words what I have learned from the stories of individuals with refugee backgrounds throughout the last two to three decades. This should not have come as a surprise to me considering not only Halleh's life story but also the fact that she has reflected on and written about the experiences of refugees for decades. In fact, my own thinking was certainly inspired by Halleh all those decades ago, not just as a student in the university course on gender that Halleh co-taught, but also through our many conversations about our doctoral work. I particularly remember a walk in the forest, during which Halleh talked about her research on the experiences of Iranian female exiles during and after the revolution that made a profound impression on me. Halleh's work was deeply personal since, to write her doctoral work, she had had to face the "shadow years" of her own past and the emotional stress related to them. I was humbled by her courage and persistence.

In what follows, I tell a version of Halleh's story following a chronological order, after which I highlight key stepping-stones on her journey from revolutionary to engaged academic. I have divided her story into two parts: her experiences in Iran—during her childhood, the Iranian Revolution and the shadow period that followed—and those in exile in the Netherlands. Although Halleh has experienced a number of transformative events, it was her physical move away from her life that had been put on hold in Iran after the revolution that began a substantially new and different phase in her life. The two periods also reflect her civic and political engagements before and after becoming an academic. These engagements had become impossible for her in post-revolution Iran, although her revolutionary activism already revealed clear academic interests and inclinations. My construction of this story is based on systematic analysis of a two-hour long, transcribed virtual interview that I did with Halleh in the spring of 2020, as well as on her key publications and publicly available lecture recordings. Halleh often uses a personal style in her academic work that presents her life story, personal experiences, and perspectives. As such, this publicly available material provided a rich source of data for understanding her story.

Coming of age in Iran

During the virtual interview conducted a full two decades after our walk in the forest in Nijmegen, Halleh shares part of her life history, starting with her childhood, which she describes as rough. Her mother was diagnosed with schizophrenia and Halleh always felt that people behaved differently toward her because of her mother's disorder. When I tell her that my project explores the strengths and potential contributions of some of those who have experienced violent conflict and authoritarianism, arguing that such experiences at times inspire people to fight for social justice, Halleh considers her own story and corrects me:

> [it is] not so much the war or suppression that was the first thing that shaped me in terms of my attention to social justice. It was more my childhood. Because I was born with a mother who became hospitalized, after I was born. She was diagnosed with schizophrenia. And

from that moment on, actually…that was so strange. I came into a world that was not very just. Not to me as a child. But also, it created a lot of moments in which I realized that my mom was different, so people treated me differently. (Ghorashi, 2020)

Halleh's parents divorced when she was nine and she was sent to a boarding school. Life there was tough. She describes herself as becoming violent after years at the boarding school, saying that she became that way to survive the harsh situation which was, she felt, anything but loving. Halleh became increasingly frustrated at the boarding school as she grew older and at times engaged in fights "for justice", as she calls them. "When I saw something happen to the smaller children, then I would fight for them. Sometimes, I really fought the people who were hitting small children and then I would start a fight and sometimes broke something, a finger or…. That was part of it" (Ghorashi, 2020).

In 1978, when Halleh was 16, one of her aunts—who was a student in Italy—returned to Iran like so many others at the time, drawn by the popular uprising that was beginning. This was the start of a transformative period in Iran that led to a major political shift and a few hopeful years that Halleh calls "the spring of freedom" (Ghorashi, 2003). These political and societal shifts coincided with momentous personal changes for Halleh.

I was fed up with the boarding school. I was really on the brink of collapsing because I couldn't deal with the situation anymore. So my aunt came and talked to my father, since he was providing for me, and they agreed that I would leave the boarding school and live with my aunt. She was one of the people in my family who was really a symbol of social justice. She was fighting against all this stupidity in the family, like keeping face, you know, keeping up appearances. I think of this often. […] I always say that saved my life. Because I started to become fully revolutionary. Coming out [of the boarding school], she gave me a lot of books. I was actually what we call a "problem child"; I was very difficult to handle. Very difficult. At that time, sometimes very violent, because I was fighting for every space, every single space in the boarding school. You learn to fight to survive. And she really trained me to become a different person, to be thoughtful, to listen to classical music, to read books…I liked to read other kinds of books than schoolbooks, to broaden my horizons. And, of course, I became a Marxist as well because of the family background. (Ghorashi, 2020)

Halleh refers to a Maxim Gorky novel about the Artamonov family living through the three phases of the Russian Revolution to explain the complex and changing allegiances within her own family. Both sides of her mother's family were old aristocrats who lost much of their wealth during Iran's White Revolution, which comprised a far-reaching series of reforms launched by the Shah in 1963 that included, for example, land redistribution (Willcocks, 2016). According to Halleh, her mother's oldest siblings were well suited to the old feudal system, whereas her mother and uncle, the middle children, struggled to fit in, feeling caught between the old and the new. The youngest generation of the family, which included the aunt who went to Italy, studied and became politically conscious. Iranian students at the time were politically well organized abroad, and two of her aunts, who were

Marxists, became very involved in the student wings of Iranian revolutionary groups in Italy.

Revolutionary activism and the spring of freedom

Living with her aunts as the popular uprising was beginning, Halleh's life changed fundamentally. She began to be politically active as a high school student. She engaged in a wide range of activities that, just a few months earlier, she could not have envisioned participating in. She describes this period in an article in 1998 (quotes from which appear in her 2003 monograph):

> We proudly called ourselves "the children of the revolution". I was 16 years old when, in 1978, the first sounds of protest were heard openly in the streets of Teheran. I remember going into the streets and seeing an ocean of people walking together and then joining them and walking as one. We felt a sense of invincibility. We weren't afraid of attacks from the police because you felt that you were now protected by your family— your big family of Iranians. In the following two years, Iranian people would witness the birth of incredible freedom and open political exchange. First, the Shah left the country, then Khomeini came to Iran. Then the people took power. What began as scattered protests in the streets would grow into a revolution, one in which Iranian women would play a leading role. (Ghorashi, 2003, p. 6)
>
> My own life, like the lives of many young women, changed radically during this time. I became politically active in a Marxist organization and started doing

things I had never dreamed I could do. I took part in political discussions and demonstrations, distributed pamphlets, and discussed politics in a group. I was making my own decisions, and for the first time I felt that I could go on to do something important in life. Before this time, I had been a high school student with a rather boring life and vague ideas about the future. Like many young women, I now felt as if my activities and plans would have important consequences for my family and my country. It was the beginning of the spring of freedom, a time when, for many of us, the feeling of empowerment was overwhelming. (Ghorashi, 2003, p. 7)

In another publication, Halleh describes in further detail what she was doing and feeling at the time:

I was brimming with energy then, and very aware that I was fortunate to be witnessing one of the most extraordinary events of the century. Sometimes I was actually afraid to go to sleep and miss out on these moments. I was engaged in politics from early morning until late at night. I became our school's student leader, put on political exhibitions, mobilized students for rallies and demonstrations in and out of school, and joined the student branch of one of the most popular political organizations of the day, a Marxist-Leninist organization. From a fairly shy girl I was growing into a fanatical political activist, dedicated to her ideals with heart and soul. (Ghorashi, 2017a, p. 139)

In my interview with her, Halleh puts these realities in context. She describes how, at that time, Iran was undergoing a significant change and, as a consequence, "everyone" became political. She says that, before 1978, if you met someone on the street, you would ask how school was going, you would ask about relationships and other things teenagers talk about, whereas during the revolution, the first question would always be, "What party do you belong to?" In Halleh's words, "everything was politics". Descriptions of this spring of freedom appear throughout Halleh's work, including in a 2017 TEDx talk on critical thinking.[7]

> The first time I came in contact with critical thinking, I was 16 years old in Iran. It was a year before the Iranian Revolution of 1979. In our house, politics was a topic of discussion. I also read a lot about the history of Iran, the history of suppression in Iran. And, also, historical books about different revolutions: the French Revolution, Russian Revolution. So, revolution, and the fever of revolution, got me. I became a revolutionary.
>
> During the revolution, the first one-and-a-half years, there was a temporary freedom in Iran. Just imagine: people who had been living under suppression, dictatorship for years…30–35 years, got the space to be free. The boost of energy in the streets of Tehran, where I was living, was amazing. They were discussing in the streets of Tehran all the books that were forbidden for years. They came to the market and we, the youth of that time, were buying and reading these books. It's a lot of thirst. I sometimes thought that I was eating the books—I wasn't just reading them. It was amazing to be part of that kind of atmosphere. Latin American poetry

inspired me and the music of Victor Jara was…we heard that on the streets, everybody was reciting them. I think that was the best period of my life. To be part of something so energetic, so beautiful— with so many ideals, so many beliefs in change—was amazing. (Ghorashi, 2017c)

And although Halleh was not yet a university student, she became part of study groups in which she held the role of teacher, mentor, or student, depending on the level at which the group was discussing the reading material. In her MA thesis (Ghorashi, 1994), Halleh describes this period in her life and recalls debates on the streets opposite the university where you could find people citing Marx, Lenin, Engels, and the Koran. Her life had become a life of politics and she joined one of the leftist groups. She explains this in our interview:

At that time one of the organizations, groups that became very active in the revolution, was a guerrilla group that…believed in, what do you say, the partisans? Actually, the partisan group believed in the armed struggle against dictatorship. And because of their approach, they were very much loved by the young people. Because, yeah, you want to be a hero [laughs], you are young and want to be…to go against the stream. Radicalism has very much also to do with youth. So at that time I was attracted to that group. And then I found a place and space for this social justice, I found a space where I could really… Yeah, I could find… an ideology that became my home at that moment. To belong, to be somebody. And being involved in the organization and reading a lot of books at that time which were very difficult. You can imagine reading *Also sprach Zarathustra* by Nietzsche at that age? [...] So that gave me a lot of self-confidence. To read, to share knowledge. Because I was a very fanatical activist, it was my identity. It gave me so much positive energy to be out, to embrace my ideals for social justice....So, in that sense... It was very interesting to see that kind of change in me. Everything that was negative in my life changed to something positive at that moment.... So fighting even became something positive, fighting for justice. They called me Halleh Bolshevik at that time because I was so fanatical. (Ghorashi, 2020)

Halleh here describes how the personal and political were deeply interconnected for her, and how crucial it was for her personally to develop ideals, something to live (and be willing to die) for, and to truly experience recognition for her contributions. When, later in the interview, I ask Halleh to explain further her transformation from "problem child" to "revolutionary", she says:

I created new ideals and I also had a meaningful surrounding in which to do something and be valued for what I was doing. At that point, I felt the power that I was somebody. And I had agency, you know. Being somebody, doing something—at least doing something I liked. Reading, talking, discussing. Fighting for justice. That came all together and gave me the possibility to embrace the new me, I think.

And the next thing, it was the role of my aunt, who in a very soft way tried to educate me, to make me understand and look at the world differently. And she was giving me a lot of love also. The fact that she chose me, she fought for me, and she was really taking care of me, was so important at that time. I was not always realizing how important it was at that moment but now I look back and see… I always say she was my mother and father at the same time.

[…] She really was a very important person in my life. This change happened because I started to have ideals, something meaningful in my life. And also began being recognized as someone who had something to offer. I got a lot of recognition from the organization because I was reading a lot, discussing points. (Ghorashi, 2020)

During the spring of freedom, the activist and intellectual sides of Halleh had not been fully integrated, but Halleh first envisioned the possibility of such an integration when she attended a lecture at the University of Tehran on Women's Day, March 8, 1980. The lecturer was Homa Nategh, one of the most respected historians in Iran at the time, who wrote about past revolutions in Iran. Nategh was also a feminist and an activist, about which she spoke in her lecture, which drew a huge crowd. Attending the lecture was, for Halleh, another transformative moment.

I was listening to [Nategh] and she was talking about the combination of, the importance of, academia and social change. And then at that time I thought, "Oh my God. This is also what appeals to me". So she became my idol. "If I can't be a partisan, I want to be an engaged academic". Because academia was always appealing to me, as a bookworm, someone who liked to read. I liked also to be an activist, but I had a problem with activism at the time, with that organization. Because people were only doing actions without thoughtful consideration and they would not read much, so their discussion was not so informed by existing knowledge. Not many were. In our group, I was the only one who was always discussing books. Irritating others in my group. But then I thought, okay, this is possible. She became a symbol for me as an engaged scholar. I learned that scholars don't have to choose between academia and action for social change. And that has been very important in my academic career. (Ghorashi, 2020)

Whereas some activists appreciated Halleh's contributions as providing essential theoretical underpinning for their activism, others did not. In her MA thesis, Halleh discusses those who were not appreciative, describing them as people who stood above her in the activist hierarchy and were either uncomfortable of the fact that she seemed to possess more knowledge than they did or perhaps thought that she asked too many questions (Ghorashi, 1994). Although for Halleh, bringing knowledge to her activism, irrespective of how others reacted, was important, she stresses that academic topics alone did not satisfy her. She ultimately wanted to integrate activism and academia.

I was reading all these books, but I thought, "OK, these are books, but what I can do now; it is quite a unique situation that I can contribute to the future of Iran. I can fight for freedom, for democracy, for all these things." And also discuss the issues…and say, "OK, with all these issues, what is needed for humanity to be more fair, to be more equal, to be more free from all these challenges?" Being, at a political, philosophical and societal level, engaged with these issues, you want to fight for a better society, you want to fight for a society that is more…equal. More inclusive, even though we would not have used that term then. But a better society that is maybe more just—that is the term we used. That has no poverty, that has no inequality. That was very important for me, to be part of that. To fight for it. These were my ideals, big ones. (Ghorashi, 2020)

Thus, already as a teenager during the revolution in Iran, Halleh was using her interest in ideas and knowledge to inform her practical efforts to achieve "a better society". However, the events that were to follow suggested that these ideals had been naive.

The shadow period

The sun was dead.
The sun was dead and "tomorrow"
was a queer ancient word meaning nothing
to children. In their notebooks they drew it
as an inky black smudge.

Forugh Farrokhzad, *Earthy Verses* [8]

Soon fear, pain, despair, and emptiness replaced the brief "spring" that, for Halleh was filled with hope, ideals, vision, and optimism. Halleh refers to this new period, which lasted several years, as the "black" or "shadow" period, terms widely used in Iran to refer to mourning, according to Halleh. The poem by Forugh Farrokhzad, quoted above, powerfully captures the feeling at the time through the image of children having no understanding of the word "tomorrow". Halleh quotes the poem because, although it was written years before the revolution, its sentiments reflect the thoughts expressed by the women whom she later interviewed about those dark years. If children live in darkness ("the sun is dead") and have no sense of a future, not even a tomorrow that can be envisioned as different, better, then ultimately, hope no longer exists.

Although the shift from the "spring of freedom" to the "shadow period" seemed sudden and absolute, cracks started to appear almost immediately. In her monograph, Halleh describes how, from the beginning, tensions existed between people who enjoyed the newly won freedom and tried to stretch the limits of the revolution and those who claimed the revolution as theirs and sought to limit civic freedoms in the name of Islam (Ghorashi, 2003). From the start, there were *hezbollahis*, street mobs of mainly men who attacked demonstrators and media critical of Khomeini, unrestrained by the police. They played an important early role in confronting counterforces during what later became known as the Islamic Revolution. At least nine different groups participated in ousting the Shah, each with a different political agenda and level of religiosity. These different groups had fundamentally different visions of the future of the country and disagreements among them grew.

Khomeini returned from exile in France in 1979 after the Shah had left Iran for exile. On April 18, 1980, Kohmeini verbally attacked the universities, arguing that they were Westernized and trained the youth in Iran to support foreign interests. That same night, the *hezbollahis* attacked the universities. The leftist protesters who had taken part in the revolution were in shock. Halleh participated in what were meant to be peaceful protests.

> When I heard the news of the attack of the base of our
> organization at the university, I rushed toward the place.
> I was not alone, I saw many followers who were there

before me. We began with a sitting strike in the street. We just sat in the middle of the street in front of the building; we slept there at night, ate there, and were resolute in protecting our center. The weather was cold, but it seemed that nobody was bothered with that. The anxiety of what would happen next was mainly in our minds. Our action was meant to be a peaceful protest against measures to close the universities and also our centers. It did not take long before groups of *hezbollahis* attacked us. We were not prepared to fight back; they had everything, knives, chains, or sticks. We just had our hands to defend ourselves. I saw wounded people falling down one by one. Everybody was shouting and I did as well. I was very afraid, I saw *hezbollahis* who attacked us with knives and other things, I noticed their faces and that really scared me. They were so ruthless, they looked so violent, and they were in my eyes in a state of easily killing people. And this really scared me. We were there helpless with our empty hands trying to save freedom, and they were there ready to kill us.

I could not understand it: what went wrong, and when? We participated with the same people in the demonstrations against the Shah, but now they were here ready to kill us. Blood was everywhere. I could not believe my eyes. This was the first time that I saw violent acts so close to me. At that point I got a slap on my head and shouted hard. I touched my head and felt a hole in my head, and my blouse became red. I fell on the ground and heard others saying, "She is dying, hurry." I could not walk, two people helped me, and they put me on a bike and brought me slowly to the hospital. When I was in the hospital, I felt already much better. My head was injured and it was bleeding terribly, nine stitches were necessary to close the wound. When the doctor saw me, he immediately started to talk about the courage of the young people. My father was of course less enthusiastic about my courage; he was terrified. All of this did not stop my feeling of resisting those actions. After two days I was again at the street demonstrating, but this time with a bandage on my head. I was determined to do my share of protecting freedom, which was the result of the revolution. But we did not succeed; dictatorship came back in yet another form. (Ghorashi, 1994, pp. 55–56, published in English in Ghorashi, 2003, pp. 102–103)

In our interview, Halleh hardly mentions the shadow period, only occasionally touching on her experiences while discussing something else. I do not ask her any questions about it, both because I do not want to push her to speak about something that may be painful to her and because I know that she has written about this past on several occasions. At one point in the interview, I get a small glimpse of the extent of the hurt and despair Halleh and many others experienced during this dark period. Halleh is speaking with great warmth about her aunt, recalling her crucial role in her life. Then, she briefly mentions her aunt's disappearance.

She was very active as a member of the organization and what she was doing was very interesting, but she… we lost her. That is a painful thing. She was…she is one of the missing persons after the years of oppression. We never knew what happened to her, we didn't find out what happened to her. She was actually working… she translated a lot. Because she knew languages, she knew English and Italian. She was translating a lot from the documents and news around the world. And also working on the newspaper for one of the… partisan organizations. For the editorial board of that newspaper. At that time, they arrested many people and activities were going on underground. Then the idea was that you should have cyanide with you and that when they attack you in the safe houses, that you just kill yourself, so you don't get arrested. We think that my aunt did that. That is one of the most plausible ideas. (Ghorashi, 2020)

Although this was a rare instance in our interview when Halleh discussed the shadow period, she has written and talked publicly about some of her experiences during this period, doing so in a way that connects with her audience. In her TEDx talk on critical thinking, for example, she briefly describes her feelings at that time.

People who were part of the revolution, started to stand against each other. When the years of suppression came, from that active person, I became a depressed person. We couldn't do anything. Fear and despair replaced hope and believing in ideals. Ideals just died. People were killing each other. People were attacking each other. Many of my friends got arrested. And for me, it was like the turn of paradise to hell. I was losing life, feeling that there was nothing else to live for. In those years, I was made an Other. Being a Marxist—I was a

Marxist believer in a revolution that became an Islamic Revolution—made me an Other. So, at the age of 26, I had to leave Iran because of my political convictions. (Ghorashi, 2017c)

In her 2003 monograph, Halleh drew on the words and experiences of the 43 women whose life stories she had collected in the Netherlands and the United States to describe the shadow period. The women she interviewed described their past, using Farsi words from that time that evoked memories for Halleh. They also used concepts like paradise and hell to describe and analyze their experiences in retrospect. Halleh found that her research contributed to her ability to work through her own experiences and feelings of betrayal, terror, loss, senselessness, and hopelessness. Through the women's stories, she saw her own past reflected.

Halleh's monograph describes how the situation in Iran became increasingly repressive: the media broadcasted news of the executions of young people, people being imprisoned, and people renouncing their former ideals (having been threatened or tortured). Publicly reporting the government's repressive actions was meant to instill fear in those who opposed the situation in Iran. Feeding the fear was the fact that the new regime encouraged betrayal, which meant that no one could be trusted. Further, leftist political activists no longer had access to education or jobs, and their lives were increasingly restricted by new laws and codes of behavior that imposed tighter social control, especially on women (Ghorashi, 2003). Many women, once very active politically, now had to stay at home, silent and passive, for years.

The women whom Halleh interviewed described an absence of light and hope in these years, as the many ideals and dreams of a bright future that developed during the revolution were brutally crushed. They called themselves "strangers in their homeland" (Ghorashi, 2003, p. 116); they had become exiles long before they fled Iran as refugees.

Life in exile: the journey toward becoming an engaged academic

Considering the impossible and life-threatening circumstances she found herself in, Halleh had to flee Iran. She arrived in the Netherlands in 1988 at the age of 26, ten years after her first political awakening. The contrast between her new life and the ten years preceding it was huge. Halleh tries to explain her hunger for action after arriving in her new home by reflecting further on her life during the shadow period.

> I had been in a kind of pause, a suspension for years. I was not supposed to—in the years when the oppression started—go to university. You couldn't. I could be arrested if I wanted to apply for university. I had a life in suspension. A shadow life, I always refer to it. A life in which you don't want to be recognized and seen. It was about eight years that I stayed that way. I couldn't study. And I was suffering because I wanted to study, I wanted to do something with my life. But I couldn't. Those years of suspension were terrible. I first had experienced something, a sense of freedom and possibility of learning and acquiring knowledge, and then the suppression. Experiencing freedom created

inspiration for me to do more with my life, more reason, more eagerness, urge, to do something. To know more, to do more. If you experience freedom and then suppression…when you know the taste of freedom, then being suppressed is a lot worse than when you have not experienced freedom before. (Ghorashi, 2020)

Having escaped Iran, Halleh gained a new sense of purpose, a new zest and energy (Ghorashi, 2016, 2017a). But at the same time, she confronted the many challenges of starting life in a new place where, as she phrases it during the interview "I wasn't seeing many people with my background in societal positions. I wasn't seeing anybody in academia with my background" (Ghorashi, 2020). I ask her about her resilience: How did she manage to continue fighting to overcome the many roadblocks in order to achieve her goal? She responds by referring to her own life but also to the life story interviews with Iranian female exiles in the Netherlands and the United States that she did for her doctoral research.

The thing is that, when you have had the experience with the revolution, the ideal that is too big, you can barely accept a simple life. Actually, some of the women—I have written about that—were saying that when you experience life in that way, so intensely— paradise and hell—that you have a crash course in freedom and suppression in two years, then your life can never be the same. I cannot actually say, "Okay, we go back and just…what we call in Dutch 'huisje, boompje, beestje' [live a conventional life]." You have been involved in such intense matters, issues, with ideals that are beyond your, or anybody's, imagination.

Things like, you were ready to die. We were trained to die, to go to the extreme for our ideals. After that experience, life can never go back to normal.

When you have had that intense experience of life, paradise and hell, you have also seen how empowered you can be as a human being…that you can have agency. One of the women said to me in the interviews, "One day, you are 17 years old and you go and give a lecture about justice for these workers on strike in a factory." Your life changes, you know that you can do that. That was something. (Ghorashi, 2020)

Halleh, like the women she interviewed, experienced deep meaningfulness through fighting for "a better society". Feeling that one can contribute to unique events in the history of one's country when one is young, as Halleh had been, can be deeply transformative. Having experienced freedom and suppression in such close succession and developing ideals about a just society and fighting to make them concrete, affected the choices the women who had fought in the revolution made afterward, according to Halleh, and made living a conventional life more difficult. This was certainly also true for Halleh. While she recounts her life story in exile to me, what comes out very strongly is her motivation to contribute to social justice practices in Dutch society.

A responsibility to engage: transforming society and self

Many of those with whom I have spoken over the 20 years in which I have conducted life histories with refugees not only managed to rebuild their lives in a new context but also felt a powerful urge—a responsibility, almost a duty, in fact—to contribute to society, often both locally and transnationally (Horst, 2018, p. 209; Horst and Lysaker, 2021) Why? Halleh explains how, for her and the Iranian women she interviewed, this sense of responsibility grew from their intense experiences—the "crash course in freedom and suppression"—and their recognition that they were involved, and playing a role—if only briefly, in "most extraordinary events". This created the urge to contribute to societal events and make a difference. When I ask her explicitly whether she feels a sense of responsibility, she recalls an earlier conversation on the topic. She tells me about being at a party and talking to a young man, whom she had met through his mother and known for a very long time. He kept asking her why she was doing what she was doing, and why she was working so hard.

> And then he says, "How are you doing?" "Oh, busy but very good." And he says, "You look tired—why are you doing all these things?" And I said, "I think it is important, my role is important, to try to change the society." And he said "Why?" I said, "I think I can continue doing it because of my research." "Yeah, but why?" (Ghorashi, 2020)

When pushed to reflect on what drives her to work so hard to try to contribute to positive societal transformation, Halleh talks about her inability to just relax.

> [...] I had to deal, actually, with the fact that there can be some evenings that I do nothing. Just enjoy doing nothing. Watching TV or doing stupid things or playing cards with friends, you know. That I can enjoy

something and not feel guilty about it. It was about the revolutionaries, people coming from the revolution, and having this idea of "I have to change the world, and there is no single moment to miss." And then being a refugee adds to that because now I am safe, and I have to show that I am worthy of being a refugee as well. So it heightens that need to really want to make every second of your life meaningful. (Ghorashi, 2020)

Halleh is explaining that she feels not just that she has the opportunity, but that she has, in fact, the duty to make a societal contribution. In telling me of her experience at the party, Halleh describes her almost obsessive need to keep going as arising from different sources. She believes it is characteristic of those who have contributed to a revolution to feel that they must contribute to changing the world and that their every action matters. She also explains that having made it to safety (when many others did not, I might add), heightens the feeling of "wanting to make every second of your life meaningful". Finally, for those who end up in exile, feeling the need to show "worthiness" in the society of residence—to demonstrate that you are deserving of the protection you receive as a refugee—plays a role as well.

Halleh then points out that not everyone with a refugee background wants or seeks to "make every second of her or his life meaningful". Structural challenges can limit or prevent one from making meaningful contributions in a new society. As important, difficulty processing the traumas experienced during years of violent conflict and/or oppression can interfere with one's ability to engage socially in the way one might wish. I see these two factors as interconnected; if one has found refuge after going through hell but cannot make meaningful contributions to society afterward, one is likely to find it difficult to process past experiences. And being unable to process the past may well make it difficult for one to engage meaningfully in society.

> I know a lot of people who have never been able to give a proper place to their past experiences… It can be a trauma that you can never get rid of. Many people with that experience, they cannot have a normal life because they feel that life doesn't mean anything anymore because of that experience, the deep experience, they have had. The past is so dominant that it overshadows everything, so that you can't see present or future. I think, for me, it really helped that I have been able to write about it, to analyze it. (Ghorashi, 2020)

As Halleh explains during our interview, her academic research and writing have been central to her effort to place her past traumas firmly in the past. Halleh talks about this explicitly when she describes her work on her MA thesis, which sought to understand why social action ends up being unsuccessful, and her doctoral research, for which she collected stories of politically engaged women during revolutionary times.

> This ended up becoming my own therapy, in a way— this was something I realized later—that writing helped me also to understand and place and analyze my own experiences. That was very important for me. To deal with the past and also the present. Because it was about refugee-ness, it was about being uprooted and in a new country, as well as feelings of betrayal, betrayal of democracy or freedom. Social justice is claimed but

never realized in the way that people expect it to be. (Ghorashi, 2020)

It seems to me that Halleh, in finding a form through which to share her experiences, was able to process the past in a way that "gave it the place it deserves"—not forgotten but not dominating her present or her future. By engaging deeply with memories of the past, not only through experiencing them again in embodied ways with the women who were part of her doctoral research but also by systematically analyzing them and connecting them to contextual and conceptual literature, Halleh's understanding of her past evolved and became more nuanced. As she explains:

My academic training put things into perspective, and slowly but surely that new perspective led me to reflect on my own past. It was by no means an easy matter to admit shades of gray into my black-and-white account of a past that held such painful memories, for when you feel pain all you want to do is to accuse those who are to blame for causing it. To put the past into perspective and context just seems to weaken it. Yet gradually I was drawn to reassess my normative judgment of the past, which helped me to acquire an important academic skill: to step back and give my involvement an academic translation. (Ghorashi, 2017a, p. 142)

[...] For me, opting for engagement meant that I wanted to seek the answers to social questions that interested me in the shared space between my personal background and the social science issues of identity and integration. So I purposely chose themes that were close to my biography. (Ghorashi, 2017a, p. 144)

Halleh thus established a strong basis for an academic career characterized both by an engagement with various themes of interest within feminist studies and diversity studies and by strong societal engagement.

Being an engaged academic: form and focus

Halleh's political and social engagement as an academic in the Netherlands integrates form and focus in an intrinsic way. She displays a willingness to experiment to find research approaches that create societal impact. A core aim of her work is to challenge both images embedded in public discourse and interpersonal encounters that are othering, especially those affecting individuals with migrant backgrounds. For Halleh, being societally engaged while having enough distance to understand her own positionality is an integral part of what it means to be an academic.

> If you are not engaged in society, your thoughts are not influencing people around you. You can do everything, but if you are not engaged in discussions, in public debates, in discussing your thoughts, what is the value of it? You need intimacy, you need involvement in societal issues. You have to be engaged to make a change. But if you are too engaged, and not distanced enough, if you cannot be reflective about your own positioning…then there is no value of you compared to others who are not academics. Anybody else can be engaged as well. Your value as a scholar when you get engaged is that you can also create distance and

reflexivity on your position and your situatedness. This is a balancing act: continuing to debate in society, for a better society …and creating distance, enough distance to reflect on your own situatedness and positioning. Doing this—juggling that involvement and distance all the time—is very important for me as an academic. This is the core: being engaged and at a distance. (Ghorashi, 2020)

After studying the Iranian Revolution and its impact on individual lives, Halleh's postdoctoral work has increasingly explored refugee experiences in exile, focusing on processes of belonging, homemaking, and civic participation in new contexts. She works from a feminist perspective, and often includes personal reflections and experiences in her work. Halleh also sees the importance of collecting and representing marginalized stories, and like me, works a lot with life stories and a narrative approach. In our interview, she explains why she emphasizes these stories, and how her use of the narrative approach stems from her own experiences with public discourse on refugees.

When I came [to the Netherlands] as a refugee, among the things that I could not understand were the images, the power of the words, and how I was portrayed as a refugee in the media. I was finding these numbers and percentages that were presented about migrants and refugees, compared to the wider Dutch population, made the refugees seem lacking. You were always on the wrong side, always doing something not good enough. And I thought, "Okay, but what does it do with me?" I just… I didn't see myself in the stories, I didn't see my development in those stories. I didn't see my opportunities and only saw challenges and struggles to make a life. I saw these numbers that only showed what was not good about being a refugee, an image of refugees as never being good enough. I thought, "Okay, I don't want to be that number, I don't want others to be that number all the time." That is why I started with refugees' stories. I had to tell the stories to show the complexity…and also to challenge the hierarchy of "the white versus the Other" in which you never catch up, you always lag behind. (Ghorashi, 2020)

As Halleh explains, she seeks to address the processes of othering that she sees in society by telling her own story and the stories of other women who had to flee their country of origin. Having experienced a society in which othering could have deadly consequences, such as being a Marxist revolutionary who suddenly finds herself in the midst of an Islamic Revolution, Halleh understands the significance of her academic work. She aims to engage critically with, and to question, images of the Other that are still common in the Netherlands. In her TEDx talk on critical thinking, she describes what happened to her when she experienced being othered as an exile:

I was seen as this woman coming from an Islamic society, so I must have been unemancipated and suppressed by the men of my family. I was a refugee, so probably pitiful, somebody who needs help and with not much to offer to society. A problem rather than part of the solution. I was feeling like, "okay, this is not new to me." I was othered in Iran and it still was painful.

But there was something different about this time. I couldn't find an enemy that othered me. There was no enemy. The people who did that, it came from the images they had of me. Normal people, normal conversations. They were like me. They were not dictators intentionally excluding me. So I was confused. In the years in Iran, being othered, being made an Other, having enemies to fight against was crucial for me. But also, it was solid; the power, the source of power, was solid, was clear. The source of solidarity was clear. Here, it was confusing. People with whom I just had a normal conversation, othered me. How could it be? (Ghorashi, 2017c)

She goes on to discuss one of the projects she developed to fight this new type of othering that was being carried out, not by an enemy and not as a deliberate plan of an evil dictator, but by "normal people" with whom Halleh and others interacted daily, going about their lives in a peaceful, democratic country. Because this othering was so invisible to those who engaged in it, many of whom even had good, not bad, intentions, it needed to be addressed in a different way. Halleh set up a meeting place for a diverse group of refugees and those working on behalf of refugees in Amsterdam to talk about the exclusion of refugees from the labor market, a place where all participants could share their experiences and stories and really listen to one another. In this safe space, the fullness and complexities of refugees' lives were revealed and the inaccuracy of stereotypical images of the Other was exposed.

An incident during one of the meetings revealed clearly to the group not only the inaccuracy but also the devastating impact of certain images; the incident was collectively transformative. Participants were asked to focus on the moment in their lives when they had felt the most powerful. Several women responded with stories, but Halleh noticed that "Sarah", a refugee from Eritrea, said nothing. When she finally spoke, her story of fighting for freedom in Eritrea and facing horrible consequences afterward silenced the other participants. When she was asked why she had kept quiet for so long when she had such a powerful story to share, Sarah described what she had felt when asked when she had felt most powerful. As Halleh recounts:

> And she ["Sarah"] said, "I was actually amazed by it myself and realized, when I thought about it, that from the moment ten years ago when I came to Netherlands, the only thing I heard was "no". "Your language is not good enough; your papers are not good enough. Your cultural competence does not fit our organization, it is not good enough." And I realized that a repetition of no's actually made me lose my self-confidence. But today I also realized that a repetition of those no's made me to forget my story. And now, here, I was able to rediscover it."
>
> And when she said that, I literally saw that the light in her eyes came back, as if there was a boost of life that went into her body. The rediscovery of her story made her live again. And that was an amazing, amazing, experience. There was this policymaker there who had been working with migration issues for years. She shared with the group that she in her work had been mainly focusing on the deficits and the lacks of migrants and refugees, so much that they were fixating

on that, wanting to help them to make them equal, to make their life better. But fixation on lack actually was so much that she almost forgot that these people also have qualities, they have something to offer to this society. (Ghorashi, 2017c)

Halleh believes the meeting place project succeeded in its aim to make people question critically the ways, which are taken for granted, that they were othering one another, and to understand the negative effect of such behavior, particularly on those of minoritized backgrounds. What was required was not an explicit, direct confrontation with the "repressive" Other, but instead deep listening and sharing in order to unveil and tackle the many preconceived ideas we have and are often not consciously aware of, and to expose and explore the ways that stereotypes harm others. As Halleh explains in her TEDx talk:

What happened was that, through sharing those stories, people became aware of these images that we have about each other. Images we take for granted. And by doing so realizing that despite the best intentions, we make the other "Other". And in doing so, in maybe the repetition of that, they actually make the Other completely passive. But something else also became very clear: that people do that with the best intentions. So, the enemy is not a dictator—that is not there anymore. Actually, the power is not in positions of suppression. The power is in all those images that we have of one another. And all those images that become so normalized in our daily life that we don't think about it, we don't think and question it, we take that for granted. So if we want to think about change, we need to think about how to unsettle these powerful images, this powerful chain of images that influences ourselves, but mainly others; that contribute to othering of people, to exclusion in society. Sharing stories, as this story of Sarah shows, is a very powerful instrument to do that. But sharing stories from points of difference, between people who are actually disconnected, becomes even more powerful because this creates mirroring effects. (Ghorashi, 2017c)

Halleh's organization of and participation in the meeting place project is one illustration of her political and social engagement as an academic. She believes that the othering that takes place in public narratives and everyday encounters is best addressed by sharing life stories in all their complexity and through experimenting with ways of communicating such stories that allow people to truly hear them. When people are seen as complex and three-dimensional, reducing them to stereotypes is difficult, if not impossible. Halleh sees the ultimate goal of this work as making a difference. Creating a more just and equal society is an ideal that she has not given up on.

Making a difference: action, impact, and uncertainty

Halleh's achievements since she came to the Netherlands in 1988 are impressive—not least in light of the many challenges she faced. She held the prestigious government-initiated chair in Management of Diversity and Integration from 2005 until 2012, and has since held the rank of full professor. She has a long list of peer-reviewed academic publications and has supervised 25 PhD students. She has established a range of collectives, including VU's Refugee Academy. She is a member of the prestigious Royal Dutch Academy of the Sciences and sits on multiple academic boards. She is often invited to deliver keynotes and has received many prestigious prizes and grants. In 2010, she was rated among the 100 most powerful women in the Netherlands; since 2018, she has been ranked among the top 200 most influential people in the Netherlands. In addition to her manifold academic accomplishments, she has an impressive list of societal contributions. Among the most prestigious is her role, since 2018, as a Crown-appointed member of the Social and Economic Council. Clearly, Halleh is committed to trying to better society through both her academic and nonacademic work, the two of which are closely intertwined.

Halleh's written and oral work clearly show a drive to change perspectives and practices with respect to refugees, diversity, and societal inclusion. She has an informal, at times conversational, style that directly addresses the reader or listener; she tries to establish empathy and thus influence individual perspectives. In Ghorashi (2016), "Wat als u een vluchteling was?" (What if you were a refugee?), she presents the story of her teenage and young adult years in Iran to illustrate how political shifts can suddenly reduce one's opportunities to zero, emptying the future of all content and rendering a present that offers only marginalization and oppression. She then argues that fleeing to a new country means having a chance to gain a new life; it is like a rebirth and can reawaken dreams and create new energy.

This article is simultaneously a call for change in the structural conditions that make it so difficult to make full use of that energy and the many contributions refugees have to offer their new societies, and an encouragement to individual readers that they can make a difference in a refugee's life. She describes her own experiences with a system focused on deficit rather than possibilities and explains that she only achieved what she did because, in addition to her own work and dedication, some people believed in her potential and ambitions in a context where that was uncommon. In her oral engagements, Halleh applies this same direct style of explaining things by drawing on concrete experiences, including her own. She also encourages her audience to engage, for example, by imagining themselves in the position of "the Other".

In one of her most influential public performances, as a speaker for TEDx, Halleh speaks explicitly about what "making a difference" means to her. Her position is clearly shaped by her experiences in Iran and her reflections on the differences and similarities between processes of othering that happen in any society. Halleh asks:

> What is the changed condition of critical thinking when the power is not the visible power of the position of dictators we fight against, but power is in the process of daily interactions where we take our own assumptions for granted and exclude others without realizing that we are doing that? So one may ask about stories like Sarah's: How can such a story change a system? Revolution changes the system! How can we change a system, structures, macrostructures? How can we change them?

I would say that the only way to go about change, and think about change, in this time, with this power, is in the normalization practices. The only way to go about it is to invest in interpersonal relationships and make them more thoughtful. Those thoughtful relationships create waves of influence, can travel all around the world and inspire others to do the same thing. This example of Sarah; can you imagine how impactful that can be, and has been, for many people who were part of that space? Most of these people shared the way that they took that story with them to their organizations, to the ministries that they were working in, to the municipalities they were part of. That story has been repeated by many. And that is the kind of impact and change that stories can bring. And the repetition of these small, small, stories, small-scale stories, can be essential in thinking big.

So we do not start with a revolution when the power is so subtle and invisible. We do not start a revolution—we start investing in each other and giving the relationship and the conversations we have more color and multiplicity. And maybe [...] then we can have some kind of revolution by just deconstructing the blind spots in our own thoughts. And by doing so, make a change. That could be the kind of change we can imagine when we think of critical thinking at a time that power doesn't work in the old-fashioned way, but through our own taken-for-granted, normalized practices. (Ghorashi, 2017c)

In academic work and while describing her personal experiences, Halleh explains that she has learned that human action and interaction may well lead to unintended change because reality is affected by the actions and interactions of millions of people, all of whom operate simultaneously within larger societal structures. Thus, Halleh is deeply aware of the fundamental uncertainty over what one's expressed speech and action can do. With this fundamental uncertainty arises a need to be humble about one's ability both to know and to create change, a humility that Halleh believes we should all embrace, especially those in positions of power. In our interview, she insists that it is important,

> to also, from time to time, embrace your not knowing. That is something that I think is very important for me to embrace as well. And that is a continuous challenge. You want to make a change, but you have to accept that you can't make changes always. You can say things that do not work out or you have ideas that are very far away from reality of the people's life. (Ghorashi, 2020)

At the same time, as Halleh knows from her own experiences, there may be people who do not want you to make a difference and who will actively try to silence you. There was a period when Halleh was frequently asked to contribute to television programs, and at that time, there were people trying to prevent her from expressing herself publicly.

> You know, when I was more in the public space, I got a lot of hate mail. Some of it was funny, some of it was scary. But once, I was threatened to death. And that was quite… I was very scared for a week to go out. And then there was a realization. I said to myself, and also to others, "yes, finally I made it, I made my opponents angry, so my ideas have impact"… I have to be very careful not to please too much. And also not to forget

that my voice does not always have to shift in different directions because I like to be liked; it has to be my voice. That is a challenge, actually, that I have. To be more conscious about the message, the change that I want to bring about. Sometimes I become maybe too strategic and forget about the value of not being in control and just saying the right things. (Ghorashi, 2020)

Balancing her strong wish to make a difference and contribute to a more equal and just society with this realization that the consequences of what she says and does are not necessarily within her control, Halleh continues to work hard, to engage where she thinks she can have an impact, and to aim to remain humble in light of the fundamental uncertainty over whether her work will lead to the change she envisions. Although the Iranian Revolution may have taught her this harsh lesson, it did not discourage her from being a highly engaged academic.

Key stepping-stones toward political action

When analyzing Halleh's story—her coming of age in Iran, her involvement in revolutionary activism followed by a long "shadow period", and her life in exile—I identify several significant themes. First, key individuals inspired and/or supported Halleh in her journey from revolutionary to engaged academic. I would argue that her life would not have been the same in the absence of these individuals; as they seemed to have played important roles in key moments. This is one entry point for exploring the importance of individual action. Second, her story shows the value of exploring experiential, embodied knowledge. Remarkably,

Halleh has managed to integrate the different parts of her story by acknowledging and exploring the experiential, embodied knowledge she has gained about violent conflict, oppression, and exile through her lived experiences. Although there are vast, seemingly unbridgeable differences among the various periods of her life—childhood, Iranian Revolution, the shadow period, and life in exile—Halleh has succeeded in creating an integrated story through deep and systematic exploration of her own and other people's experiences. Doing so, I realize, required both the courage to brave psychological strain as well as a questioning attitude that enabled her to resist academic as well as social conventions.

Role models and supporters of dreams

In our interview, there are two moments that Halleh indicates were crucial in her life. The first was when her aunt managed to free her from the boarding school before the 1979 revolution. The second was when she attended the lecture by Iranian historian and activist Homa Nategh right after the revolution. Her aunt played a key role in Halleh's engagement in revolutionary activism. Nategh inspired Halleh's ambition to become an engaged academic. Both women arguably altered the course of Halleh's life. On Nategh's inspirational role, Halleh reflects:

> I was, as I mentioned, a bookworm. I loved to study. But I was thinking that academia was too abstract, too far away from the activism. Especially when you are in the middle of activism, you don't see any space for academia in the future…The thing is that when I saw her, I saw a possibility. I saw a possibility of combining

both my passions: reading and activism. That was a very important moment in my life. You need to have idols, some form, some examples that help you imagine the future for yourself. And she became one. (Ghorashi, 2020)

Role models can be understood as people who are greatly admired and who provide a vision of a future for oneself. In a way, they offer an image of how individuals might lead their lives beyond present-day realities. Halleh's role models were strong women. Interestingly, both Halleh's aunt and Homa Nategh went abroad to study and became members of Iranian student organizations outside of Iran, where they developed their social and political activism. (Nategh was in Paris for graduate studies from the late 1950s to the late 1960s; Halleh's aunt was in Italy in the 1970s.) Both were active in leftist organizations, and Nategh was an active advocate for women's rights. More so than Halleh's aunt, Nategh was a real front runner as a woman studying abroad, and she was one of the first women to join the Confederation of Iranian Students, a civil society organization that served as a student union for Iranians abroad in the 1960s and 1970s. The group was particularly active in West Europe and the United States and comprised different factions of students opposed to the Shah.

Halleh says that her aunt probably died as a consequence of the oppression that followed the Iranian Revolution, whereas Homa Nategh had to flee the country. Neither woman achieved her dreams for a just society in Iran. And yet these two women played crucial roles in the lives of others, transforming the course of life for Halleh and others.

In exile, Halleh found herself facing, on the one hand, an opportunity to build a new life after a decade of restrictions and invisibility and, on the other hand, many structural challenges and obstacles to the building of that new life. Again, a few individuals played crucial roles in her life. Although Halleh does not identify particular role models, she does mention a number of key people who supported her ambitions, believing in her abilities and talents and encouraging her never to give up on her dreams. As I highlighted earlier in the chapter, Halleh says that as an exile in the Netherlands, all that one hears is "no, no, no". The constant focus on deficiencies can lead to a damaged self-image and the abandonment of ambitions. Such an outcome for those who have experienced violence and oppression may not seem surprising. However, such a result can be particularly damaging for people like Halleh for whom societal engagement is a strong part of their identity and holds the potential to heal and offer meaning.

Experiential knowledge

Throughout her academic career, Halleh has understood that her experiences in Iran were crucial to her ability to grasp fully the topics she explores. She has always followed this understanding to its logical conclusion and explored her own experiences in her academic work. In her MA thesis, Halleh stated, "I find that my participation in the Revolution is essential to do this research. I have learned a lot from the Revolution and I find this critical as background for this thesis" (Ghorashi, 1994). Throughout the thesis, she includes short reflections on her personal experiences during and after the revolution. She also explains, however, that, due to her experiences, she was initially too close to what happened to make sense of things and that she needed to gain distance. She describes the method she used as something close to, but not the same as, participant observation, the most common methodological approach of anthropologists. In Halleh's case, she first participated (in Iran), and then conducted analysis (15 years later, in a university in the Netherlands). In her book based on her doctoral research, she describes her approach as that of a "reflective outsider":

> I became more aware of the difficulty of the path I had chosen, and did my best to travel it. The ups and downs were part of the research. Nevertheless, taking all of these difficulties into account, my shared experiences with these women have been a crucial part of this book. [...] By being aware of this position I tried to create a reflective outsider position, even when I felt very much an insider. By reflective outsider I mean not just being able to place the interviews in a broader context, but also, through those other stories, re-evaluating my assumptions based on my personal memories and experiences of the past and the present. (Ghorashi, 2003, p. 15)

As Halleh notes in her monograph, her path was difficult. I believe this was for at least two reasons. First, trying to understand the human consequences of violent conflict and authoritarianism through a combination of academic research and exploration of one's own personal experiences of violence and oppression seems likely to place anyone under significant emotional and psychological strain. Second, seeking academic knowledge by systematically analyzing and integrating personal, embodied experiences is seriously frowned upon in most academic disciplines. Halleh makes a similar observation when she writes, "It was not only dealing with personal emotions that worried me, but also the constant need to defend my work from accusations that I am not distant or "scientific" enough" (Ghorashi, 2003, p. 14). Halleh must have needed courage to continue to pursue her inquiry when the road to finding answers was so painful both for herself and the women she worked with. Her questioning attitude, developed at an early age, may have helped her to resist the significant pressure to conform to mainstream academic practice.

Halleh's persistence may have been bolstered by the fact that, as mentioned earlier, she believed that her approach would ultimately improve her academic insight and was crucial to her restoring her mental well-being after such deeply traumatizing experiences. When we discuss this further during our interview, Halleh reflects on the fact that writing about her experiences and analyzing them both helped her to process her traumatic experiences but also deepened her knowledge, with the two going hand in hand.

> That is why I say writing about revolution—my experience of revolution—in my MA thesis was essential. At that time I was writing and crying behind the computer most of the time. But that helped me, by writing and analyzing, to distance myself from it, to understand it, to analyze it. And later, when I was analyzing the life stories of women like myself in the Netherlands and their struggles to belong, it became

too overwhelming and I became sick actually. It was so intense to analyze those lives and also to be confronted with my own life through their stories. Then the past and the present became so vivid, my old struggles and nightmares and sense of non-belonging in the present…

You know, in all these phases, I have been able to give the past the place that it deserves. Not ignoring it, but also not letting it overshadow my life—my present and my future. In that sense, I think I was lucky in my choices. And the fact that I was stubborn enough to include my life in all the phases of my academic work and writing helped me. (Ghorashi, 2020)

Halleh's reflections suggest that analyzing, processing and sharing experiences of repressive times in conjunction with academic research can benefit not just the individual involved but also the academic field and society. As Halleh makes clear, doing so enabled her to put the past where it belonged, so that it did not dominate her and allowed her to see both the present as well as the future. At the same time, knowledge based on embodied, personal experiences that have been sufficiently analyzed and put in context is vital in gaining an understanding of the human consequences of violence and oppression. Such knowledge is, of course, positioned and partial but that does not make it unique. However, if developed through a process that is systematic and involves a questioning, open attitude, such knowledge can contribute vital insights not easily gained through other means.

I could not escape the fact that I had an emotional involvement in this research. But the joy came when I realized that this does not have to be a barrier, but can actually become a key to approach such emotionally charged research. (Ghorashi, 2003, p. 14)

In conclusion: narratives of change

How have experiences of war and oppression inspired Halleh to engage in political action aimed at challenging injustice? Halleh highlights that the injustices she experienced as a child—as a consequence of living with a mother with a mental health disorder and of her years in an oppressive boarding school system—have shaped her identity. Beginning in childhood, Halleh possessed a questioning mind and a strong sense of (in)justice. At the same time, being a witness to and participant in extraordinary events changed her life profoundly and became a driving force for her later work. The long-term transformative effect that experiencing and participating in a revolution had on Halleh and other Iranians at the time, including those who subsequently fled the country, become clear from both Halleh's life story and the stories of the women in her research. For many, their lives were forever altered, as they were unable to resume a conventional life after having experienced freedom and brutal oppression in quick succession. This experience led many to want to continue to contribute to the world in substantial ways.

Halleh's story furthermore highlights the importance of youth to periods of resistance. It was as a teen and young adult that she and many others engaged in politics and were shaped by these political engagements. In the early years of the revolution, when Halleh was a teenager, she experienced radical shifts in her life world. She, at this young age, was in a position where she could contribute to the struggle for a better society in Iran, giving her a deep sense of meaningfulness. This experience of meaningfulness derived in part from having a strong sense of agency and belonging, feeling able to contribute to important events in the history of Iran, and being respected for her contributions and strengths. When people are young in such times of change, Halleh says, they are often also more radical in their perspectives than they would have been if the experience had taken place at an older age.

Throughout her academic career, Halleh has been dedicated to fight against what she terms "othering". In much of her academic work, as well as in her interview with me, she describes the devastating impacts that othering stereotypes have on individuals. She draws clear lines between the processes of othering she experienced in Iran after the revolution, and those she experienced in the Netherlands. The fundamental difference lies in the very explicit, open ways that othering occurred in Iran after the revolution, which made it clear to her whom to fight and how—in contrast to the more implicit and often subconscious ways that it occurs in the Netherlands, requiring her to develop a different strategy to fight it. Intersubjective exchanges through the sharing of stories across difference is one vital strategy, in Halleh's view. Besides writing and speaking about practices of othering, Halleh has also facilitated such intersubjective exchanges in order to put her ideas in practice and work on transforming individual perspectives, one individual at a time.

This is one example of how throughout her academic career, Halleh has wanted, and been able, to combine academic work and civic activism. Throughout her story, her interest in knowledge gained from books and discussions is always linked to concrete transformative action. Halleh is only able to integrate knowledge and action fully, I would argue, as a result of rigorous explorations of her own life history and the stories of women like her. Having taken ownership of her story and having worked with a range of academic tools to understand it fully, Halleh is currently an engaged academic. This painful process has enabled her to transform her own story in ways that allow her to draw on it as a source of inspiration to fight for social justice and enabled her to have an impact on the many individuals she inspires, whether they are students, women whose life stories she writes, or key stakeholders in the public debate in the Netherlands on inclusion and diversity.

4

Diala Brisly: "The braver you are, the more you will see"

Diala Brisly is a Syrian artist whose artistic practice spans a variety of media, including animation, painting, comic books, illustration, and murals. Recurring themes in her work are social justice, freedom, and the voices of children. I got to know Diala Brisly and her work in the spring of 2019, when she was invited to Oslo to participate in a seminar series organized by the PRIO Centre on Culture and Violent Conflict (CCC). Diala was asked to present her work and then to discuss the inspirations and responsibilities of artists and academics whose work focuses on violent conflict with then senior researcher Kjetil Selvik and myself. Over lunch before the event, we started to get to know each other a bit. I had already read a transcription of a life story interview with Diala.[9]

"The braver you are, the more you will see", which is Diala's motto on her Facebook page, powerfully sums up my impression of Diala at that first meeting. I was instantly dazzled by both Diala and her artwork, and my sense of awe has only grown. Reflecting on why this is, I can think of several reasons. First, as I noticed immediately when she first presented and talked about images

Image 4.1

of her artwork in Oslo, she conveys a unique combination of extreme vulnerability and strength. The openness with which she communicated the trauma of war and of working with refugee children affected by war impressed me deeply. To present such powerful artwork on the human consequences of war without hiding the traumatic effects of violent conflict and exile on oneself requires incredible bravery, it seems to me. Similarly, it takes courage to see clearly what is going on, to refuse to flinch or turn away, in order to visualize and illustrate those human consequences of war. The braver Diala is in her art and her presentations of her work, the more fully the eyes of others will be opened, I suspect.

Second, Diala stubbornly insists through her art on engaging with beauty and playfulness in dark times (Image 4.1). The result is images that simultaneously encompass ugliness and beauty. There is a lightness and a playfulness in her drawings of children with missing limps, for example, which affects me as a viewer of those images. Having studied the human consequences of war for decades, I am familiar with the themes Diala represents, and yet they somehow become more visible to me because of the unfamiliar motifs and styles that Diala uses. The contrast between, on the one hand, the ugliness of the consequences of war and, on the other hand, the warmth of the colors and the careful detail with which she presents humanity, forces me to pause and look with an openness and curiosity that I rarely feel when faced with the suffering of others.

And finally, the extent of Diala's productivity is very high as is her creativity in employing different materials and styles to grapple with and convey social justice issues that she cares deeply about. It is difficult to get a complete overview of her work because there is simply so much of it. Although I will not be able to present here the full variety of her artistic and human contributions, I aim to offer parts of her life story in a way that affords insight into her creative practice and her commitment to issues of freedom and social justice in Syria and beyond. After describing the development of her artistic engagement since the 2011 Syrian uprising and while in exile, I will focus on the interconnected themes of inspiration, trauma, and responsibility that emerge from her life story and work.

Art as a safe space: Diala's childhood and young adult years

Listening to Diala talk about her childhood in Syria, it is clear to me that she faced many challenges. She tells a story of a stubborn young girl who always questioned the many things that did not seem right to her and whose artistic work created a safe space in an environment that offered her no sense of belonging, comfort, or stability. Outside her home, she was always made to feel different because she was not born in Syria and had a grandfather who had come to Syria seeking refuge. At the same time, her home situation was problematic for her. Her parents often fought and Diala's relationship with them was strained. On top of this, they left Diala with the responsibility of taking care of her younger siblings when she herself was barely an adult. These experiences as a child and teenager shaped Diala's life in important ways, as did the Syrian uprising.

A challenging childhood: questioning what it means to belong

I was born in Kuwait, and I stayed there for ten years. Then I went back to Syria in 1990. I was ten years old. It was really a big move for me. Especially because when I went to Syria, we had a different accent. So at school, kids were making fun of us, because we talked differently. And at the same time we had this really weird family name. So everyone asked us, "What is this family name, because it doesn't sound Arab?" Because my grandfather, he's originally from Turkey and he went to Syria because of dictatorship in Turkey at that time. And he got married to a Syrian woman, so he became Syrian. So I'm the third generation in Syria on my father's side. And that made me think a lot about what citizenship really means, and what belonging even means.

So when I became a teenager I heard a lot of things here and there, like "Where are you from?" It's the same in Europe, we are not really that different. Sometimes you even have racism in the middle of Damascus, you know. In Damascus, they try to be more polite sometimes. They don't really talk about it, but they give you hints. I always felt kind of alien in a way. Imagine being Palestinian or Kurdish there! So that made me really think a lot about this, and I decided not to think about belonging and care about nationality and things. (Brisly, 2019a)

While Diala was struggling to find her own answers to big questions such as what it means to belong or to be a citizen, her home situation did not provide the comfort or stability she may have needed at such a time. When we talked in 2019, it had been ten years since she and her siblings had been in touch with her mother. Initially, they stopped talking to her to protect themselves mentally; later, political differences added to their reasons for breaking off contact. Yet Diala's story makes clear that her relationship with her parents was already troubled when she was a child. Diala describes herself as leading a "double life": one at home, which was full of strife, and one outside the house with friends, which was happy and revealed no trace of her homelife. She also identifies herself as strong-willed.

> I am a very stubborn person, ever since I was a kid. Everyone knows this. My mom hated this in my personality. Everyone did. Because I was like, "I wanna do it!". No one can stop me, you know?
>
> I had a very tough time with my family at home. That's what made me someone who does not want to give up. I really had a double life. My life at home was very sad and stressful, and outside I was very active and energetic. I just wanted to play, I just wanted to go around with my friends. So I had a double personality: I was very quiet and shy around my family and my family's friends, but with my friends I was really crazy.
>
> I didn't want to give up on having a happy life. Sometimes, I remember, I used to go out of my house crying because of a fight that happened between me and my mom. But once I went out to meet my friends, I always wiped the tears off my face and said, "I have to be happy, because we live once." So I always had these two lives because of this. And I think that, just because of my relationship with my parents, I became

more stubborn to hold on to all these opportunities in life with my teeth and hands and everything. So yeah, I didn't want to give up on having a normal life like others, just because I have a shitty situation at home. (Brisly, 2019a)

From an early age, one activity that she could retreat to while at home—"escaping her own life", as she describes it—was art-making, specifically, drawing and painting. As far back as she could remember, Diala was "the artist of the family" and wanted to create art. Her mother did not appreciate her artistic engagement and wished that Diala would take up science, a subject Diala also liked. Yet it was her artwork that offered Diala a crucial safe place where she could relax, a way to escape from her homelife. Responding to a question about what inspires her art, Diala reflects:

In the very beginning, I knew I could be good with this. And I knew that I had this passion. I used to wake up at three in the morning to draw when I was still living with my parents, because it was the most peaceful time when everyone was sleeping at home. When I was a teenager. So it was my…do you know this movie *Being [John] Malkovich*? […]

For me, it's an amazing movie and it's very important. It's about a secret floor between floors. It's really small and secret, and when you go inside of it, you find yourself inside Malkovich, the actor. So I always try to find my secret floor and live my own life, far from other people. Waking up at three in the morning was like *Being Malkovich*. I always wanted to have this very private time, and I felt like I really had. Maybe without even knowing, it was my escape from all this mess in my life since I was a teenager. It made me feel really relaxed to do art. I think it started this way. (Brisly, 2019a)

Diala remembers that her parents quarreled all the time, hosting many parties and then fighting. Diala describes a particular occasion when she was about 17 years old. It was lunchtime and her parents were fighting, as they often did. Her younger sister spoke up and told them that she and their other children were fed up with the quarrels. She suggested they divorce rather than stay together for the sake of their children. Shortly afterward, Diala's father moved out and her parents divorced. Within a few years, both had remarried, her father immediately and her mother after two years. Before she remarried, Diala's mother was away from home for increasingly long stretches at a time.

Then finally she left when I was 20 years old. And my younger sister was in love with someone and during the time my mom was increasingly absent, she just wanted to leave home. So she got married, and had already left home. Just to get rid of the situation. So yeah, I had to be responsible for my other two siblings. My sister was 14 years old and my brother was 10 years old. So it was a really tough time for me, because I had to work. I had to find my way in this cartoon company as well. I was working on something to make my living and getting my training in that company while studying civil engineering and taking care of my siblings. So it was such a tough time. (Brisly, 2019a)

Reflecting on this period, Diala says that, although she is now very close to her sisters, she at times feels guilty that she did not do enough for them in the past. She says she tried her best, but they needed more: "They needed real parents, and I wasn't a real parent" (Brisly, 2019a). At age 20, Diala carried a heavy emotional burden and her responsibility for her siblings shaped the choices available to her in terms of study and work.

Young adulthood: study and work

For about five years after high school, Diala moved between the arts and the sciences. She studied mechanical engineering for some months, then Arabic literature between 1999 and 2001, and after that, civil engineering from 2002 to 2004. Although she was interested in studying fine arts, when she finally had the chance to study them, she decided not to because she worried that formal education in the subject would result in her developing the same style that all the other students were taught. "Afraid to be put in a box", she decided instead to teach and train herself.

It was in her years at the civil engineering institute that Diala discovered the level of corruption in Syria. At times, examiners failed to mark exams properly and professors expected students to pay them for passing grades. Diala was unwilling to provide the bribe required to receive a passing grade on a final exam in civil engineering.

> I didn't graduate, because I had one subject to graduate, but professor wanted a bribe, which is totally normal in Syria. Totally normal. And I didn't want to do it. I was already working in Spacetoon channel, a cartoon channel in Syria. That was in 2001. So I went there and

I remember I told the secretary, I told her: "Could I ask you a question?" and she told me, "What?" and I said, "How come I scored a zero in my exam? If I write just a few words, I would get more than a zero, so how come I got zero?" She told me, "Well, you can apply again for the exam", and I told her, "I did it eight times already. I really don't need the certificate. I am already working". And I was very angry and I just left, and she was like, "Nooo, you have to think about your future. The certificate is really important." And of course, socially, people consider you a loser if you don't graduate. But I just didn't care. My friends, they were against me about this, and they thought I have to pay. But I was really frustrated to do these wrong things. I know there is no other way even. But I just didn't want to do it. And what strengthened me at that time is that I already had a job. Like we say in our expressions, "I had a big head and I didn't want to do it." (Brisly, 2019a)

By that time, as Diala indicates, she was already working. In 2001, she took a position as an animator at Spacetoon channel. Her story about how she got the job reveals her stubborn insistence on doing things her own way. She had applied to work as an artist for the company and was given a chance, but after a week, she was told that her style was too realistic and not a good fit for the company. However, during that week, she met a very good cartoonist and he was willing to teach her what she needed to know in order to work for the company. After training with him for seven months, during which she studied and worked elsewhere, an opportunity arose for her to contribute to one of Spacetoon's TV programs.

So I was training for seven months, without getting any payment. Usually they train people and they give them small payment until they become really good. But I didn't get any payment from them. And one day after seven months, they had a really urgent episode to be shown on the TV. And the artist who was doing the layout had troubles and didn't do it. So I told them, "How about me doing this? You can just have a break and I will do it." So I stayed there for two days and two nights without even sleeping and I worked on it. The director said, "Yeah, it's really a very nice episode. Who did it?" There were two artists and they were not available, and they said it's me and she was like, "How come? She is not even employed here." And she said, "Yeah, but she did it." And then I got my first payment. So I became a very important artist in the company, finally. (Brisly, 2019a)

By late 2005, after working at Spacetoon for about five years, Diala became frustrated that all the projects looked so similar. Wanting to be involved in different types of projects and to practice different kinds of art, she decided to work as a freelancer. For the next five years or so, she illustrated children's magazines and worked artistically on a host of other things, including video games, film, animation, and advertising. In the run-up to the 2011 Syrian uprising, Diala was again experiencing frustration because she felt that she and her colleagues were not sending strong messages through their work at a potentially momentous time in history.

The 2011 Syrian uprising: activist and artist

Protests against the Syrian regime began in the spring of 2011, as part of the wider Arab Spring, to demand democratic reforms and the resignation of President Bashar al-Assad. These protests have been described as the civil uprising phase of the civil war that followed, or are sometimes referred to as the Syrian Revolution. Diala became an activist. She began by helping set up field hospitals. As she explains:

> I started doing this in the beginning of 2011 when Daraa, where the revolution started, was under siege. A friend of mine was living in Damascus, but she was originally from Daraa. And she knew the city very well and she had relatives and her brothers there. She said, "I want to send them some medical supplies and food. Who is with me?", and I told her, "I will be with you." So I started doing this because I had a car; it was really easy. I went to a pharmacist who I knew was from Daraa originally. So I asked him for help, and I told him I want to buy this and that. And he gave me everything I needed. I filled my car to the brim. It was really full. It was really crazy to do that, because if someone had stopped me at the checkpoint…it was really crazy. But in the very beginning they were not checking cars.
> But he took me aside outside of the pharmacy and he told me, "Listen, I gave you everything you need now, but do not ever come back here. It's really dangerous and that will put me in trouble." And I totally understood this, so I talked to someone else who was arrested

for 18 years for political reasons, who was working in a pharmacy. I told him, "I want to do this and we can do it secretively. I won't tell about you." And he was paranoid to do this. He refused. I told him, "Okay, you can think about it." After two weeks he told me, "Okay, I will do it." Because he had real anger from being arrested for 18 years and getting tortured for a long time, underground. We know Syria has two separated lives: under the ground and above ground.

So he told me, "I will do it, but please be really careful. Don't mention my name." I have forgotten his name now. We were really good at forgetting each other's names. Most of the time we were working with nicknames. So that if you are tortured or something and you are forced to talk, you have no information to provide. (Brisly, 2019a)

Diala explains why well-equipped field hospitals were crucial to support the civil uprising.

Because protesting in Syria, you know, it's really very dangerous. And it never happened without blood, people either get beaten or you find shooting everywhere. And if someone gets injured, it's really dangerous to go to any hospital in Syria.

Being injured after a protest is really dangerous in Syria, and you can't go to any hospital. Because you might go in with a bullet in your leg and you go out with a bullet in your head. So nurses in Syria, they are really scary for us. Because that is part of our history. When the massacre happened in Hama in 1981, many people got killed in hospitals. And that happened also in the beginning of our revolution. So activists started preparing field hospitals that are hidden in shelters and buildings and secret places. (Brisly, 2019a).

Asked why she decided to take on a dangerous task like delivering medical equipment when she could have chosen to do nothing, Diala answers:

> I knew about all the corruption in Syria. I was never satisfied and happy, especially with my studies and everything. It's not easy to make your own way in Syria… And anyone who is really smarter than usual, he might be in danger and get arrested and things. So I knew that we had a dictatorship and our life wasn't really fair for us. We were isolated, living in a bubble. We were not even allowed to travel. Everything was not okay. So when the revolution started, I wanted to be involved. I got really involved in preparing field hospitals, so I gave it priority because that gave other people who were doing different kinds of activism sustainability.
>
> So I gave it priority over going out to protest. I was protesting in the days that I didn't have delivery. I remember there was a big protest in 2012 and it was snowing in Damascus. It was so beautiful. And there were like 3,000 people in the streets. That was so rare to happen because it's not allowed for us to protest. We do a protest for five minutes and run away, and we have to survive, you know. But that was really big. I was afraid that there will be shooting in the protest and I had delivery that afternoon. So I didn't go to the

protest. But I was dying to go there. For me, it was a part of history. And there was shooting, indeed, but maybe I wouldn't be injured.

But I wanted to be sure I would be safe and not be selfish to go there just to have this feeling, this amazing feeling. And I gave priority to do this delivery. Because that helps many people. I always try to think in a practical way… I don't want to do this protest because I help thousands of people with preparing field hospitals. Sometimes you can't really follow your feelings, you have to be rational and do the right thing. As much as you can, of course. That's why I was preparing field hospitals, because there are many people who were doing amazing things and they need this. They need to survive. They need these field hospitals. (Brisly, 2019a)

Contributing through art

Diala also increasingly found ways to contribute to the uprising as an artist. Prior to the civil uprising, artists were very careful, recognizing that there were many things that they could not articulate without risking trouble. The uprising created an opening for new forms of expression. As Diala explains at a public seminar at PRIO in 2019. "After the uprising we had the right—in a way, we gave ourselves the right—to express our opinion about other things" (Brisly, 2019b). The uprising thus enabled Diala to express things that before she could not and to do things that felt meaningful to her, she tells me.

When the Syrian uprising started in 2011, I always felt that what I'm doing in general about work is not satisfying for me. Because I wasn't working on interesting topics, let's say. Especially in Syria you can't really…really express much by your art or whatever, because of the dictatorship that we have. So when the Syrian uprising started, that was a very big boost for my art, and for many other people as well. Many other artists and journalists, writers, and musicians. In 2012, I created my first art to express what is happening in Syria. It was coming from frustration. I wanted to say anything that could really express what was going on. Then, because we didn't really have journalism—we had alternative journalism—some journalists started sharing my artwork to support their reports. So that encouraged me more to do art and I got a good impact. I just started because I was really angry but then I felt it was really, very… It's stronger to express it through art because people pay more attention to this. So that literally encouraged me to do more and more.

[…] I wanted to give meaning to my art. But it was really hard to express other things, because there are many things that are not allowed to talk about in Syria. So the revolution helped me a lot and gave me a big boost to do a lot of things that are meaningful. I wanted to talk about everything that wasn't allowed to talk about before. When I realized that art could really help, it's not just a picture on the wall, I wanted to discover more about this. (Brisly, 2019a)

When, in 2011, Diala decided to use her art to express how she felt about the Syrian situation, she began with a collection that she called Leave Us. To communicate what was happening in Syria, she experimented with different images and metaphors. Leave Us comprises eight images drawn in sepia after which

Ecoline® red watercolor paint was blown onto the image. Each image is accompanied by a text that says "Leave [something] and leave us". Examples include "leave my last hand and leave us" and "leave our doctors and leave us".

At the seminar in Oslo, Diala presents some of the images (Images 4.2a, b, c) in the series and explains:

Images 4.2a 4.2b, 4.2c

This collection I call Leave Us. Whenever something happened in Syria, I wanted to express it in a different way. There were a lot of kids that…got involved in the war even though they were not decision-makers.

[…] [T]here was a field in Damascus suburb, it was full of cactuses, and the government was afraid that people would go there to hide some weapons, so they destroyed the whole field. Different things happened. Of course, journalists and doctors were targeted by both the Syrian government and ISIS later on in 2014. Syrian activists were in the middle, actually. (Brisly, 2019b)

Realizing she had an impact through her art, and that journalists, civil society organizations, and activists were displaying her images to support their own work, Diala continued to produce art about the situation in Syria. Her artwork supporting the hunger strike in the Adra prison (Image 4.3) became the featured image of the movement, and her illustrations were used for fundraising by the White Helmets, a Syrian humanitarian organization, for whom she later created an animation video about cluster bombs. She also worked on a commission for Amnesty International and a range of international organizations. At the same time, Diala was confronted with skepticism and doubt by people who questioned the relevance of art to "real life" and world politics.

Once I was talking to a really young man in FSA, Free Syrian Army. He told me, "Yes, your art is nice and beautiful, but do you think it will change anything in our situation or bring down Assad? This is not going to happen." I like challenges. My life is based on challenges anyway. When people tell me "Do this", I do the opposite. Just like, it's me. Now I listen more, I'm getting

Image 4.3

better at that. But I don't like to know that something is impossible. It drives me crazy. So when he said that, I started to try to find more useful ways to create my art, and give it a bigger role than just expressing what is happening. (Brisly, 2019a)

The issues of relevance and making a difference have always concerned Diala, and questions related to these themes inspire the art she creates as much as her own creative drive does. Her drive and ability to make a difference have always influenced her career choices; it would soon influence her geographical location as well.

Choosing exile in order to contribute

An armed insurgency followed the civil uprising and lasted for about a year. Beginning in the summer of 2012, a new, intensified phase of the conflict began as internal divisions grew and international interference increased. For Diala, the escalation of the conflict led to an increasing sense of the futility of the ongoing civic activism. She decided to leave Syria, as did so many others at that time or in the years that followed.

> I left for Istanbul in 2013, because of the revolution and because the situation became harder to protest. I was preparing field hospitals as well during this time. Then it became harder and more dangerous to do this. I had a car so I was delivering [medical supplies] by myself. But then, because of the checkpoints, Damascus became an island (Image 4.4), so it was really hard to do this. So

I felt I'm useless there. We can't do any kind of activism anymore. So I decided to leave.

In 2013, I felt like we were living in a waiting room and everything was going backwards. We didn't really achieve anything with this activism and this revolution. It became really dangerous to stay. So I moved to Istanbul. And I thought from there I could really meet other activists and we could work on things maybe from outside. We tried to meet and organize protests and such and do things. But then I felt like we were doing these things just to feel good about ourselves. I felt like we were not really achieving anything. We just didn't want to forget what was happening. (Brisly, 2019a)

Diala had trouble finding work in Istanbul and sustained herself through her savings until she finally was forced to sell her car. Her financial situation was extremely precarious and she had a

Image 4.4

lot of time on her hands, so she began following the news from Syria very closely. This inspired her to create more art about the situation there, and led to increased recognition of her work among Syrian activists and others. She created art for campaigns and for a children's magazine that was distributed in Syria. These engagements were meaningful to Diala, although they did not provide the financial support she needed. Then, after a year in Istanbul, she landed a project with a Turkish cartoon company. Although her financial situation started to improve, she decided to leave. She ended up in Lebanon, working with Syrian refugee children.

> My life started becoming better in Turkey, I started to have a stable life. But I don't know, I thought it's better to go to Lebanon to try to help there. Maybe it's crazy. But I don't regret it. I feel like I did the right thing because it kept me closer to the Syrian situation and more involved with what is happening. Which was really very important for me. It was my priority.
>
> But for some reason, it was really good for my career as well, which is something I didn't expect. I just wanted to help in a way and just survive with my living. But I don't know, it helped me a lot. I got really good exposure and recognition, for example, in Europe. And I helped to get some attention to these kids. I see now a lot of people try to help prepare school tents or alternative education in Lebanon. So I think for both me and the kids, it was really successful and helpful, you know? But it wasn't the plan. The plan was just to feel like I really can help and be useful in a way.

I was lucky that I lived in Damascus but these kids paid the price because they lived in different places. I mean, Bashar Assad didn't want to destroy Damascus because he lives there. He can't destroy his home, you know. But he didn't really care about destroying all over Syria. So I was just lucky that I lived in Damascus. So I felt that it's not fair that other people pay the price and we just don't support them and we forget about them and try to have our own life. It's not really fair, you know? (Brisly, 2019a)

Diala left Turkey because she felt the protests she was engaged in there were meaningless. They were not gaining the attention of audiences they wanted to reach—passersby would just stare at the protesters—and they were not achieving their goals. Diala's decision to leave was also prompted by the death of her brother, who stepped on a mine in Syria while trying to avoid a roadblock. Diala shares in a later interview what her family was told about the circumstances of his death:

My brother was forced to go into military service, from which he tried to escape. From my side, I talked to someone related to the Free Syrian Army to help smuggle my brother out. But we lost contact with him; apparently, he was in jail because of trying to escape. When he was released, a big conflict was raging in the north of Syria, close to Deir Ez-Zor, where he was stationed. He could have escaped then, but he decided to stay to help his friends provide first aid. So he left his post to deliver medical supplies. When he came back, he could not find a direct way, so he went through a minefield and he stepped on one of the land mines, which exploded…and he died there. (Brisly, 2021b)

Diala could not attend her brother's funeral because she learned that she was blacklisted and would have problems at the border if she tried to cross into Syria. Her sister in Damascus took care of the funeral despite her own tough circumstances. Both her brother's death and her inability to return to Syria left Diala with feelings of guilt.

> I feel guilty, yeah. Sometimes my guilt feelings come from my siblings because I feel like I didn't do well for them…And losing my brother always gave me this guilt feeling as well. So that's what motivated me to go back to Lebanon to work with kids. Because I wanted to do something instead. Because I felt like I can't really protect my brother and save his life, so [her voice trembles] … It's really tough for me to talk about this. (Brisly, 2019a)

A month after her brother's death, Diala created a painting (Image 4.5) that she says symbolizes the losses that Syrians experienced and also expresses how such losses can promote empathy and mutual support. The painting does not just reflect her own loss, she says, but recognizes the collective nature of Syria's loss as a consequence of the war.

> This is…it means a lot to me. It looks kind of kid-style and simple. I drew this one month after losing my brother. I call it "I will be your arm". It is about when many of us have lost, we know what losing means and we can really support each other. It is not just about losing limbs, it is about…losing anything in your life.

Image 4.5

When that happened, I had a feeling of course of a big
loss for me, and it was really sad, but it was another way
to understand what other Syrians are losing in the war.
(Brisly, 2019b)

Diala has moved a number of other times since leaving Syria in
order to be able to contribute to the situation in Syria or to help

Syrian refugees (see also Horst, 2020) or, more generally, to be able to engage meaningfully in something bigger than just her own livelihood.

Creating art with and for Syrian kids in Lebanon

Becoming more financially stable in Turkey did not mean much to Diala on a personal level and remaining in Turkey did not allow her to try to improve the situation in Syria or help those affected by the war. So she moved to Lebanon to do something to support the many Syrian refugee children stranded in camps there.

> I noticed how many kids were now displaced and had to skip school. They are really the part of the Syrian people who pay the heaviest price for this. And I was really depressed in Istanbul that I couldn't do anything from there. So I decided to move to Lebanon. Because people in refugee camps there, they need everything. I think Syrian refugees in Lebanon have the toughest circumstances compared to other refugees. So I decided to move there and to work with kids. (Brisly, 2019a)

Diala offered art workshops that she hoped would be therapeutic for the children. She had not studied psychology, but she started reading about (arts-based) therapy and experimenting with different approaches, communicating in the process with friends who were therapists. Her workshops grew out of her own experiences and ideas, but she always asked her friends for expert help and advice.

While working in the camps, she observed that Syrian children in Lebanon had limited access to regular education. Unable to attend regular school, they were offered alternative education projects in the refugee camps. Diala was inspired to make murals for these refugee schools (Image 4.6). At the seminar in Oslo, she presents images of some of these murals and explains:

> So, I started doing this in refugee camps, where there are alternative education centers. And school tents. Because most Syrian kids study in school tents, which are really very small, it could be one classroom or two, maximum. They are really very small. It is super cold in winter because it snows there in the Beqaa valley. And it is super hot in summer. So, I really wanted to make it attractive for them to go there. (Brisly, 2019b).

In the life story interview, Diala discusses her work in Lebanon at length, explaining her inspirations for pursuing this work on her own with very limited financial support. To Diala, creating art in the refugee context was crucial both to inspire the kids to go

Image 4.6

to school and to challenge the reality of people in the refugee camps not being treated as fully human.

> I started doing murals in education centers around, so kids get encouraged again to go to school. My first mural was in 2014 in Aarsal town, at the Lebanese-Syrian border. It was for a public library that was established by an activist called Diana Yakub, who did so much to provide kids some help. So I offered to do this mural for her. And when I saw the response from kids, how they really liked it and they were amazed, and said, "Wow, this is the best thing we saw, ever. It's not like Micky Mouse, it's not like...and it really looks like us", because they saw kids flying with books and they felt like it's them. It touched them more than Micky Mouse, of course. So when they told me this, it really encouraged me and I wanted to do it more and more. Of course, it was my personal initiative and I was doing this as volunteering. Because local Syrian organizations, they mostly have a lack of...funds. Because they are based on donations. That makes their projects not sustainable. So I wanted to offer this to local organizations and I told them, "You cover the materials and transportation, and I do this for free." It is really not expensive to cover the materials. Because I know how to do it in a cheap way.
>
> Then I had a reputation of doing this. So sometimes I went to the organizations and offered them, sometimes the organizations asked me for this, which is really helpful because you need partners to do it in this refugee camp. You can't just go there and show up and do it. At least they have connections with people there.

Because people there, they need to have their own privacy, they need to feel like they matter to others, because sometimes it gets like tourism: going to refugee camps doing projects. This is not really comfortable for refugees there. They feel like they are immaterial, in a way. I don't blame them, actually. So yeah, that was really my biggest project that kept me very busy for two years in Lebanon. (Brisly, 2019a)

Working creatively with and for children has been a central part of Diala's work for decades. Much of her artistic work in Syria and Turkey since the 2011 uprising has engaged with the plight of children as victims of war. Her artistic work before the uprising was often directed at children; then, she was simply creating art to entertain them and make them feel happy. Much of her work in Lebanon was driven by her wish to give Syrian refugee children the childhoods and feelings of security that they had lost as a consequence of the war and life in exile. For example, Diala tried to redirect their imaginations, as reflected in art, to bring back memories of childhood from before the war.

In the beginning when I started working with kids, it was even traumatizing for me since they were drawing just about war, because it was still fresh in their memory. It was red, blood, blood, blood. That is why I have all of this red in my drawings, because I got it from the kids. Then, when I saw this…that when you give them the free space to draw whatever they want, they draw a lot about the war…So, after that I started working on different things just to support them. To draw themselves, what they think about themselves, what they think about each other. Kind of replacing concepts in their memory, for example, about flying. When they think of flying, it is just jet fighters, but there are many things that fly that are more beautiful than jet fighters and rockets. (Brisly, 2019b)

Although Diala went to the refugee camps to use art to help children, the experience was also therapeutic for her. She says that she felt useful in a way that she had not while living in Istanbul. She also learned a lot from the children. Working with them, in her view, forced her to look at herself and how she was handling her trauma and exile compared to how the children were. At both the Oslo seminar and in one of our interview conversations, she talks about what she gained from working with children.

> I got all my strength from them because…they can forget about what is happening and what is going to happen and they live in this moment. This is really something very helpful that adults do not always succeed on achieving. (Brisly, 2019b)
>
> Because kids have more strength, and the ability to live in the moment. So I learned this from them. And I thought, if they have this, they adapt their way of living. They have a really hard and tough life. They have trauma because of the war and they get trauma every day from their life in refugee camps.
>
> But despite that they still…whenever they live any good moment, they live it to the max. They go insane, they go crazy. They are full of life. So when I compared myself to them at that time, I was like, "What the hell am I doing? I am trying to help these creatures, but they are really stronger than me. And then I refuse to go out

and have fun." This is a contradiction I'm going through.
(Brisly, 2019a)

Living in Lebanon for two years helped Diala in many ways. It allowed her to believe that she could contribute in meaningful ways, on whatever scale was possible for her, to alleviate the consequences of the civil war for the children she worked with. It enabled her to challenge her feeling that she could not or should not enjoy herself because of the injustices that had befallen so many in her country. And her artistic work began to be noticed not just by fellow Syrians but also internationally, as she began interacting with international NGOs and journalists in humanitarian environments. Then, in 2016, knowing that her passport would soon expire and her legal grounds for staying in Lebanon would be shaky, she applied for asylum in France.

A visa to Europe—living in France

Although Diala had tried to travel outside Syria before, she had never received the necessary visas (Image 4.7). This time, however, she was granted asylum and moved to France. She recognizes her good fortune: her current permit allows her to stay in France for ten years and to continue working as an artist without worry about her legal status. Further, having asylum in France means that she can travel freely in Europe. Before the early 2020 global lockdown in response to the pandemic, Diala traveled extensively across Europe at the invitation of various organizations and individuals with whom she was working or who were simply interested in her work. These opportunities increased her international visibility and profile. But having asylum in France meant that traveling back to Lebanon would not be as

Image 4.7

easy as it had been and that meant, in turn, that she could not be involved in the projects she had initiated in Lebanon. However, Diala found new solutions.

When I moved to Europe, it was really hard for me to get a visa again to go to Lebanon and do murals and the tents there. That was really sad for me and gave me a guilty feeling, but since I used to do it on a canvas already, because the tents were made of fabric, I thought, "Okay, I will build a big wall and make murals and fold them to send them back to Lebanon." The only thing that is missing is the interaction with kids. But at least it is better than nothing. (Brisly, 2019b)

Diala was able to continue to be involved because of her collaboration with two other women. Diala sends the murals to Jacqueline Flori, a friend who lives in Munich and runs Zeltschule, an organization that sends school tents to the refugee camps. Jacqueline takes Diala's murals to Lebanon and builds new school tents with them. In Lebanon, Tandem Ibrahim, who is Syrian, runs a local organization called Alphabet Alternative Education, which provides education to children in the school tents. In this way, the three women work together on the project. Jacqueline also fundraises in cooperation with German schoolchildren. When Diala, after receiving her French permit, was finally able to travel to Europe, she created a mural in the school in Munich to thank the children for the many tents that had been purchased as a result of their fund-raising.

We had this connection between German kids and Syrian kids, just by videos and some projects. And they never met, so I wanted to do this project to thank them. And the theme was: "You help kids from far away but you never met them, so if you imagine that these clouds spin around the planet that we live on and you want to send messages to these kids, what kind of messages might you put in these clouds?" So, they really put a lot of nice things. Some of them, they put a crocodile, but I do not know what they meant [laughs]. But they put really nice messages about peace and "I hope you have peace in your life", safety and things. (Brisly, 2019b)

In the last few years, Diala's work has been in high demand, so she is busy with many different types of projects. She works a lot with and for children in Syria and Europe and also tries to raise awareness about the situation in Syria and about Syrian refugees.

What I do is either work for Syrians inside of Syria or in the refugee camps, or I do my work to European audience so I can raise awareness about the situation. Because people really have no idea what's going on in Lebanon especially. Of course, definitely there are hard circumstances as well in Zaatari camp in Jordan, but I don't have experience there because I never managed to get a visa there. So I talk about my own experience, which I feel like I really know what I'm talking about. So yeah, wherever I go, if I have a talk, or presentation, or a festival, I try to talk about this.

Because once I had an art symposium in Austria with a few artists and they were all from Europe. One of the artists told me, "I don't understand; if you are in Lebanon and you are safe there, why do all Syrians want to just leave and come to Europe?" And I told him how we are not really safe there. We have to face racism. And a lot of people get arrested, get tortured, get beaten in the street. We have this situation and that situation. And then I knew that European people don't really have a clue about what we have to face in Lebanon.

So I felt like, since I managed to come to Europe and I know that some of my friends are still stuck there and they couldn't manage to get asylum anywhere, it's my responsibility to raise this awareness about what is going on there. Lebanon is not a country of refuge. It's not really prepared for this. And they already have a lot of troubles of their own and they can't really deal with it. So they can't really afford hosting more people. It's really hard. I mean, even Lebanese are not really comfortable there, so what could they give anyone else? (Brisly, 2019a)

Although living in France has given Diala many opportunities to strengthen her international profile as an artist, she finds aspects of her increased visibility deeply problematic. In a follow-up interview she describes her feelings.

Now we are labeled as Syrian artists and that really scares me and makes me have a lot of doubts about all that I am doing. It was a really long struggle, the last three years I struggled with this idea… Especially when sometimes I got invited by curators to exhibitions and I saw the collections of the art works of other Syrians and I see that some of them are not really artists, I know they cheat, and I felt like…it made me have more doubts. Maybe people just look at my work because I am a part of this label "Syrian artist".
[…] It is really a very small room. Category. First it comes from a Syrian, second it comes from a refugee, or maybe first refugee, Syrian, then artist. I am not good enough. But I want to be first categorized as an artist and then the rest comes after. (Brisly, 2021a)

This reductionist labeling of artists who have experienced life in contexts of violent conflict and authoritarianism is deeply problematic. Both the creative aspects of the artwork and what the artist wants to express are at risk of getting lost if the main reason of paying attention to the art and the artist is that the artist is a refugee or comes from a particular country. Individual artists often create art about issues that occupy or engage them. For artists, such as Diala, who are in exile from countries experiencing violent conflict or oppression, this may mean they focus on themes related to that violence or oppression. This does not mean, however, that Diala's art can be reduced to these themes or that she should be understood primarily as a "refugee" or "Syrian" artist. Diala's art, for example, plays with contradictions and challenges conventions by making them explicit in new ways. This is unrelated to her status as a refugee or her country of origin. For instance, in one of her paintings she suggests that some traditions in Germany—a country she has visited regularly since her move to France—are misogynistic.

> I was really shocked because I had never been in Europe before and I did not know that there is still sexism in some places. We had really high expectations to go to Europe, to come here. And I was like, really? (Brisly, 2019b)

From this sentiment of being disappointed in European social realities, Diala developed a painting where she depicts a woman dressed in a German traditional costume meant for men in order to challenge fixed gender roles. Diala's art reflects her critical perspective and her ability to use themes, patterns, symbols, colors, and techniques both to engage her audience's emotions and to make them pause, become more aware, and question that which is taken for granted. She deals with a wide variety of themes and often manages to create artwork in which others recognize themselves. Becoming aware of the inside world as well as the outside world is important, Diala believes, because this awareness helps one to understand others. As she says, "You become less judgmental, more open to others when you understand yourself"(Brisly, 2021a). These are just some examples of aspects of Diala's art that would be overlooked if, as an artist, she is labeled in a reductionist way and if her art is seen as the product of a single aspect of her identity, such as her nationality or her legal status.

Trauma, responsibility, and change

In Diala's story, her sense of responsibility to make a difference and to take care of her own mental state seem, to me, to be intertwined. A belief that what one is doing is meaningful can contribute significantly to mental well-being (McAdams, 2008). At the same time, the line separating a wish to make a difference and unhealthy feelings of over-responsibility and guilt is very thin. For Diala, finding a healthy balance between feeling responsible to challenge injustices and oppression and taking care of herself has meant being realistic about the scale of the contributions and realizing that her work is having an impact on some individuals' lives.

Personal and collective trauma healing

In talking to Diala, I realize that the things that have happened to her, both before and as a consequence of the Syrian civil war, and her direct observation of the suffering of other Syrians, both children and adults, have affected her profoundly. In our follow-up conversation, she talks a lot about the need to take care of oneself, which she sees as a personal responsibility for those who want to help others as she does. This self-care has been difficult for Diala and she has struggled to deal with her knowledge of the realities of war while living a "normal" life in exile.

For a very long time, Diala says, the inspiration for her art came from outside of herself, and she had no desire to engage much with her own feelings or experiences. Then in 2018 she painted four self-portraits which visualized her own experiences. She called the collection Survival Mode and the individual paintings were named *Shattered*, *Break*, *Solitude*, and *Integration* (Images 4.8a, b, c, & d). She mentions this series when I ask her about the most powerful work she ever created. By "powerful" I meant the sense of power that arose in the process of creating a piece of art.

When Diala worked with children, she asked them to connect with themselves and their emotions before expressing themselves creatively. One day, she asked herself why she had the children do this but had never dared to do it herself. As she says, "If I encourage kids and others to do it, I have to go through this experience as well" (Brisly, 2021a). Diala talks about the importance of concentrating on oneself and acknowledges that she tells others to do this but does not do it much herself. At the same time, she believes making a peaceful connection within oneself is essential before one begins working with

others. Gaining a better understanding of herself has become increasingly important for Diala.

> Some people are very well educated, but they don't have self-knowledge. We learn about everything in the world, but we don't look inside. I always say I don't get bored because there is no time. It is not just because of being busy with projects. But just to understand myself; it is a lifetime job. (Brisly, 2021a)

Images 4.8a, 4.8b, 4.8c, & 4.8d

Diala explains that the Survival Mode series means a lot to her because she created it from the inside out. These first in-depth artistic explorations of her inner world inspired Diala to develop a new project.

> I want to make a collection, a painting collection, that is based on trauma. I am reading a lot about trauma now and I am trying to process my own traumas, reading a lot. I am doing this in different ways, so it was very

interesting for me as well to go through the process and the healing and how…why, what are actually symptoms and what is actually the problem. Because the concept sometimes is very mixed for others. Sometimes people think [something] is the problem but actually it is the symptom.

[…] I want to work on this project now, just to raise awareness about the situation. To not judge people from their behavior. Because sometimes…some people have been through a lot and you just see a simple thing and you characterize them according to this behavior. I want to raise awareness…it's not just refugee traumas or people in war or…trauma in general… For me it started because of my experience, not just the war experience but also my experience in childhood. When I talk to my friends here in France or somewhere else, sometimes we feel related in a way, even if it is not on the same level. I think it is very important to raise awareness for this. (Brisly, 2021a)

Diala experienced trauma and substantial levels of insecurity as well as radical breaks in her life long before the start of political developments in Syria as of 2011. She discusses the importance of moving on, something she learned at an early age. It is clear from listening to her that her challenging childhood, the insufficient presence and later absence of her parents, and the resulting responsibility she had for younger siblings, while she herself was still young, affected her deeply. And yet, Diala also describes these experiences as teaching her a valuable lesson: that it is possible to start over.

And I decided to get over it and move on and start all over again. So I always believe that we can start again, and we can look forward. And I think everything… sometimes you get trauma, but you really have to learn from it, more than thinking about the trauma itself. (Brisly, 2019a)

A closely related theme is the importance of trying to live a normal life, both as a way to express defiance and as a way to move on and not become overwhelmed by trauma. This was difficult for Diala and others in exile, and even harder for those in Syria, living in the midst of the war. She recalls how others, through their examples, helped her to make an effort to normalize her own life.

A friend I used to communicate with, he was under siege, and I heard [the friend's] interview with the BBC…: "Once the shelling stops, we immediately gather and we play cards, we have fun and we try our best to really socialize." And that was so inspiring for me. And the kids were very inspiring for me. And I thought, we really have to do it this way. We have to remind ourselves how to live normally. (Brisly, 2019a)

In her first years in exile, Diala did not go out much. She experienced feelings of hyper-responsibility and guilt, and wanted desperately to contribute positively to the situation in Syria. But she says she came to understand the importance of living a normal life, despite how hard this was for her. This required a conscious effort, and was challenging.

As a human being I have rights and responsibilities, and one of the responsibilities is to keep my mental health really good if I want to help other people. Because if I am not good, how could I help other people? So I started really to push myself to go out and meet people. But that was with some anxiety. I wasn't really feeling well when I'm out. (Brisly, 2019a)

Diala's story shows that one's mental health and one's ability to contribute are intrinsically linked. Diala realized that she could not make a difference in the lives of others if she did not take care of her own mental health. At the same time, knowing that she was helping others was essential to improving her mental health, according to Diala. Diala was able to integrate self-care and helping others only when she left Turkey, where she had felt she could not really contribute to improving the situation in Syria or of Syrians, to live in Lebanon.

So when I went to Beirut, that really helped me a lot. Because it made me feel like I'm doing something useful. I'm helping other people, so that helps me in return. And really, working with kids taught me a lot of things. (Brisly, 2019a)

I note that when Diala describes the situation of refugees in Europe, one of her main concerns is that most of them are in no position to make any meaningful contribution to society. While she herself has been fortunate enough to be able to produce meaningful art on themes that she has relative freedom to choose, most refugees are not so lucky. Many are made passive by bureaucratic systems.

But in Europe, you mostly wait [for an answer to your asylum application] for a year and a half or two. So it's a long time…And when you have all this background of the war and depression, you really spend a lot of time inside of your head, and you might go insane. Some of us manage to work in the black market so we get ourselves busy, which is something I know is illegal, but it's healthy. I think it's illegal to leave us without work. We need to work. Not just because of money. We need to work because it's healthier for us. We will have crazy mental issues. Many Syrian people really went insane and some… I have a friend of a friend who committed suicide just because he couldn't have any jobs for two years. That drove him crazy. He felt useless. European countries have to take this into consideration. It's not really good. (Brisly, 2019b)

Again, Diala mentions the interconnections between contributing to society in a meaningful way and people's ability to cope with traumatic experiences. Although she mainly refers to the importance of refugees being able to contribute to the societies they live in, such societal contributions are, indirectly, contributions to their societies from which they have been displaced or have fled. For example, if a Syrian refugee lacks the ability to earn a living and thus establish a place in European society, helping those left behind in Syria is difficult. Thus, local participation is important to enable transnational contributions.

A sense of responsibility

Diala loves making art, and at one point in our interview, she says that art is her life. She elaborates: "I have a lot of things to say. So it's my language and I want to use it. And I don't think it's a luxury to do this. It's part of our responsibilities as well" (Brisly,

2019a). This sense of responsibility comes through clearly in the interviews and the seminar with Diala. My colleagues and I have noted that this sense of duty is often expressed by individuals who have lived through violent conflict (Horst and Lysaker, 2021; Stapnes, Carlquist and Horst, 2020). This sense of responsibility has the potential to become overwhelming, but it can be made manageable by scaling back expectations about what is achievable. As Diala explains:

> I know maybe it's a drop in the ocean, but it's better than nothing. What was depressing in the beginning when I was in Istanbul was that we had way bigger dreams than we could achieve, and when you feel like you can't really achieve what you are doing, you feel depressed. So I decided to make my goals smaller so I can at least be rational and achieve them. So now I think, even if we can work with a few kids and change a few kids' life, it's better than nothing.
>
> I remember once I was talking to someone who was a musician in the north of Syria. He told me—"If there are just five kids I'm working with, I'm not going out of Syria. I want to work with them. It's a waste that we go and leave them alone when there are many fighting groups around and ISIS and the regime and everything"—and that really gave me more strength. He's right. We can't really change the war. We can, but it's really a very, very slow process. And we might not see the results of it. But if we surrender and we pull back, there won't be enough balance. We can't really let these people control everything. We have to resist. At least we can resist, you know.

So, I don't know. Maybe we can't really change anything about Syria, maybe Syria will become another Afghanistan. Obviously, it's going in this direction, but there are still a lot of Afghan people, they are doing amazing things. They are doing activism, so that some people survive. So it's still better than nothing…better than just surrendering.

Once I met an Italian guy and he was like, he wasn't really nice, and I think he was ignorant and he told me, "You think you are going to change war by your art. You are going to achieve nothing. You are just a drop in the ocean." And I told him, "Okay, I don't want to be a mountain." Like I was aware of what he is saying, because I've thought about this three years ago, you know. I already had these questions in my head, and I answered them. So I told him, "I don't want to be a mountain. I want to be a drop in the ocean with other drops in the ocean." Because there are a lot of people still trying. I'm not alone. (Brisly, 2019a)

What Diala describes here so eloquently, is that for her and many others, ceasing to resist is simply not an option. To discontinue doing what they are doing—whether it be teaching music to children in Syria or making murals for and with kids in Lebanon— would, to them, be to surrender, to give up on Syria's future. At times, Diala says, all the terrible news out of Syria and the lack of progress saps her energy and makes her feel "down". She explains how she copes:

We have to remind ourselves all the time that there is still much to do. But just to keep it rational. I try to do initiatives that I really can achieve. Because when you can't achieve… For example, when we started the revolution it was …in the beginning it was really something like a dream. It was very dreamy and amazing and emotional. It was romantic for us. So then we started seeing that we are failing with this. I became very down, like many other Syrians. So then you feel like, "okay, set small goals and achieve them. Do them well." It is better than nothing. Because some people, they need you. (Brisly, 2019b)

Repeatedly, Diala asserts the importance of setting achievable goals. She explains that this is "because we need to take care of ourselves and we need to feel that we are doing something. If we aim for something very far, that we can't reach, it puts us down" (Brisly, 2021a). Diala also mentions often that she is not alone in her work, that many people are trying to make a positive difference in the lives of others. This knowledge is crucial in providing strength to those who are fighting for an end to the war and for a better future. Diala is in touch with artists and activists inside and outside Syria, who both inspire her and humble her and, at times, help her continue when she loses motivation and feels depressed.

I told you about this man who was still in a refugee camp, he lives in a tent under very hard circumstances. He is the director of a school that is just one class and there are many shifts that come to it. And he got asylum in Germany but refused to go. That made me feel very ashamed when he told me this, because I got my visa at that time when he was saying he was not leaving. So I feel that these people are really handling the situation, under the shelling and in the refugee camps, and doing all this…

So yes, at times we feel down, I get depressed, but I feel really ashamed. How can I, with these amazing heroes in my life? And we are still in touch all the time. So yeah, I think we really have to keep in contact just to remind ourselves of some people who do not give up. But it is kind of circular; we have to support each other in a way. (Brisly, 2019b)

How and where Diala hopes to make a difference has changed over the years based on (her understanding of) societal needs and where she believes she can best contribute. Her goals have also changed based on what she has believed was achievable. As an artist and activist since the start of the revolution in 2011, Diala has continued to feel a sense of responsibility to make a difference in the lives of Syrians. She has been able to maintain this consistent engagement both by scaling back her expectations of the extent of the changes she can effect and by staying in touch with other artists and activists who are doing the same. Throughout the years, though, what has kept her going is not just the work of others but also the realization that she is, in fact, making a difference in the lives of others.

Seeing real impact

Diala first started illustrating the human consequences of war at the start of the civil uprising in Syria. Journalists who were writing alternative news stories to the ones condoned by the state used her work to illustrate their stories. Diala suggests that drawings and paintings touch people in a different way than do photographs and can push people to take their actions further than they might otherwise. Many artists in addition to her have used their creative skills to express the human consequences of war. That this had an impact was plain from seeing how the Syrian government reacted to the art, which it treated as a real threat.

> I was really surprised about how many artists we have in Syria, and we never knew anything about each other. This is exactly what scares the government...
> Drawing about the war itself, the kids that are suffering, this is scary for the government. Everything, anything we express about what is happening, it could be scary and threatening the...authority of the Syrian regime. Even this blood, the red thing, everything could be scary. All the symbols in the drawings, not just in my artwork, but in general in all Syrian artwork. And yeah, many Syrians...I never heard about them, I never knew that we had this much creativity. (Brisly, 2019a)

Diala describes how, in her art, she works with facts as well as with the feelings that accompany those facts. She believes it is important to create something that people recognize; she wants people to see her art as expressing their experiences and to talk about them. She seeks to find the style that will best express a particular message, always keeping in mind her audience so that her artwork will have the biggest impact.

> I change a lot between styles. It depends on the audience. When it is, for example, for Syrian kids, I give them something with a lot of hope. It is very dreamy.

But…for example, a Western audience, if I want to raise awareness, I show them the bad reality. (Brisly, 2019b)

The main way that Diala tries to contribute to bettering the situation in Syria both now and in the future is by focusing on Syrian children. She has done and continues to do this both by creating murals for school tents and through workshops with children and youth. Rather than protesting the situation in Syria on the streets of Europe, she believes she can do more by supporting education.

Even if we got Syria back, who will go back to it? The generation that is coming after us, that is now falling apart and being shattered? Syria is not just a piece of land; the kids of today will be the Syria of the future. So if we did not really help them and we only wanted this change for ourselves, then what would really be achieved from this revolution? Nothing! (Brisly, 2019b)

Thus, for Diala, focusing on children and on their education is focusing on a future for Syria, as she shows in an animation video of that title (Brisly, 2020). Diala works from the understanding that art is essential to society and not simply an indulgence.

Yes, art is maybe something soft, it is not like building a city or…but it is building something from inside. It is no less important. I know it looks like a luxury to do art, but it is not like something you just hang in your living room, just for decoration. It is more than this. (Brisly, 2021a)

According to Diala, it is not a luxury to create, view, hear, or sense art. Rather, art is essential as a language of expression that can build something from the inside, move the senses, open up feelings, and build intersubjective recognition of experiences among individuals. At the same time, in contexts of violent conflict, art can open up space to express—through symbols or colors, for example—ideas and information that the authorities may want hidden.

Connecting inside and outside, individual with collective, Diala's artistic work and creative practices have had real impact. For the most part, Diala never sees how people react to her work in real time, except when she meets her audiences during workshops and exhibitions. But she does occasionally receive feedback on digital platforms, in private messages, and sometimes in person. When I ask whether she has any sense of the impact of her work, Diala explains that she does by providing some examples.

> The closest to my heart are the people who started doing murals in schools or tents of education in the north of Syria, in different places, inspired by my work in the refugee camps. They told me, "We saw what you did and we really liked it and we started doing this in our schools, in our tents, and the kids really love it." Because for me, the first time when I wanted to do a mural, I just wanted to impress my small audience, the kids there. And I found it really challenging to do it with the kids in the refugee camp, they really have a lot of trauma and maybe it won't interest them to look at an artistic thing. But then when I saw people are doing the same in different places….

And also, I met a guy through Facebook, he was in Daryaa under siege, and he said "I want to inspire others and make something that could really look positive to others, but the buildings are all destroyed." So he started doing murals but on destroyed walls. They were all on the ground, but yes...We talked a lot, we became really close friends, and we never met. So…yes, he was asking me how to use these materials and [such], and that created a relationship between us on a different level. He was saying, "It will be a pleasure for me to die for a cause I believe in." And I also felt responsible for our relationship so I tried to support him; "we fight to live, not to die." And now he is in the north of Syria and he continues with his art. For him now, his art is for pleasure and kind of like a treatment. Not for other people. And he showed me his room is full of paintings. He gets his training by an artist there, but it started from just small talk and now he is doing a big effort just to treat himself through art. So yes, I was inspired by others as well and I feel it is a chain, it is contagious. (Brisly, 2021a)

I ask Diala how this makes her feel. "It's just like...really sweet power. It is really beautiful", she replies (Brisly, 2021a).

These examples show the ripple effects of Diala's art, many of which she may not be aware. They illustrate the importance of individuals inspiring others to make unique contributions, that themselves will touch others in a ripple-like effect. When Diala inspires people inside Syria to create murals for local schools, these initiatives affect the lives of children there. These examples also illustrate the importance of creative practice for individuals and how it can serve as a kind of therapy for dealing with the psychological effects of war. Again, it is difficult to know the ripple effects of art practices that focus on individual healing. Regardless of the exact nature of all these ripple effects, it is absolutely clear that Diala, through her creative practice, has transformed the lives of others. This fact, in itself, provides inspiration for her to carry on contributing—on whatever scale she can.

In conclusion: the courage to see

How have experiences of war and oppression inspired Diala to engage in political action aimed at challenging injustice? As in the case of Halleh, Diala's inspirations started before the civil uprising, and go back to her childhood. Both being treated as an outsider in Syria and facing an unhappy childhood and neglectful parents at home may have contributed to Diala's sense of (in)justice, which is very strong. Throughout her story, the understandings of justice and fairness affect the need to act that she feels. For example, when Diala describes her work in refugee camps in Lebanon, she says she was fortunate enough to have lived in Damascus, which was not damaged as badly as the areas of Syria from which the people she met in the refugee camps had come. Mentioning the issue of fairness explicitly, Diala says, "So I felt that it's not fair that other people pay the price, and we just don't support them, and we forget about them and try to have our own life. It's not really fair, you know?" (Brisly, 2019a). With these words, as elsewhere in her life story interview, Diala reveals a great depth of caring, a feeling of solidarity with others, and a strong sense of responsibility to address the injustices created by the war in Syria, even though they have not affected her to the extent that they have some others. At the core of these feelings is a deep love and empathy for the world and its people, which I see reflected in her artwork, as in this drawing of an old woman in her neighborhood in Istanbul (Image 4.9).

A related theme that appears in her story from childhood is her strong need for autonomy and freedom. The stubbornness that Diala describes as one of her core characteristics is connected to her wish to do things her own way. This trait has not always made her life easy, she acknowledges. However, her authenticity and sense of autonomy seem to constitute the driving forces behind some of her most important explorations. From an early age, art helped her maintain a sense of self, by allowing her, first,

Image 4.9

to imaginatively escape her difficult homelife and later, to express and explore her experiences of war in Syria. More recently, she has been exploring, through her art, how external factors affected her inner life. For much of her life, Diala had little room to maneuver, as other people determined crucial parts of her life, but creative practice—propelled by an inner drive—opened up space for her. Sometimes the space was real and at times, it was space within her own mind. When Diala says that flying—a theme that appears often in her art—is a symbol of freedom, she clarifies, "We can't really change the kids' situation in the refugee camps. We can't get them out of there. But at least we can give them imagination. That is the strongest thing, freedom is there" (Brisly, 2021a).

In her artistic practice, her sense of injustice and need for autonomy materializes in work that questions the realities around her through contrast, contradiction, and play. As Diala's story reveals, throughout her life, she questioned things, not taking anything for granted. She challenged what people said and what was understood to be the norm, exploring the world with an openness and curiosity that may have naturally led her to a questioning attitude. Her work offers others access to her ways of seeing and understanding the world. She manages this in several different ways. Diala has a wide array of styles and forms at her disposal and a surprising way of visualizing realities. When she describes her creative process to me, she offers an example: when she is asked to draw something based on a story, she pays attention to the feelings that the story provokes in her. These feelings are transformed into images in her head, which she then sketches. I find the way she works with contrasts and contradictions—of style, color, symbol, and/or theme— especially compelling. The contrasts problematize that which seems "normal" in ways that go beyond the intellect and affect me viscerally. Thus, her images reflect her lifelong habit of questioning, inspiring others to do the same. After all, "the braver you are, the more you will see."

At the same time, Diala's work communicates a strong love and care for the world and people within it. Her art shows that beauty is everywhere, and she clearly takes great care to draw in detail the beauty that she sees. To me, her art provides an inspiring vision of the world and its people; it is focused on goodness and kindness in the midst of cruelty and brutality, qualities that it supports and promotes. Diala continues to engage with a vision of a better future for Syria despite her disillusionment with the impact of the civic uprising. She does this in a way that is still focused on contributing to social justice, but the level at which she does this has changed.

In the initial phase of the Syrian uprising her aim, together with many others, was to contribute to a revolution in order to challenge corruption and oppression and radically transform Syrian society. In later years, she recognized the need to create more modest goals for herself if she intended to continue to persist in her resistance and activism. The work she does with children allows Diala to be engaged in ways that have a direct impact on individuals without giving up on the larger vision of a better future. By working with children, making sure they receive an education and learn to express themselves creatively, she works on building that future, one child at a time. This work can influence what the future looks like for each child at a personal level, but it also has the potential, through the children, to impact collective futures. And her drive to work toward a better future is not limited to her work with children. Diala acts to make a difference and effect change in other ways as well. Through creative practice as well as speaking engagements across Europe, she aims to create more awareness of the unsatisfactory living conditions and the indeterminate status that regional refugees endure. Diala gains strength from knowing that she is not alone in her desire for and work on behalf of a better future for Syria and Syrians, and that she is in fact "a drop in the ocean with other drops" (Brisly, 2019a).

Diala's current personal interest and creative work relates to trauma and healing. The oppression and war that she experienced were deeply traumatic, both on a personal level for her and on a collective level for her society. They thus continue to affect her life, even though the events she experienced are now in the past. Healing is a slow process. Art, I believe, has played a significant role in this healing process for Diala since, through her artistic creativity, she has been able to express her perspectives on the Syrian situation and also to begin the process of exploring her own experiences and inner life. Diala's reflections on the painting she made after her brother's death and on how creating it enabled her to gain new understandings of loss and support suggested to me the importance of engaging with trauma and healing on both the individual and on the collective level. Connecting the individual to the collective—expressing deeply personal experiences and feelings that are recognizable to others and thus create meaning and feelings of connectedness—seems to be crucial to Diala's personal healing process as much as to those with similar experiences. Such individual healing is essential, it seems to me, for initiating processes of collective healing.

5

Can stories inspire response-ability?

I know maybe it's a drop in the ocean, but it's better than nothing...

I remember once I was talking to someone who was a musician in the north of Syria. He told me, "If there are just five kids I'm working with, I'm not going out of Syria. I want to work with them. It's a waste that we go and leave them alone when there are many fighting groups around, and ISIS, and the regime, and everything". And that really gave me more strength. He's right.

We can't really change the war. We can, but it's a very, very slow process. And we might not see the results of it. But if we surrender and we pull back, there won't be enough balance. We can't really let these people control everything. We have to resist. At least we can resist, you know...

I don't want to be a mountain. I want to be a drop in the ocean with other drops in the ocean. [10] Because there are a lot of people still trying. I'm not alone.

Brisly, 2019a

The life stories of Monirah, Halleh, and Diala make clear the wider relevance of unique, individual stories. Life stories provide a level of detail about people's everyday lives—their social relations, their families, their homes, their larger community—that is recognizable to anyone. The traumatic experiences and the courageous actions revealed in these three stories are not unique. All around the world, individuals confronted with a range of man-made atrocities resist and fight for social justice and a better future. They do so out of a complex range of factors, including a strong sense of justice, a deep sense of caring for their communities and the people within them, from a commitment to the larger collective, and in the belief that they can make a difference, however small.

This book aims to support the process Diala describes, through which the work of like-minded others provides strength to those who work for social justice but might get demotivated by the sheer magnitude and apparent lack of impact of their work. There are many individuals who continue to resist inhumane conditions—not just by challenging such conditions but also by maintaining their humanity and expressing that which is silenced. I believe that learning about such individuals does not just benefit other social activists but can also inspire response-ability in those who do not yet engage in political action for social justice. By exploring in depth the life stories and work of Monirah, Halleh, and Diala, I have aimed to highlight the many "drops in the ocean" that do exist. This was possible because these women allowed me to share their deeply personal stories in this book. They did so with the understanding that this book is about more than just them and that others might recognize themselves in their stories or be inspired by them.

In this chapter, I return to my original questions about inspiration, action, and impact, and I draw attention to key characteristics and circumstances of individuals who seek to promote social justice that emerged from the research for this book. In what follows, I will provide insights into what **motivates** people to resist by drawing on the three stories and conceptual work on normative identity and the ethics of care. Here, I provide more substance to the concept of positioned agency by connecting it to reflections on marginalization and privilege. I will then describe the **type of action** Monirah, Halleh, and Diala engage in, and analyze it through Hannah Arendt's work on political action in repressive contexts and conceptual work on courage and prefiguration. I conclude this chapter focusing on **impact** by exploring the role of storytelling in transformation, circling back to the theme that opened this book and considering it in greater depth. While I discuss these topics consecutively, they are intrinsically linked. People's particular motivations can shape the type of action they engage in. Political action in Arendt's conceptualization consists of both individuals acting and others following that act—intrinsically linking action and impact. Storytelling about political action can amplify its ripple effects, thus creating new motivations in others to resist.

Inspiration: exploring "a sense of responsibility"

> I think she somehow made me understand this from early childhood, that it is our action, it is our words that can create circumstances, can create situations, change situations…But yeah, I think it is my mom's teaching that made me believe that, as a person or as a woman who has access to some platform, to some resources; then I do believe that it is my duty…to bring up this discussion. (Hashemi, 2021a)

The stories in this book take place in contexts in which grave injustices occur and many individuals are implicated in systems of violence and oppression, if only through their silence. Many of the individuals with lived experience of war and exile, whose stories I have heard, display awareness of the need to speak up or act, in some cases in the midst of violence and oppression, and in others, in exile. So what factors made Monirah, Halleh, and Diala engage in political action rather than accept the status quo? Clues to an answer can be found in their life stories. They each describe themselves as stubborn, curious to learn, outspoken, interested in new ideas, "difficult", and/or as having a fighting spirit. They see their questioning attitude as innate or as a characteristic that developed at a very young age. In addition, they each describe a childhood in which they felt different or excluded. Then, these women experienced social and personal upheaval—revolutions in Iran and Syria, war and oppression in Afghanistan, exile—which, rather than crushing them, heightened their determination and their critical, questioning spirit. It seems likely that personal traits that developed during childhood and youth—stubbornness, outspokenness, and a strong sense of justice—sustained and aided them in the face of social and personal transformative events.

Yet the actions of individuals cannot be understood outside of the social context in which they occur and without acknowledging that individuals evolve in relation to others. Courage can be easier to muster when one feels that one is not alone but among like-minded others who challenge social conditions. Monirah and Halleh had clear role models who inspired them to question and stand their ground. It helps to feel that one is not just fighting for oneself but also for the good of the collective and for generations to come, doing something that is "larger than oneself" (Tellander, 2022). The realization that what one does is for the good of others and can stimulate the actions of others can lead an individual to overcome a depressive sense of disempowerment and to do something despite experiencing fear. Many of those who fight for social justice under repressive or violent circumstances do not survive. This can increase the sense of responsibility to persist of those who do survive, as they strive to give meaning to the deaths of loved ones and comrades. Thus, the personal suffering that results from loss can drive action.

It could be argued that the sense of responsibility revealed in the stories of Monirah, Halleh, and Diala is psychologically necessary to these women's actions, both for themselves as well as to their relationships with others. Monirah in the quote opening this section expresses a sense of **duty**. Halleh describes how some people who participated in the revolution—where they glimpsed what it meant to play a role in historical events and then received a "crash course in freedom and suppression"—feel that they **must** change the world and make every second of their lives meaningful. Diala argues that creative expression provides her with the language to say the many things she wants to say, and that expressing herself through art is not a luxury to her but a **responsibility**. According to Beausoleil (2015), who uses the term response-ability, to be responsible means

> To be accountable; answerable. Put differently, it is the ability to answer when called. From the Latin *respondere*, "to respond". Bound up in the term is a notion of responsibility as responsiveness. (Beausoleil, 2015, pp. 1–2)

The concept of "responsibility" is an important component of normative identity, which Swedish philosopher Per Bauhn (2017, p. 1) defines as a person's "identification with values and norms and their connecting a conception of who they are with a conception of what they ought to do". Normative identity "provides us with direction in our lives, guiding our actions and strengthening our resolve" (Bauhn, 2017, p. 18).

Normative identity

Personal narratives can have a strong influence on individual action if connected to normative identity, which takes the form of "because I am, I ought to do" (Bauhn, 2017). Aiming to occupy the storyteller's position with respect to one's own actions allows an individual to move from "is" to "ought", as the story of one's life is always embedded in the story of those communities from which one derives one's identity. What one (chooses to) tell oneself and others affects one's actions and ultimately the world. A person's belief in an orderly, reliable, and just society that rewards people for behaving morally, for example, has powerful real-life implications as it strengthens one's ability and will to act, as psychological research on post-traumatic stress has shown (Lev-Wiesel *et al.*, 2009).

Monirah, Halleh, and Diala all display strong feelings of responsibility to advance social justice, to interrupt and change oppressive patterns and behaviors in society by making them visible and offering alternatives. What is the origin of this strong sense of responsibility? For Monirah, it seems to have been the combination of having injustice inflicted on her and seeing it imposed on those around her, beginning when she was a small child, as well as having a mother who encouraged her to speak up and address injustices when she was able. Monirah repeatedly recalls her mother's words that taught her that once she was powerful enough to do so that she must speak up against perpetrators. Both her mother's and grandmother's realities—as well as her own—showed them the need to be strategic when speaking up. Done in the wrong way or at the wrong time, such outspokenness merely led to being silenced (or worse) and could negatively affect others as well. Monirah's story reveals the long-term nature of critical awareness and social justice practices, which can be latent but passed on through generations.

Similarly, Halleh's strong sense of justice and responsibility seems to have been shaped by the combination of personally experiencing injustice as a child and having a female role model, in her case, her aunt. Growing up in Iran with a mother with a mental disorder and living in the harsh environment of a boarding school imbued Halleh with a strong sense of (in) justice from an early age. Halleh's aunt, who rescued her from that environment, also played a crucial role. She cared for Halleh and facilitated her education while she was, at the same time, active in the communist resistance during the revolution. Additionally, being a teenager during the Iranian Revolution seems to have been significant in shaping Halleh's normative identity and strong sense of justice; it was in this context that she learned that she could fight for big ideals and aim to play a role in history. Interestingly, Halleh never relinquished that belief, despite the failure of the Iranian Revolution to bring about the society that she and those around her had envisioned and the resulting oppression and suffering. Halleh continued to work for transformation where she could, but redirected her focus from the national level to interpersonal relationships.

Individuals, in accordance with their dignity as moral agents, aim to contribute, to the best of their ability, to the common good of a community by exercising self-control and refraining from behavior that could damage their dignity as autonomous agents (Bauhn, 2003). Dignity is defined as the capacity of the individual to remain a subject with free will. In violent and oppressive contexts, achieving or maintaining dignity can be difficult. Research, largely carried out by psychologists, on those who engaged in rescue activities during the Holocaust also shows that those involved in rescuing acted in response to a normative identity (Fogelman, 2011; Monroe, 2008). What mattered most to them was behaving in a way that maintained their integrity. As Lev-Wiesel *et al.* (2009) point out, desperate times may also create opportunities to live up to higher standards.

A strong sense of moral responsibility clearly has an immense power to influence action. It requires a person to recognize that some things are more important than one's own personal well-being (Tellander, 2022). A first implication is that a person's "sense of moral responsibility may well be sufficiently strong for her to face both danger and death" (Bauhn, 2003, p. 71). Monirah explicitly discusses how she calculated the risk of losing her life before deciding to go into exile. She concluded that her death would do great harm to the young women she had trained over the years, possibly curtailing their opportunities to continue working creatively with film and theater. She argues that those who tried to intimidate her commonly used the threat of harming loved ones as a way to control women who speak up against injustice.

> Because these women in Afghanistan who are working for change at the front line, are not thinking about themselves. They have thought that this path will be dangerous, full of threats and death, so they decided that, yeah, they are ready to die any minute. But they don't want their work to put their family in danger, to put their students or colleagues or loved ones in danger. (Hashemi, 2019a)

Psychological research on the Holocaust seems to confirm that, at least in times of war, a positive causal relationship exists between being involved in socially meaningful work and being able to control one's fear of losing one's life (Fogelman, 2011). Feeling a responsibility to fulfill duties toward others—having a strong sense of moral responsibility—may in fact enable one to control one's fear of death. Thus, sharing a common good with others can create a sense of meaningfulness in times that may appear utterly meaningless and alienating, and it can thus also lead to courageous acts.

Intersubjective responsibilities: the ethics of care

> Even if we got Syria back, who will go back to it? The generation that is coming after us, that is now falling apart and being shattered? Syria is not just a piece of land, the kids of today will be the Syria of the future. So if we did not help them, and we only wanted this change for ourselves, then what would really be achieved from this revolution? Nothing! (Brisly, 2019b)

Normative narratives are created and embedded within a community, shaped by intersectional positionalities (Crenshaw, 1991; Kearney, 2022). Individuals come into an existing moral world and adopt, modify, or reject particular narratives and beliefs, and individual positions and standpoints interact with collective stories (Bauhn, 2003). At the same time, an individual's normative beliefs influence those of others, which, in turn, can influence individual acts, group practices, and, ultimately, public narratives. Halleh identifies two clear role models whose beliefs and actions determined the course of her life. Monirah's stories show the powerful role that her mother's strong normative identity played and continues to play in her ability to manage life and make brave choices. And each of the three women has influenced the lives of numerous others, thus creating further ripple effects.

Exploring the intersubjective dimensions of normative identity is thus essential to understanding the role of morality in inspiring everyday resistance in violent and repressive times. As is clear from these examples and throughout this book, individual intentions and motivations are never created in isolation and they cannot be studied as such. Parents and educators shape perspectives and behaviors, which are further influenced by role models and key societal events. Morality is intrinsic to human character formation and is created within the context of collective moral tales and influenced by one's intersectional positionality through relationships with others in social, cultural, religious, and/or political communities. Morality is largely practiced in interactions with others, and moral practices cannot be disconnected from other social practices (Robinson, 2018).

In most cultural contexts, individuals are understood to be intrinsically interconnected with others and as integral to collective life (Chabot and Vinthagen, 2015; Letseka, 2012; Murithi, 2007). Similar perspectives can be found within feminist approaches to the ethics of care. In her research on moral perspectives and actions, Carol Gilligan (1993) developed alternative conceptions of morality based on human connection rather than on neutral principles of justice and a system of rules. She describes how the women and girls she studied understood "individual lives as connected and embedded in a social context of relationship" and, how, in this way of seeing the world, responsibility includes both self and other entities that are "different but connected rather than separate and opposed" (Gilligan, 1993, p. 147; 1995). Care requires attentiveness, responsiveness to the needs of others, and the ability to understand a situation from the point of view of the other (Held, 2006). Recognizing interdependence, this ethics of care starts from the belief that we all have the responsibility to look out for each other while also acknowledging the gendered, classed, racialized, and otherwise positioned nature of understandings of care and responsibility.

The ethics of care holds that interpersonal relationships and care are central to moral action; it starts from an understanding of human beings as dependent on one another. It recognizes, as political theorist Fiona Robinson explains, that caregivers are also care receivers and that they too are vulnerable, needy, and sometimes incompetent (Robinson, 2018). Approached in this way, morality is a "socially embodied medium of mutual understanding and negotiation between people over their responsibility for things that are open to human care and response" (Walker, 2007, p. 9). Central to this approach is the idea that ethics are located in practices of care rather than in abstract principles of duty or utility (Robinson, 2018). It moves beyond the study of individual motivations to focus on the work involved in care and results of such care activities (Held, 2006).

Bauhn (2003, p. 160) argues that acts of caring for others, "although they express a moral position of an agent, are often done without explicitly invoking moral principles—done because the agent cares, conceiving of their well-being as an object of her responsibility". This perspective requires us to understand the individual as already part of the social collective. A critical feminist ethics of care rejects the narrative of human beings as "separate, atomized individuals" (Edkins, 2003, p. 256). It counters this individualist approach with a relational one that challenges dichotomies such as victim/perpetrator or care receiver/caregiver and explores the relational nature of these roles—through which individuals may express love, responsibility, power. Instead, the ethics of care examines "the messy reality of responding to the multiple, diverse, and often conflicting needs of particular others, and judging with care—in ways that seek to balance attention to competing needs, and find the least harmful ways of responding to impossible moral decisions" (Robinson, 2018, p. 6).

Key contributions of ethics of care research are its critique of common conceptions of "the political" and its problematizing of the dichotomies of private–public and individual–collective (Robinson, 2018). Acts of caring can be seen to extend well beyond relationships with relatives and friends "to the social ties that bind groups together, to the bonds on which political and social institutions can be built" (Held, 2006, p. 31). Understood in this way, caring goes far beyond the interpersonal caring for and about family members, as in the case of Halleh and her aunt, and extends to more abstract collectives, such as the fellow Iranians whom Halleh expresses care for in their struggle against injustice and poverty during the revolution. Professor of international politics Jenny Edkins (2003, p. 256) argues for moving away from the idea of "a separate, sovereign individual, who has to surrender some of that sovereignty to take part in social practices" toward acknowledging that individuals exist in and through relationships with others. This will mean that:

> It is no longer surprising that people feel compelled to respond to those in distress, since their own existence as subjects depends on the dignity of all and the continuance of the social order. What becomes surprising and in need of explanation instead is why sometimes people see others' suffering as none of their business. (Edkins, 2003, p. 256)

Robinson (2018, p. 7), drawing on Edkins, argues for thinking politically "about how and why this moral voice—of care, connection, and context—had been systematically silenced". Adding "where and when" to Robinson's "why" is vital today when alternative perspectives that lead to greater social and environmental sustainability are so desperately needed. The empirical stories in this book offer a counterweight to this silencing, revealing the depth of caring shown by these three women and those they share stories about. Halleh's stories about her teenage years during the Iranian Revolution reveal her strong sense of community and her belief in the importance of fighting for something larger than herself. As she phrased it:

> You want to fight for a better society, you want to fight for a society that is more…equal. More inclusive, even though we would not use that term then. But a better society that is maybe more just—this is the term we used. A society that has no poverty, that has no inequality …that was very important for me, to be part of that. To fight for it. These were my ideals, big ones. (Ghorashi, 2020).

Diala likewise dreamed of a better society, and she approached this by working with the next generation, whom she teaches not just creative expression but also the freedom of imagination. Many of the Syrian children and young people with whom Diala has worked over the years live in regional refugee camps where they lack basic freedoms. By encouraging them to use their minds to experience freedom in these restricted spaces imaginatively, Diala provides a crucial form of care. Her inspiration to depict the human consequences of the war in Syria includes feelings of empathy, love, and concern for Syrians who have become victims of the war and end up in regional refugee camps.

> I was lucky that I lived in Damascus, but they paid the price because they lived in different places. I mean, Bashar Assad didn't want to destroy Damascus because he lives there. He can't destroy his home, you know. But he didn't really care about destroying all over Syria. So I was just lucky that I lived in Damascus. So I felt that it's not fair that other people pay the price, and we just don't support them, and we forget about them and try to have our own life. It's not really fair, you know? (Brisly, 2019a)

In our conversation, Diala talks about the people she admires who are still inside Syria and continue to care for others, for example, by supporting children in their education. Diala's story teaches me that caring for others is hard and demanding work and can only be sustained if those providing care manage to care for themselves and receive care and inspiration from others.

Monirah also works with the next generation, and her work in Afghanistan was meant to contribute to the realization of a better future society. By creating space to discuss relationships of power inequality and abuse, whether in the domestic sphere or in society at large, she worked to change realities. She provided training for young women (and men), in an effort to give them the tools with which they could express themselves, and to use art to work toward greater equality and justice. Choosing to work with a younger generation revealed Monirah's focus on the collective, aiming to build the foundation of a more just and equal future. Her mother and grandmother had done the same before her, raising their girls to speak up against injustice whenever they had the opportunity to do so. The intersubjective nature of responsibilities is clear in all these women's expressions and acts of resistance.

Marginalization and privilege

In chapter 1, I defined "positioned agency" as,

> the degree of power and choice individuals have given their position—through both material realities and personal and collective narratives—in a particular time and place and given their gendered, classed, racialized, embodied, and other identities. Positioned material realities determine how a narrative can be shaped. Yet narrative also shapes realities, enabling or constraining particular forms of action by influencing both someone's own sense of power and choice and how others judge one's level of agency.

One's positioned agency is closely connected to processes of marginalization and privilege, which have both a material and narrative dimension. The stories of Monirah, Halleh, and Diala show, for example, how being a woman—which often brings with it forms of marginalization—influenced their degree of power and choice in myriad ways. Monirah's story provides insight into the different types of sexual and gender-based violence to which she was exposed while also illustrating how being Hazara and being an artist intersected with the reality of being a woman. The three stories also discuss how narratives and practices of responsibility play out in gendered ways. Diala's story of taking on the care of her younger siblings when her mother left shaped the choices she made afterward in profound ways. Halleh's story of growing up in the absence of her mother seems to have taken a turn when her aunt stepped in and showed her the power of political activism, while Monirah's mother shines through her story as playing a key inspirational role in her continuing to express herself despite the risks and fear involved. These stories show, then, (gendered/intersectional forms of) marginalization as inflicting trauma, shaping responsibilities, and inspiring resistance.

Those who are marginalized in one way or another and know what it is like to have an outsider perspective are more likely than others to see the status quo with critical eyes, and thus may be more inclined to feel response-ability and act politically. After all, as political theorist Iris M. Young (1989) has pointed out, those who speak from marginalized perspectives, experiences, or positionalities are always understood as highly political because they challenge what is considered the norm. Several factors can contribute to shaping an outsider perspective. Religion, ethnicity, nationality, gender, sexuality, political opinion, and a range of other individual characteristics can, in particular contexts, define individuals as outsiders. Personal experiences unrelated to the collective traumas common to violent and repressive societies can give an individual the feeling of being an outsider as well, as the childhood stories of Halleh and Diala illustrate. The very choice to become an artist can lead to an outsider status, as Monirah's story exemplifies. Artists are often placed on the outskirts of society, and female or minority artists are particularly exposed.

Returning from or living in exile can also foster an outsider perspective. Professor of English and comparative literature William V. Spanos (2012) draws on the work of both Hannah Arendt and Edward Said to claim that those who question publicly are more likely to be exiles, people who already do not belong. Individuals living in exile may gain new perspectives and learn about different ways of being and doing things; this may make it difficult for them not to question the things that are taken for granted "at home". Individuals living in exile may be treated badly by those who see them as foreigners or refugees, giving them the experience of being Other. When Monirah talks about her degrading experiences as a refugee in Iran and how they affected her choices later in life, she explains how being born and residing in Iran—which she describes as living with lots of limitations, always at the margins, and excluded from society—imbued her with a wish to reach for that which was not allowed.

Outsiders of all kinds play crucial roles in periods of violence and oppression because they have an interest in demanding space for alternative perspectives and ways of being not commonly visible in the public sphere. Authoritarian and violent contexts repress plurality; those most likely to recognize this repression are "marginalized others" who feel unrecognized and lack resonance with the collective narrative. This may lead them to want a space where they can be different, or rather, just be themselves. Whereas in some cases, this wish can be satisfied in deeply private ways, at other times it can lead to an expressed demand for such a space. Such a demand may be made, not least, when these individuals understand that their experiences are, in fact, not unique to them. Public engagement by marginalized outsiders creates an awareness of a greater plurality of perspectives and ways of being than originally believed possible, especially in dark times. Thus, such public engagement opens up the possibility that others in marginalized positions are inspired to express themselves publicly in ways that counter the dominant, homogeneous public narrative.

Whereas marginalized individuals and groups thus play a crucial role in questioning—both because the injustices they challenge are likely to affect and be visible to them and because they may have never really identified with the societal norms that privileged populations take for granted—their marginalization also makes it difficult for them to question and challenge. Marginalized groups are less likely to have access to means of public expression, and even if they do, they are less likely to be listened to. Thus, they must develop ways to influence the perceptions of others. They are often more likely to focus on trying to influence ordinary people rather than power holders, and to seek creative arenas, such as art, as the example of Monirah's engagement with community theater shows, rather than attempt to gain access to formal channels. Researchers interested in civil resistance thus need to pay attention to forms of resistance beyond those usually studied, such as those deployed through the arts, humanitarianism, or education (Berman, 2017; Groves, 2012; Tellander, 2022).

Those in privileged positions do not face the same mismatch between their private world and public narratives as those who are marginalized as Others. Dominant public narratives are easily taken for granted, as "the particular impact of discursive power—especially of the discourses that are most salient at a given time and in a given space—is that it works through normalization" (Ghorashi, 2017b, p. 2428). Discourse disciplines action and interaction in largely subconscious ways, not only through its content but also through the language that is used and the manner in which it is uttered (Lakoff, 1987). As a consequence, people in dominant positions, whose experiences and perspectives are well reflected in dominant discourse, more often hold unreflective positionalities that reproduce the status quo. Although those in privileged positions are less inclined to recognize the social injustice from which they benefit, privileged individuals not only have more choices, as they are freer to say and do more than many others, but also have a greater extent of power simply because, as a result of their positionality, they are more likely to be followed by others. Questioning underlying structural inequalities may require hard work from those in privileged positions. And yet, there are several ways in which privilege can create a sense of responsibility as well.

Whereas Halleh largely explains her feeling that "every second must be meaningful" as deriving from her experiences in the Iranian Revolution, she also feels a great responsibility to others in her privileged position as a professor at a renowned university. She recognizes that she has the resources to create impact, and this adds to her belief that she should contribute. For Diala, her engagement similarly derives in part from her realization that she has been lucky and in part from her feelings of injustice about the fate of Syrians who, unlike her, did not come from Damascus and have lost everything. There is often an inherent skepticism toward the social justice actions of those in privileged positions; there is an assumption that these people would not engage in political action if it truly threatened their privilege. Additionally, examples of situations in which privilege, in fact, leads to silencing and inaction are numerous. However, transformation requires involvement from both—people who understand marginal perspectives and people who have decision-making power and resources. I would argue that we need to understand the particular, situated power of people's positioned agency.

When agency is explicitly understood as positioned, it is possible to explore marginalization and privilege in new ways: as relational and dynamic. At the same time, the concept of positioned agency makes it possible to elaborate on the important roles that those in marginalized and privileged positions play in resisting and in fighting social injustices. As the material in this book shows, those in marginal positions are more likely than others to be aware of oppression and its impact because the oppression affects them at a personal, embodied level. Although marginality often means a limited degree of power and choice, some individuals in marginal positions have a sense of agency and a capacity to interrupt and change oppressive patterns and behaviors. This sense of agency can arise, for example, when one's positioned agency changes.

Monirah's mother understood the dynamic nature of agency very well when she told her,

> "you are not the guilty party here. But if one day, probably, if you grow up and you get the power and if you stay silent, then you can feel some guilt about yourself because then you have the choice, you have the freedom to…" She always used to say "drag down", drag down the perpetrators. "When you can do it, then do it". (Hashemi, 2021a).

Monirah's mother argued that the extent of one's power is always positioned somewhere and depends on one's circumstances. The choices one has are not static but depend on one's position at any given time. She argued that the moment Monirah could speak out against her perpetrators, she should. Whereas this quote from Monirah highlights the notion that individuals' agency changes over their lifetimes, depending on time and place, the life stories presented in this book reveal that personal characteristics influence (one's sense of) the extent of one's power and choice. These individual traits—including age, gender, sexuality, class, ethnicity, skin color, religion, professional position, nationality, and legal status—influence how one is positioned in the larger collective. Individual and collective storytelling play important roles in positioned agency too because they can both reproduce and question the status quo.

Acknowledging positionality makes it possible to regard gender, race, class, and other aspects of identity as markers of relational positions rather than essential qualities (Alcoff, 1988). I thus understand positioned agency as meaning that the extent of one's power and choice is shaped relationally, in interactions with differently positioned people; it is not predetermined or innate. And as Monirah's mother stressed, one's positioned agency can change over time, either because a malleable individual identity marker, such as class or legal status, has changed or because the context in which one finds oneself has changed. A change in external conditions can, for example, occur because the norms of an individual's society have changed or because the individual, as a result of migration to a new place, lives in a different society with different norms.

Understanding positioned agency as relational and changing opens up possibilities for exploring the many gray zones that exist in concepts like "marginalized" and "privileged". People whose life stories reveal numerous experiences of marginalization but who are currently in privileged positions—as Monirah's mother told her she might be some day—have a lens through which they can see structures of inequality that once affected them and continue to affect friends and loved ones. At the same time, they now have more tools for challenging social injustice and for holding its perpetrators to account. They may even be in positions to challenge underlying structural conditions. People who were once privileged only to find themselves later marginalized may be sharply aware of their changed position and must mobilize all their resources in order to adjust to their new status. Whether having lost or gained privilege, or privileged in one context and marginalized in another, these groups have the potential to make important societal contributions. They illustrate clearly that "marginalization" and "privilege" are not fixed characteristics but relational and context-specific attributes that we all, individually and collectively, need to be highly aware of and learn to both challenge and build on.

Political action: the key role of questioning individuals

Even in the darkest of times we have the right to expect some illumination, and such illumination may well come less from theories and concepts than from the uncertain, flickering, and often weak light that some men and women, in their lives and their works, will

kindle under almost all circumstances and shed over
the time span that was given them on earth. (Arendt,
1968, p. ix)

The stories of Monirah, Halleh, and Diala tell of individual loss
and suffering in the face of violence and oppression, but they
also reflect concerns for social justice, caring for others, courage
in acting in accordance with these concerns, and a sense of
responsibility. How did these women seek to advance social
justice under, at best, trying conditions? One of several key
components to the answer, I believe, is that all of these women
persistently asked questions about the world around them
instead of taking things for granted. They engaged in practices
of questioning, in the sense of providing both critique of the
present and visions of an alternative future (Horst, 2022).

During my work on this book, I got to know individuals who—
often out of curiosity and openness—are used to asking
questions and challenging rather than accepting the status quo.
They think critically and imagine alternatives to the here and now.
I realized that each of them tends to question societal realities
and to speak up and act in the face of injustices. Their stories,
as well as those underlying the larger research of which this
book is but a part[11], show individuals who desire to openly and
publicly challenge injustices in repressive and violent contexts
and to imagine alternatives to a situation that offers little hope
for a better future. For example, these individuals question the
consequences of war or the way that society treats women or
minorities. But above all, they question the absence of the right
to free and autonomous self-expression. Sociologist Nechama
Tec (2013) shows that the people who rescued Jews from the

Holocaust, while comprising a socially heterogeneous group, had common traits—a strong sense of individuality, an incapacity to fit into their social environments, and independence in acting in accordance with personal convictions. Her research suggests, as does mine, that authenticity and autonomy are both important to political action.

The precise way that Monirah, Halleh, and Diala question varies. Throughout her artistic career, Monirah has questioned taboos in society. Taboos are implicit prohibitions on saying or doing something based on a cultural sense that such doing or saying is repulsive (or a violation of the sacred). Monirah continuously searches for ways to speak about what is silenced, as she explains in discussing the metaphor of lighting the stars in her theater play. These stars can shine light on dark spaces that cannot otherwise be seen because no one shines light on them. When she asks, "who lights the stars?", her answer, I believe, is that no one does and that she thus has the responsibility to do so, to the extent that she can. Previously—although obliquely—in Afghanistan and now explicitly in Sweden, she shines light on domestic violence and other taboo issues, using the tools that theater offer her.

Diala's art promotes questioning by presenting contrasts and contradictions in an almost playful way, forcing the viewer to stop and think. It is focused on goodness and kindness in the midst of cruelty and brutality, and captures beauty and compassion when focusing on the ugly consequences of war—like in her drawings of children with missing limps. Diala also encourages her audience to think critically by using themes that express autonomy and freedom in contexts where there is very little real freedom. For example, she understands her work with children in refugee camps to stimulate imagination, as a crucial counterweight to the lack of freedom in confined settings such as camps. Imagination offers alternatives to everyday reality, it can allow one to disconnect from that reality, and it may also stimulate questioning of the here and now and the envisioning of future alternatives.

For Halleh, who has followed an academic path, questioning has been central to her critical and engaged work. Halleh has combined action and reflection since she was young. During the Iranian Revolution, she stressed the importance of thinking, debating, and reflecting while engaging in oppositional action even though some of her comrades were skeptical of this. Later, as an engaged academic in the Netherlands, Halleh continued to combine action and reflection, although mainstream academia tends to dismiss engaged scholarship. Thus, both in her activist and academic practices, she has challenged norms and done things her own way irrespective of the skepticism she faced. She still engages critically with societal issues of importance and encourages her students and wider audiences to do the same.

Initiating "new beginnings"

According to Arendt (1960, p. 44), writing in the wake of the Holocaust, "historical processes are created and constantly interrupted by human initiative". Totalitarianism, in her view, aims to stifle initiative and spontaneity, and depends entirely on automatic processes in the political arena. In any authoritarian context, as we also learn from the stories of Halleh and Diala, engaging in autonomous action and authentic expression can come with great risks. Thus, resistance is often only expressed among a small group of trusted others "at the kitchen table" (Goldfarb, 2006) or in hidden ways understandable only to a select group (Scott, 1990). Yet despite these conditions, some of those who have experienced the inhuman and undignified treatment common in these contexts are more inclined than others to question the status quo and speak up and act against it.

Arendt assigns great importance to the human ability to act in new ways rather than just to repeat what others do or to follow norms. Her controversial work on the banality of evil argues that, although totalitarianism functions to take away the agency and creativity of individuals, there always exist thinking and acting individuals willing to challenge the status quo (Arendt, 1973). According to Arendt, all human beings have the potential to insert themselves into the world through unique speech and action and thus have the potential (if others follow) to set in motion new processes and thereby create new beginnings (Arendt, 1958). In ancient Greek and Latin, two different but interrelated words mean "to act". In these languages, action is seen as "divided into two parts, the beginning made by a single person and the achievement in which many join by "bearing" and "finishing" the enterprise, by seeing it through" (Arendt, 1958, p. 189). In the classical world, then, action was seen as dependent on both the person beginning or leading it, and those following or joining in.

In understanding power as the capacity to make a difference in the course of events, I prefer to explore "power with" or even "power through" others, rather than "power over" others, so as to underscore that Arendt's "new beginnings" can be set in motion by individuals but never advanced without the support of others.

Ultimately, the process set in motion by such new beginnings is not directed by any individual and thus its course and outcome are uncertain. This is clear, for example, from Halleh's descriptions about the Iranian Revolution that show that she realized at some point that what she and others had participated in and set in motion had led to events far different from that they had wished to achieve. Further, as Arendt warns us, new beginnings can also become old routines, structural properties that are both constraining and enabling of other people's actions. Established paths and their expected outcomes seem to guide or limit the unlimited options an individual has, and it takes a questioning person—a brave, conscious, and critical individual—to create new paths.

Academics and artists can play key roles in creating new beginnings. Art serves to connect the inner world of the artist with the outer world (Jackson, 2016). The back-and-forth between interiority and exteriority occurs in a world in which we always appear to, and are recognized by, others according to what we disclose about ourselves through what we say and do. The public, critical stance of artists has the potential to prompt their audiences to question publicly as well as to push at the boundaries of what individuals can imagine themselves thinking and doing. Through their creative practice, artists can criticize, create space for open exchange, stimulate thinking, and envision alternatives (Grabska and Horst, 2022; Horst, 2022). Artistic processes can "create something with the potential to question society and engage people in political action" (Manresa and Glăveanu, 2017, p. 45). Art can—both publicly and in indirect or hidden ways—"creatively expose the norms and hierarchies of the existing social order and injustices perpetuated by state or nonstate actors" (Horst, 2022, p. 215).

This function of art as critique is described by Diala when she discusses the new forms of visual arts that appeared during the Syrian uprising in 2011, and how this was perceived by the Syrian authorities.

> Drawing about the war itself, the kids that are suffering, this is scary for the government. Everything, anything we express about what is happening, it could be scary and threatening the…authority of the Syrian regime. Even this blood, the red thing, everything could be scary. All the symbols in the drawings, not just in my artwork, but in general in all Syrian artwork. (Brisly, 2019b)

During the Syrian uprising, Diala learned about many artists whom she had not known existed and was amazed by the level of creativity in Syria. These artists moved from only publicly displaying state-approved art to creating and presenting work about what was happening in Syria at the time and expressing their individuality publicly for the first time. Diala herself produced increasingly critical work, addressing the ways women were silenced and exposing the suffering created by the war in Syria. She stresses that, before the uprising, space for critique was lacking as the government had not tolerated it. With the uprising, people found new space to express themselves critically despite government disapproval.

Academics similarly have a role to play in objecting to illegitimate authority, and in striving to advance social justice. For example, academics can record what is happening in society with the aim of enabling society to remember atrocities. As crucial as the creation of knowledge is the communication of that knowledge to a variety of stakeholders. Some argue that academics and educators have an important role to play in helping the oppressed and marginalized to understand the larger context of their life situations and to act to transform their reality (Freire, 2017). By communicating research findings, members of the academy can also contribute to fostering dialogue or influencing public opinion on certain matters. Finally, academic institutions play key roles through teaching and providing access to higher education to all those interested in obtaining it. Indeed, when it comes to resisting oppression, students often take the lead in protests, with universities providing a vital space for expressing resistance (Ghorashi, 2003; Stapnes, Carlquist and Horst, 2020; Sapiie, 2016).

Since the academy is also a space of privilege and authority, sociologist and philosopher Zygmunt Bauman argues for the need for academics to remain at the margins, as Halleh explains:

> Bauman (2000) paints a picture of the scholar as an exile who must venture into social engagement to have an influence, while preserving the marginality of a scholar to be able to reflect and abstract. This margin where the scholar dwells is not a state of isolation but a precondition for maintaining a relative distance from being overtaken by the power of the dominant discourse. To opt for the margin is to choose to slow down while everyone else around you is running around, and to choose to raise questions while others are certain of their answers. (Ghorashi, 2017a, p. 143)

As professor of literature Edward Said (1991) argues, the critical academic is a traveler, someone with a willingness to explore and discover new worlds, idioms, and rhetoric who can abandon fixed positions, in a ceaseless quest for knowledge and freedom. However, several authors demonstrate the many ways in practice that the academic world, through a range of, inter alia, gendered, racialized, and class-based norms, limits diversity and reproduces privilege, and thus uniformity (Brown and Strega, 2005; Locke, 2017; Smith, 2013). Indeed, although academic freedom can contribute to and disseminate new knowledge, and although the academy can play an important role in checking authority, this does not mean that the academy is a free and open institution that offers a full range of ideas and viewpoints. The modern university is, by nature, hegemonic and conservative, a result of its history as an institution called upon to promote a national culture in service of domestic needs, such as nation-building as well as international, imperialist ones (Azoulay, 2019).

For Halleh, questioning has always been part of her academic inclination, evidenced by the high value she placed on reading and thinking when she was engaged in political action during the Iranian Revolution. Through the role model of Homa Nategh, who was both an academic and a political activist, Halleh discovered the possibility of being an engaged academic. After she established herself in exile, Halleh moved from a life in hiding to one of hyper-visibility. Unable to develop academically during the years that followed the revolution in Iran, Halleh in exile became a highly outspoken academic, writing extensively about the experiences of women political activists in Iran and contributing to Dutch society in myriad ways. Her current social engagement extends to issues of migrant inclusion in Europe and structural racism in academia.

The stories of Monirah, Halleh, and Diala show that they continuously questioned societal realities and did not remain silent or passive when confronted with injustices—thus aiming to initiate "new beginnings". In contexts with limited space for alternative viewpoints, many may question the status quo, but far fewer express their challenges publicly. Fewer still actively try to change these realities. The innate fear of questioning, which is related to the fear of failure and of social or physical death, makes people passive, according to Bauhn (2003). Furthermore, many sociocultural and civil–political mechanisms expressly deter people from openly raising questions. In the stories shared in this book, those mechanisms include the threat of arrest, torture, and death, but also measures that may seem less punishing, such as social criticism. For example, when Monirah received letters criticizing her involvement in film and containing lies about her behavior, her neighbors and community members pressured her and her family to stop her from engaging in her creative work. Had Monirah succumbed to the pressure, she would have relinquished a crucial tool that she now uses to speak out about a range of societal injustices.

Displaying courage

In authoritarian contexts, engaging in autonomous action and authentic expression is risky. "[A] willingness to act and speak at all", ultimately "leaving one's private hiding place and showing who one is, in disclosing and exposing one's self", requires courage in democratic as well as in authoritarian settings, according to

Arendt (1958, p. 186). It is the only way to initiate something new and (if others follow) to set in motion a larger process. Addressing a key question related to action and nonaction, Arendt (1960) asserts that both fear and mindlessness prevent individuals from acting when the status quo demands that they do. In situations offering little space for a plurality of perspectives—for uniquely individual, autonomous self-expression—presenting a challenge to the status quo through expressions or conduct requires real courage.

Courage is not the absence of fear but rather the ability to act in spite of fear. It is the ability to face and confront fear, not danger (Bauhn, 2003). One may fear failure, loss of life, or victimization, or one may believe that whether or not one acts does not really matter. Whatever the reason for the fear, it breeds passivity (Jarstad and Höglund, 2015; Valentino et al., 2011). Courage is required to be in the world authentically, unhampered by one's fear, and to maintain or restore a "sense of autonomy even in the face of adversity" (Bauhn, 2003, p. 42). It is thus an important agency-supporting disposition. Both Monirah and Diala describe a transformative moment or phase in their lives that seems to have fortified their courage. For Monirah, it was when, after she had been silenced, her mother insisted she resume her artistic self-expression. For Diala, it was during the Syrian Revolution, which created a space for expression previously closed due to censorship, and made visible the many creative artists and the diverse perspectives within the country.

What Bauhn (2003) calls "the courage of conviction" is directed by the individual's sense of moral responsibility and focuses on supporting the common good. The courage of conviction is "the courage of men and women who die for their nations or their religious beliefs, who go to jail rather than making a deal with injustice, who sacrifice popularity to principles and who prefer a life in poverty to one sullied by corruption" (Bauhn, 2003, p. 89). Halleh talks about this type of courage explicitly when she states that she and her comrades, believing in big ideals that merited sacrificing one's life, had been willing to die for their cause during the Iranian Revolution. This form of courage can also be found in those who support others facing injustice and mistreatment; it is made possible because of a sense of moral responsibility for the common good of one's community, nation, or humanity. Perceiving oneself as sharing certain interests, rights, and duties with others—and thus recognizing a common good—gives meaning to people's lives. This may enable people to persist in conditions where speaking up could lead to imprisonment or death (Selvik, 2021).

Expressing oneself can put oneself and one's family at risk, not just locally but also transnationally. Monirah and her family received threats and felt unsafe after her performance in Sweden came to the attention of the Afghan authorities. Participants in the revolutions in Iran and Syria became the targets of the government as well as government-affiliated groups both during and after the political upheaval. Halleh describes experiencing fear as a teenager after taking part in a peaceful sit-in and being struck in the head by Hezbollah street mobs who were silently endorsed by the government and, in Halleh's eyes, sought to kill people. Many of Halleh's and Diala's friends and fellow activists disappeared into the prison system of their countries. Both Halleh and Diala themselves faced the frightening possibility of imprisonment, the attendant risks of being tortured, disappeared, or killed, and their families being unable to find out what happened to them. This risk haunted Diala for many years after she left Syria.

> It was my fear to be arrested in Syria, it was the scariest nightmare. It's weird because I still have nightmares— now I don't have it anymore, but I had it for a long time after leaving Syria—that I go back to Syria and I get arrested but then the nightmare stops. I don't know what happens then. Always, it stops at the point I got arrested and after that it is blank. (Brisly, 2021a)

Courage is also needed because to explore and share one's inner world after traumatic experiences—which may be filled with anxiety, sorrow, anger, and other strong emotions—is difficult and can make one feel immense vulnerability. Halleh explains both the incredibly tough work of doing this as well as the crucial role this process has played in her life:

> At that time I was writing and crying behind the computer most of the time. [...] Then the past and the present became so vivid, my old struggles and nightmares and sense of non-belonging in the present... You know, in all these phases, I have been able to give the past the place that it deserves. Not ignoring it, but also not letting it overshadow my life— my present and my future. (Ghorashi, 2020)

Displaying courage, both when engaging in dangerous activities that challenge the status quo and when facing one's wounds and trauma, is central in forms of resistance and can be crucial in inspiring others to develop their response-ability. Thus, I would argue that displaying courage is not just a personal trait but also, in fact, a part of political action.

Creating visions of the future and acting prefiguratively

Political scientist, sociologist and public intellectual Carl Boggs (1977) coined the concept of "the prefigurative" after more than a decade of research on social and political movements for equality and social justice, including the civil rights, women's, and gay rights movements. He defined it as "the embodiment, within the ongoing political practice of a movement, of those forms of social relations, decision-making, culture, and human experience that are the ultimate goal" (Boggs, 1977, p. 2). Prefiguration developed from a critique of movements in which the means of struggle were in tension with the ends (Leach, 2013). Critics of these movements argue that it is impossible to achieve a peaceful, non-hierarchical society through a hierarchical organization that uses violence. They further assert that by making sure the means are in line with the ends, political action, regardless of its outcome, is meaningful (van de Sande, 2017). Research on prefiguration provides interesting examples of the transformative mobilizing power of narratives, and how visionary perspectives of a future beyond what is possible today are central in keeping everyday resistance alive in dark times.

Political action through narrative work can focus on sharing visions of a future that contains "a good beyond what is presently given" (Robbins, 2013, p. 458). The transformative potential of this visionary future orientation has been extensively explored in the literature on everyday resistance and social movements, and in particular, in work on prefigurative action. Those who engage in everyday resistance often stress the importance of presenting alternative societal visions and living according to those visions. This is maybe even more essential in oppressive contexts, as Jeffrey Goldfarb explores in his work on resistance movements in eastern Europe in the 1980s.

> In the words of the most articulate leader of this movement "they acted as if they lived in a free society", and a free society resulted. They represented themselves to each other as independent citizens and in the process they created an independent public. (Goldfarb, 2006, p. 33)

In Czechoslovakia in the 1980s, Václav Havel encouraged people to "live in truth", believing that to end totalitarianism, people had to stop replicating the official narrative and instead start independently to define and live their own truth. Authoritarian politics has social limits that are structured by ordinary people interacting with each other outside of official definitions, prefiguring an alternative future. This was, for example, experienced during the 1979 Iranian Revolution—as Halleh explains—when university and high school students took to the streets and openly debated a new, free, and equal society within an Iran that experienced high incidence of political prisoners, torture, and death penalties. Both creating an alternative narrative and acting in accordance with it are crucial modes of everyday resistance that build on the transformative power of storytelling.

Besides (higher) educational spaces, artistic spaces and creative practice also play crucial roles in the contestation over the definition of reality (Goldfarb, 2005). Art can help citizens produce images of a more hopeful future after war by creating a truly public space of engagement. It can also create civic conscience through stimulating open debate about models of cultural and social reconstruction (Arsenijevic, 2010). Although cultural production is often deeply embedded in societal realities, it is also free to envision and imagine far beyond such realities, thereby stimulating hope and visionary imagining. Diala's art, and especially the art she produces for children, offers examples of work that presents freedom from the restrictions of a confined everyday reality. Art can also visualize alternative ways of living together that can play a prefigurative role by encouraging people to live their lives as if the society they wish for is already in existence.

The psychology professor Vlad Glăveanu (2017) argues that one of art's most important qualities is its capacity to make us wonder. Wondering, creativity, and imagination are needed to envision a better society (Horst, 2022). Art presents new questions and perspectives. These do not automatically lead to social change, but they can stimulate empowering experiences that offer the possibility of change (Glăveanu, 2017). Diala's art is a powerful example of this, I believe. In the drawings, paintings, and murals she creates with and for children and in her artwork for adults, Diala uses colors, detail, and contrast—between her warm style and the horrific and unjust consequences of war and oppression—to inspire feelings of wonder. Diala also uses symbols in her work and she plays with concepts, ideas, and materialities that are not normally juxtaposed. Altogether, her techniques challenge her audience to look closely, absorb, and reflect.

Artists also play an important role as creators of spaces for free exchange in a context in which such spaces do not exist. Artists in Serbia for example used political humor to cleverly create space for criticism—without suffering repercussions—within a context in which the government limited alternative perspectives (Sørensen, 2017). In situations where public space is unavailable, artistic practice can offer a legitimate way for people to come together in a semiprivate space. For example, Monirah created a safe space for young women in Afghanistan to share their own perspectives freely with one another. As Monirah describes the training sessions, the girls and young women talked about their experiences of oppression or exclusion and discussed strategies and role-played ways to handle such situations. Through community theater, Monirah also created a space for visualizing and talking about taboo subjects in public. Through artistic means, she carefully carved out space for discussion within the community about a practice that people generally disapproved of but could not talk about.

Impact: the transformative power of storytelling and narrative

Expressing oneself through speech and action against violence, oppression, or other types of social injustices affects the collective because doing so—whether verbally or through other means—brings out into the open thoughts, feelings, and perspectives that many may in fact share. When one person speaks out, it may inspire others to express themselves and to act and resist. This is what Arendt refers to when she explores political action as both consisting of a person beginning or leading it, and others following or joining in. But in order for people to be able to follow potential "new beginnings" (Arendt, 1958), beyond those few who were present and witnessed them, these political acts need to be transformed into narrative—their stories need to be told. Storytelling that focuses on social injustices, as well as on the actions of those who try to challenge them, is crucial for individual action to have an impact.

Given the many pressures—applied by society or internally generated—to remain silent about the human consequences of war and exile, rather than resist its causes, the need to create supportive communities of listeners is essential. Expressing oneself in front of a witnessing audience can be crucial to one's process of healing from trauma. For storytelling to have this effect, it helps to share complete, detailed personal stories, not generalizations or abstractions. This is essential to evoke embodied understanding in the audience and to show that personal experiences are complex and multiple, and should not be reduced to singular stereotypes. Listeners need to find ways to witness commonly silenced stories, as the systematic silencing of lived experiences can easily undermine communities. These listeners need to learn to hear the personal stories of those who have experienced violent conflict, oppression, and/or exile in a caring, respectful way without judgment or political agenda. For the storyteller, sharing deeply personal stories can be important as it helps them to recognize that their unique story is the story of many others. As Halleh so beautifully phrased it, "understanding that the pain is a common pain does not necessarily take it away, but it does enable individuals to feel strengthened, knowing that their experiences are shared" (Ghorashi, 2008, p. 121).

In what follows I will explore the transformative power of storytelling and narrative by first describing core themes in stories of violence and oppression and then exploring the process of witnessing stories as central in individual and collective healing. It will become clear just how closely interrelated the individual process of coming to terms with experiences of violence, oppression, and exile, and the collective healing process is. Not only is individual healing essential for being able to share such vital stories, but witnessing them also addresses intersubjective aspects of trauma and healing, and can encourage a wish to explore historical and collective trauma more profoundly and to acknowledge a universal responsibility in order to inspire response-ability. I will conclude with observations from Monirah, Halleh, and Diala on some of the ripple effects that they have understood their political action to have had.

Stories of violence and oppression: loss, pain, suffering

> I am a teller; a storyteller. Telling is a kind of breathing. I can't stop myself. I can't stop breathing. I am a storyteller who would like to light stars in dark spaces, to attach stars at a dark sky, at a dark roof. Still there are endless black spaces that need endless stories.[12] (Hashemi, 2020b)

Although storytelling is "a kind of breathing" for Monirah, talking about violence and oppression—whether they occur in the privacy of the home or in public in the context of war or authoritarian rule—is not easy. Powerful interests wish the stories to remain untold and those who seek to share them face strong internal and external pressures not to. In *Who lights the stars?* Monirah presents two voices in her head, one that argues for the merits of and need to tell her stories and the other that warns of the dangers of doing so. The first voice explains that to help humans get along and survive, our brains suppress what has happened, but that talking assists in regaining the "forgotten" information. This voice tells Monirah to share her story and trust that she will be fine. Yet the second voice insists that she cannot possibly tell her story, as doing so will provoke unbearable pain and will plunge her into a fearful uncertainty as to what lies ahead.

> My heart beats fast. I am certain of my death and I feel the trembling in my bones and veins. If I open my mouth, I will not survive. It's going to kill me. I'll be crushed, ground, shattered like a broken glass that can never be repaired. I won't be able to put myself together, ever again. I am acquainted with faking myself. I have learned how to stand up when my whole body screams in extreme pain. I know how to smile when tears flow inside me. I know nothing about a world, where everyone knows everything about me. Me! That's an unknown world. It's dark, cold, and I know nothing about people there. (Hashemi, 2021c)

Despite this fearsome scenario, Monirah, after ending up in hospital, chooses to listen to the first voice. When we spoke, she was in the middle of what would undoubtedly be a long and extremely painful process of not just recovering the details of her own story and learning to share it but also of dealing with the consequences of sharing. Halleh, on the other hand, has already gone through much of this painful process, having become convinced many years ago that telling her life story would be crucial for dealing with her traumatic past. Writing became her therapy; it helped her to understand, place, and analyze her own experiences. "The stories of other women made my own past revive. I started having recurrent nightmares, because the past, despite my efforts to forget it, had come to life again. Yet, my confrontation with the past gave me the chance to build up a new relationship with the memories" (Ghorashi, 2008, p. 121). Halleh argues that storytelling helped the women who shared their life stories with her, and at the same time, it helped her, the listener. Sharing traumatic stories about one's past, in a safe environment with someone who is empathetic is a way of "giving the past a place in the present" (Ghorashi, 2008). It is thus a part of healing.

While storytelling is painful and can lead to traumatization, not least in an unsafe environment, an additional risk of storytelling is that the listeners have preconceived ideas about the storyteller that limit what they actually hear. Monirah debates whether to release certain parts of her personal story at a time when political interest in Afghanistan is high and her story could be co-opted to fit certain ethno-national narratives. Diala describes occasions in which she felt she was invited to contribute not as an artist, but as a Syrian or as a refugee. The reality that people are so readily categorized before their stories are even heard makes those who have much to teach others about the human consequences of war and oppression understandably reluctant to express themselves.

One could argue that this reaction is an unfortunate side effect of the tendency to categorize and to place people in preformed boxes; or it could be argued that this is actually the desired effect, an efficient way of silencing marginalized individuals. I believe that the pressures on women to not share their stories are particularly strong, as their narratives are often construed as affecting the honor of a larger entity, such as a country, an ethnic group or a nation (Korac, 2006; Schrijvers, 1997, 1999). Thus, it is unsurprising that Monirah consciously deliberates about whether or not to speak up. As she explains:

> I had only one digital performance with *Who light the stars?* and there were lots of discussions raised amongst certain groups of people and my friends, and that was after only showing it once online. And if I start a tour, a discussion, I am going to talk about incest in our society, that is a very important issue. It exists, we cannot deny it. And if I do that, I would like to talk about my experience. I would like to give examples. How it exists, in what way we are part of these things going on. So all of these things will come out, it is not only that this book is going to put it outside. It is going to come out. And I think I need to make myself ready for many things.
>
> [...] And I am a little worried about whether it is the right time to perform. Or should I wait because what is going on, Hazaras have been killed everywhere. If I put this play ...if I talk about this issue, will Hazaras be more targeted? I have been accused that I put the life of Hazara in danger. I have been accused of this many times publicly. That I do it willingly, since I have a safe refuge here, I have a safe haven, I don't care about others' lives.

I do care about others' lives. But…I am afraid that the right time never comes. Especially for Afghanistan, Afghan women. And if we are going to sacrifice, if we are going to change, I have to do it. I will be condemned in different ways; I am ready for that. But I think finally I need to make peace with myself, I know this, I am fully aware of that…but somehow it also burdens my heart that I will be held responsible for many things. (Hashemi, 2021b)

Stories told by people who have experienced violence and oppression often include many experiences best described as traumatic. Such storytelling can thus lead to fragile interpersonal situations in which the teller struggles both with a painful memory and with putting the recollection into words, and often with an audience who lacks experiential knowledge of the kinds of incidents being described. As a listener, I struggle in a different way. On the one hand, I strive to maintain an openness in the interpersonal relationship so that the teller of the story feels secure in continuing and understands that I am listening respectfully. On the other hand, I try to cope with my own strong emotions as I hear stories about the horrible suffering that people are capable of inflicting on others and the unfathomable grief caused by loss—of loved ones, of a home, of an identity, of a future, of trust in humanity, of "dreams and ideals" (Ghorashi, 2003).

Loss, pain, and suffering are central elements in the stories these three women tell about the human consequences of violent conflict and severe oppression. They leave powerful imprints. I remember the fear and uncertainty that followed the "spring" of the Iranian Revolution, when peaceful protests became extremely dangerous. When friends, family and comrades disappeared and becoming invisible by going into hiding was the only way to survive. I would rather forget the little girl who was sexually abused by her father, who learned firsthand that, in the world she inhabited, the options to be herself—as a woman, refugee, and Hazara—were extremely restricted. I recall the minefield where a brother was lost, leaving behind a sister who, with both fragility and strength, reveals the human consequences of the atrocities taking place in war.

Enumerating the many painful experiences suffered by Monirah, Halleh, and Diala, and then generalizing from their experiences onto those of millions seems inappropriate, as does identifying "key characteristics" of the human consequences of violence and oppression and analyzing them abstractly. Instead, I am impelled to wonder how I put the unspeakable into words and whether academia affords any space to do so in a respectful way. How do I make sure that putting into words the suffering caused by violence and oppression does not invite voyeurism? That it does not contribute to creating an Other that is evil, nonhuman, or pure victim? That it does not turn me into the protagonist as the conveyor of the story?

In processing the stories of people who have experienced conditions of violence, abuse, and extreme coercion—not just for this book but for research I have done over the last 25 years— I have struggled to find a balance between, on the one hand, maintaining my faith in humanity and not succumbing to severe psychological strain and, on the other hand, resisting the urge to protect myself by suppressing my feelings and emotionally distancing myself. One "strategy" to find a balance between caring too much and too little has been to allow my emotions to wash over me on a regular basis, and to feel the anguish, pain, and loss. I let myself cry as I read interview transcripts and, sometimes, while talking to the storytellers. I give myself space to feel, understanding it as a very normal part of this work. And I try to hear all aspects of the stories I am told, to not just focus on the suffering, but to recognize, too, the tremendous courage and strength the stories convey.

I have also struggled with my strong urge to change the false narrative "out there" because expecting my academic work to lead to visible societal transformation can easily lead to feeling naive, hopeless, or cynical. Trying to maintain a balance between despair and detachment while continuing to engage in witnessing, I have experimented with forms of communication that have the potential to reach nonacademic audiences, including comics, animations and an online exhibition.[13] Most people who have no lived experience of violent conflict, authoritarianism, or refugee life have little opportunity to listen to stories of these experiences in their interpersonal relations or even in mediated forms. This lack of opportunity contributes to maintaining the status quo; it also comfortably impedes the development of feelings of responsibility or the need to witness. My response to Edkins's question of "Why sometimes people see others' suffering as none of their business?" (Edkins, 2003, p. 256) is that the narrowness of public discourse promotes the idea that the listener or viewer has no responsibility for the everyday realities in the faraway places presented to them, which is a luxury the privileged (falsely assume they) have.

Violence and oppression take many forms. The stories of Monirah, Halleh, and Diala clearly illustrate that some of the processes that they have undergone and experienced as deeply violent, persist in exile. The anthropologist Veena Das and her colleagues (2001) argue that suffering results from devastating injuries inflicted on humans; it can also be appropriated in ways that inflict further violence (Kleinman and Kleinman, 1996). Suffering, in this anthropological perspective, is the result of the social violence that local, national, or global social orders bring to bear on people. Das (2006), Kleinman (2000), and others have written about how everyday forms of violence impact societies, interconnecting private and collective realities and social, political, and economic factors. Not just practices toward, but also narratives about, others can be experienced as violence, for example, when others seem to have the right to impose a simplified label like "refugee" on one's complex, multifaceted identity. This can augment trauma, as the underlying processes of othering replicate those experienced within the context of violent conflict.

Life history research provides personal narratives, such as Monirah's, that reveal the connections between the here and there and the then and now. It thus makes it possible to explore positioned agency across time, to chart its fluctuations as individuals and societies change or as individuals move to new contexts. Although changes occur, the past is carried along. Seeing the connections between the here and there and the then and now in each of the three stories in this book, I identify one particularly striking element: all the women experience continuity between what they underwent in their countries of origin and what they experience where they live currently. In exile, all of them continue to fight against stereotypes, labeling, and processes of othering as they did in their home countries. Monirah had to deal with the stereotypes of Afghans while a refugee in Iran and with those of Hazara while living in Afghanistan; in exile, she deals with Western media stereotypes of Afghan women as vulnerable and passive victims. In Iran after the revolution, Halleh experienced political and religious oppression; in her life now as a professor in the Netherlands, she actively fights labels and implicit bias. She describes being othered in the two different settings and her feelings of confusion:

> I was feeling like, "okay this is not new to me". I was othered in Iran and it still was painful. But there was something different about this time. I couldn't find an enemy that othered me. There was no enemy. The people who did that, it came from the images they had of me. Normal people, normal conversations. They were like me. (Ghorashi, 2017c).

The various forms of othering that Monirah, Halleh, and Diala faced in exile as they were labeled "immigrant" or "refugee" have augmented their trauma since the processes of othering they experienced in their new lives replicate those that were so familiar and damaging to them in the context of violent conflict from which they escaped. These forms of othering appear in all the stories, at times prominently, and thus need to be included in processes of witnessing and healing. In short, when refugees and others affected by violent conflict and authoritarianism share stories of violence and oppression, their stories do not necessarily end when they leave their home country or even when they arrive in their new country of residence. The nature of the violence and oppression changes, and may become less obvious to those who enjoy the privilege of not being exposed to it, but it is often closely connected to everyday processes of othering.

Witnessing and healing

Each of the women featured in this book notes that the othering they experienced in their country of origin—on the basis of ethnicity, nationality, religion, political beliefs, gender, or some other trait—also occurred in exile. Halleh is confused when she discovers that, upon moving from Iran to the Netherlands, she is still the Other but that she can no longer identify an enemy who is responsible for this othering. As the stories presented in this book illustrate, labeling someone as "Other" reduces a complex individual to a set of particular, largely negative, traits. Everyday resistance to violent narratives and practices is thus not just necessary in contexts of violent conflict and authoritarianism; it is just as essential within functioning democracies that see themselves as exemplars of values such as freedom, inclusiveness, equality, and consent. In reality, marginalized individuals and groups in democratic contexts are othered on a daily basis, and this happens in ways that are largely invisible to people in positions of relative privilege.

Within such realities, as several of the stories presented in this book show, interpersonal relationships that involve fully seeing one another—instead of merely seeing "the Other"—shape how lives evolve. Such relationships can play a key role in supporting individuals in marginalized positions in their fight for social justice. Halleh's story suggests that her life would have been very different had it not been for her aunt, and the love and care and political education that she offered her, and for those individuals who recognized her as a full human being–rather than "a refugee"–when she first came to the Netherlands.

I am interested in the interpersonal because it is the first level at which respect for individual authenticity and autonomy as well as collective well-being and care can be (re)established in a society damaged by war and authoritarianism. This is especially true if deep interpersonal relationships cut across boundaries of privilege. The interpersonal is also an important level in democratic contexts in which othering occurs: when injustices become visible to those not directly affected by violence and oppression, demands for structural changes become inevitable. Halleh makes a similar point when she explains her belief in the transformative power of storytelling:

> The power is in all those images that we have of one another. And all those images that become so normalized in our daily life that we don't think about it, we don't think and question it, we take that for granted. So if we want to think about change we need to think about how to unsettle these powerful images, this powerful chain of images that influences ourselves, but mainly others; that contribute to othering of people, to exclusion in society. Sharing stories…is a very powerful instrument to do that. Sharing stories from points of difference, from people who are actually disconnected, becomes even more powerful because this creates mirroring effects. (Ghorashi, 2017)

However, if sharing stories among people in different social positions is to have transformative power, people in marginalized positions must first share their stories and those in other positions must hear them and truly acknowledge the lived experiences these stories speak of. Given that these stories involve the human consequences of violence and oppression, telling them, as well as listening to them, requires time, patience, and much hard and often very painful work. At the same time, telling these stories and witnessing them can be healing, inspirational, and transformational—facilitating connection and a sense of meaningfulness.

As I have argued, there are many internal and external forces that prevent storytelling before, during, and after traumatic experiences. These include direct or indirect political or social oppression, feelings of shame and guilt, fear of misrepresentation, loyalty to a marginalized group, and a range of other factors. I have also shown how such silence upholds the status quo, benefits those in privileged positions, and comfortably prevents "bystanders"—such as citizens in democratic countries that host refugees—from feeling responsible. In her essay, "We Refugees", first published in 1947, Arendt (2017) illustrates the many ways in which refugees—in her case, Jewish refugees across Europe in the early 1940s—are urged to be invisible and silent about their past:

> Once we could buy our food and ride on the subway without being told we were undesirable. We have become a little hysterical since newspapermen started detecting us and telling us publicly to stop being disagreeable when shopping for milk and bread. We wonder how it can be done; we already are so damnably careful in every moment of our daily lives

to avoid anybody guessing who we are, what kind of passport we have, where our birth certificates were filled out—and that Hitler didn't like us. (Arendt, 2017), p. 269).

In a recent article, my colleague Odin Lysaker and I draw on Arendt's work and ask, "How do some individuals with refugee backgrounds still claim their identity and history, show who they are and make their appearance in the world, when there are such strong forces encouraging them not to?" (Horst and Lysaker, 2021, p. 72) This book, I hope, provides some further answers to that question. Monirah's mother, for example, instilled in her the responsibility to speak up if and when she had the power to do so. And Monirah—like the other women in this book—did not maintain silence about uncomfortable—taboo—topics that most people prefer not to hear about. When we meet up again after she has read the first full draft of this book, Monirah explains just how intertwined her own personal healing is with her desire to contribute to helping others. She says that she speaks about her experiences not just to help others but also because doing so is the only way she can help herself:

> Because the more I talk, the more I understand myself; the more I realize what has happened and how it affected me, how it changed me…When you are living in so much censorship you have to give probably a weaker version of the reality, something that could have been but then, no, the reality was something else. Within all this censorship one does not realize how much we are changing; we are manipulating ourselves.

We are making ourselves to see and get along and then finally it becomes the only way.

[…] And now reading this, I realized that this is also part of the healing, talking is very important. And we do it for ourselves. I think the first step is to do it for ourselves. And then, when you pass it, you stop shivering, you stop shaking, you stop crying, then you can share it with others. And that's where the collective healing comes in.

[…] I mean, I need to get over this to be able to help others. For me thinking that it is happening, I mean… what I have experienced, whenever I imagine it, whenever I go to my psychologist, I talk to her and I imagine, feel that "is there any other child going through this, right now, when I am talking about it…and am I in that position to change it?" I know that probably one year ago, two years ago I was not in a position to do anything. Cause I was so much into my own pains and troubles and sorrows and past and traumas…but passing that phase I knew that I have to pass this to be able to help that child. (Hashemi, 2021b)

One can improve one's current life situation to the extent that one can tell one's co-citizens a story, expressing oneself narratively (Benhabib, 1996, quoted in Horst and Lysaker, 2021). For Monirah, telling her story is important not just because it draws attention to the abuse and violence occurring in Afghanistan but also because by telling it she refuses to be defined by her personal trauma. Storytelling is a means of helping her process her trauma; the sense of responsibility that her story engenders is what gives the story meaning in the first place.

The listener as well as the storyteller is central in creating this potential transformation, as listening to marginalized and traumatic narratives requires a respectful presence and may entail a responsibility to engage in more active witnessing that goes beyond mere listening to include acting upon what one has heard; for example, by sharing the narratives with others. This is especially the case when stories have been actively silenced, resulting in the repression of experiences and identities, as can happen to women in a range of different contexts and situations. Monirah is saying that telling a marginalized personal story publicly has particular value because doing so meets the needs of both the storyteller and the listener.

> I think through telling, through talking about our experience, we can also create a tolerance in the society to just listen. I know it is very weird, it is very uncomfortable for a patriarchal society that has only listened to men…And I think for me storytelling is not only empowering women, but it is also helping the society in developing a tolerance towards women's experiences. (Hashemi, 2021a)

Thus, the combined need of telling stories and developing a tolerance to hear them is central, I believe, to both individual and collective healing. Although Monirah illustrates this through the example of women's stories in a patriarchal society, I see this as true of a wide range of marginalized stories in any society. Feeling that she has "a moral duty" to share her own and other women's stories, Monirah, in her theater work, takes women's stories out of the private, domestic sphere and sets them firmly in the public sphere, where they become the collective responsibility of all those "witnessing" the play and the everyday stories it tells.

Witnessing or bearing witness is a theme that has been explored in a range of fields, including nursing, education, and journalism (Bunkers, 2014). Professor of implementation science and nursing Rahel Naef defines bearing witness as "a human way of relating, a mode of existence, an ethical obligation. It involves listening to, writing about, and speaking of the stories of immense suffering experienced by the other/others through atrocities, violence, and war" (Naef, 2006, p. 149). She continues by arguing that "bearing witness becomes a testimony, and it is a gesture of ethical resistance toward suffering that has already taken place. Bearing witness happens face-to-face, but also through rituals, testimonies, documentation, literature, story-telling, and art." (Naef, 2006, p. 149) In the field of journalism, bearing witness has been understood to consist of both "a mode of address that consists of an appeal to the audience to share responsibility for an event", and "a site for the transmission of moral obligation" (Tait, 2011, p. 1227). Witnessing in this sense involves enacting and inspiring "response-ability".

Thus, witnessing is listening (or seeing, reading, feeling) and responding. In the case of the stories told of the human consequences of violence and oppression, witnessing is sharing responsibility based on the knowledge and insights gained. One of the most devastating realities for storytellers who share their experiences of injustices with others and the world is the lack of response that often follows. An interpersonal relationship between storytelling and respectful, caring listening is crucial to the process of personal healing. And even when storytelling occurs in a more public way, such as when Halleh wrote about her own experiences in her MA and PhD theses or when Monirah created a play based on her own experiences, such storytelling can and often does include interpersonal exchanges—as when her Master's supervisor read Halleh's story and encouraged her to share it, or when Monirah told her full story in several sessions to friends, as a preparatory step to writing her play. The processing of the story, "giving the past a place in the present", as Halleh puts it, can be facilitated with the support of others. Ultimately, sharing the story with others who are not just listening but also witnessing can aid the healing process.

This process of sharing silenced stories is as important for the listener as it is for the storyteller. In "We Refugees", written during the Second World War, Hannah Arendt describes the lived experiences of refugees in a way that is still relevant today. She also warns of the consequences for the position of privileged bystanders when no one responds to the plight of the refugees. "The comity of European peoples went to pieces when, and because, it allowed its weakest member to be excluded and persecuted." (Arendt, 2017) What does ignoring the suffering of others do both to those who painstakingly worked to tell their stories and to those who listened to them? I would argue that personal healing as well as collective healing are impeded by the lack of response-ability. A first step toward creating response-ability may be to recognize that experiential and embodied knowing, in all its diversity, is a source of knowledge and collective wisdom.

Observing and sharing one's impact on the world

The effect of one's actions cannot be known in advance and may be quite different from that which was intended, and tracing the effect retrospectively can be difficult. It is not possible to know with certitude that a TEDx talk, for example, will affect the audience's future actions. But it is clear that the three women whose stories I have shared profoundly affected the lives of others. Halleh has mentored hundreds of students and inspired many more while also exerting immeasurable influence through her appearances on TV and radio, on government commissions, and as a contributor to a range of policy reports. That she has had an impact has been publicly acknowledged as she has, on several occasions, been identified as among the most influential people in the Netherlands, most recently in 2020 by the Dutch newspaper *Volkskrant*.[14]

Monirah speaks of several occasions when people who watched her performances came up to her afterward and told her that she had moved them profoundly. Hazara women were deeply grateful that their history was being told, whereas male members of the audience told her that she had opened their eyes to various forms of oppression from which they had benefited. Monirah is proud to note that some of the young women she trained are still active in the fields of art, culture, or media, and a few are now successful artists in their own right, working as photographers, filmmakers, theater producers, or providers of creative workshops for others. Thus, her work creates further waves through these students–as is the case for Halleh.

Diala says that the artists who emerged after the Syrian uprising "gave themselves the right to express themselves about other things", whereas before, the regime determined what could and could not be expressed. Through their daring actions, these artists inspired others to express themselves as well. Diala describes how the regime was particularly unhappy with the outpouring of expressions about the war and the suffering it caused. Diala has also had a profound influence on the children she works with and for as well as on the diverse audiences for her art and her presentations about her work. When I ask Diala whether she has any sense of the impact of her work, she provides the example of those who have been inspired to replicate her work with murals for schools:

> The closest one to my heart is the people who started doing murals in schools or tents of education in the north of Syria, in different places, inspired by my work in the refugee camps. They told me, "We saw what you did and we really liked it and we started doing this in our schools, in our tents, and the kids really love it."
> Because for me, the first time when I wanted to do a mural I just wanted to impress my small audience, the kids there. And I found it really challenging to do it with the kids in the refugee camp, they really have a lot of trauma and maybe it won't interest them to look at an artistic thing. But then, when I saw people are doing the same in different places…. (Brisly, 2021a)

Diala illustrates well the ripple effects of individual action taken by the individual as part of the collective. She has inspired others to seek to improve Syrian children's lives and knowing of this impact has helped Diala to persist with her own engagement despite finding it tough to do so and struggling with trauma. She describes the ripple effect as a chain of people who inspire each other in a way that is contagious, leading to "really sweet power" Brisly, 2021a). That is the collective nature of agency and why it is so important to tell stories about these less visible forms of political action and everyday resistance, as I will explore further in the next section.

In conclusion: storytelling, response-ability, and positioned agency

Set in the context of war, oppression, and exile, the life stories shared in this book include several moments of great loss, pain, and deep suffering. All three women encountered situations or periods in their lives in which they faced violence, experienced dehumanizing treatment, or witnessed others in such circumstances. They also suffered tremendous losses, whether it was loss of a home, a peaceful life, or loved ones. Such experiences can be deeply traumatic and difficult to discuss. And yet, already before we met, Monirah, Halleh, and Diala had all found ways to share some of their experiences publicly, sometimes soon after a difficult experience, and at other times, only after decades and with the help of artistic or academic tools. The work that these women did prior to my reaching out to them for interviews aided me tremendously in my research for this book.

The first phase in the sharing of their stories—telling their stories to me for this book—seems to have benefited Monirah, Halleh, and Diala. In their telling of their stories to me, and in my listening to them carefully and seeking to render their stories truthfully and compassionately, a meaningful interpersonal connection was forged. The feedback I received from the women after they read my drafts of their chapters suggests too that the process of reading about one's story, although it makes one vulnerable, can be helpful and validating. For example, Monirah, who read her chapter while processing the most difficult parts in her own life story, told me "our conversation has been part of my personal healing" (Hashemi, 2021b).

The second phase of sharing stories—in which you, the reader, encounter these stories—extends the chain of interpersonal connections and thus of learning. Storytelling is inherently risky and takes place in a landscape where stories are often politicized for particular purposes. When there is little room for diverse experiences and perspectives and complex individual realities are often reduced through processes of labeling and othering,[15] to tell one's story entails risks: of being treated without respect, of being disbelieved, of being dismissed as irrelevant, or of being effectively ignored. Or worse still, the risk that one's story is used for political purposes, as Monirah feared would happen when the situation in Afghanistan again made headlines.

This book advances several claims. First, when understanding agency as positioned, relational, and changing, appreciating the narrative and interpretational dimensions of agency are crucial. Although changes in the extent of one's power and choice can occur over time due to individual or societal shifts, the stories that individuals tell about themselves often take time to adjust. Further, individuals can only approximate the perceptions, motivations, and intentions of others. Through the in-depth sharing of lived experiences, the gap between the reality of the individual and the perception of it by others, can be reduced. The kind of story one tells to oneself and to others influences individual and collective action. For example, when Diala responds to the comment that "she cannot really change anything" by asserting that she is happy to be "a drop in the ocean with all the other drops", she preserves the possibility of action, which a purely fatalistic perspective does not.

Second, the categories of marginalized and privileged, and of victim and perpetrator, are defined narratively in relation to each other. Common representations of war and exile often focus on particular stories of victimization, adopt black-and-white understandings of the people and positions involved, and ignore other stories that might challenge these simple categorizations. This is disturbingly similar to what people do who aim to create essentialized ethno-national states. The narrative requirements of mainstream storytelling encourage the labeling of people as villains, victims, or heroes. But such categories do not accurately describe reality. For example, they cannot accommodate certain people, such as Serbian anti-war protesters and men who desert rather than fight in an ethno-national war (Korac, 2018). And yet anti-war protesters and military deserters who are crudely classified as "belonging to the aggressors", in fact, play crucial roles in challenging injustices and aggressions that are carried out in the name of the group to which they are seen to belong. Silencing the variety of stories that exist and elevating only narratives about victims and perpetrators, marginalized and privileged, creates a dominant narrative that, ultimately, benefits those with a stake in preserving the status quo.

Stories told about reality are always a reduction and approximation of that reality rather than complete and full narratives of people's lived experiences. For example, in describing a lived experience of violence and oppression, academics might focus on the trauma and victimhood that the experience entailed and the resulting feelings of powerlessness. The same lived experience could be told with a different focus, however, one that emphasizes everyday forms of resistance. In any given reality, both elements can be found. The choices we make as to what aspects are included in the narrative determine how the story develops. Integrated, complex stories aim to include all these different elements, including the trauma, resistance, and courage as well as moments of powerlessness, guilt, and shame. Given how important narrative dimensions are in determining one's positioned agency, the nature of individual and collective storytelling matters. This is why I began this book by stating that we know a great deal about the devastating effects of war, oppression, and forced migration but know far too little about the transformative potential of such experiences through the everyday resistance they also generate.

To shift the balance, this book shows how the stories of those who resist in whatever form they can— such as Halleh's aunt and Monirah's mother—have inspired the women in this book. I also hope and believe that the stories of Monirah, Halleh, and Diala will inspire others as well as encourage response-ability. While being well aware that the stories told here can only be partial, I nevertheless chose to highlight the remarkable words and work of these women in order to provide potential inspiration to others, in the realization that narratives influence the stories we tell about ourselves and our everyday actions.

Witnessing these women's stories and the many others that I have listened to over the last decade has raised for me difficult questions about voice and privilege, which I have tried to address through shared forms of knowledge creation. To witness a life story, especially one that describes lived experiences that the listener has not had, requires a willingness to accept that one witnesses the world from a particular position that is different from that of the storyteller. One can only approximate the position of the teller of the story by listening deeply and then observing and reflecting in conversation with the teller. Through this dialogue, a new, cocreated story emerges. This mode of witnessing builds on the realization that systems of domination and subordination shape our understanding of the world and that we must engage in a continual process of unlearning these systems and relearning alternatives (Azoulay, 2019). This lifelong process, one hopes, will lead to a greater diversity of voices, perspectives, and stories as well as to more initiatives that both hold individuals accountable for their actions and address oppressive structures.

Notes

1 The role of storytelling and narrative in transformation

1. Most recently, I have, for example, made use of excerpts of Monirah and Diala's story for an article on questioning individuals (Horst, 2022).

2. Valuable research on related topics has focused on the Second World War (Braun, 2019; Finkel, 2017; Monroe, 2008; Semelin, 1993; Semelin, Andrieu and Gensburger, 2011; Tec, 2013).

3. I will also touch upon some of this work within the humanities, where it has been of central influence in debates among social scientists. What follows is not intended to be yet another comprehensive overview of narrative methods (Andrews, Squire, and Tamboukou, 2013; Czarniawska, 2004; Goodson et al., 2016; Maynes, Pierce and Laslett, 2008; Riessman, 2008; Squire et al., 2014); rather I focus on those methods most relevant to my own approach.

4. This name is a pseudonym to protect the identity of this research participant.

5. This research took place in the context of a larger research project (TRANSFORM) on what motivates individuals to take action for social justice in societies at war or facing severe oppression, although doing so involves great risk and uncertainty. Several of the findings I present in this book are also supported by data for the larger project (Selvik, 2021; Selvik and Groves, 2023; Stapnes, Carlquist and Horst, 2020; Tellander, 2022).

2 Monirah Hashemi: who lights the stars?

6. This first interview was conducted and transcribed by Trude Stapnes, who provided assistance to the seminar series and is currently doing a PhD in psychology on the role of artists in resistance in Myanmar after the 2021 coup d'état.

3 Halleh Ghorashi: from revolutionary to engaged academic

7. Available at: www.youtube.com/watch?v=OtU8vidBYF8 [Accessed 3 March 2023].

8. Quoted in Ghorashi (2003, pp. 18–19), although this translation is from *Sin – Selected poems of Forugh Farrokhzad*, edited and translated by Shole Wolpe, University of Arkansas Press, 2007.

4 Diala Brisly: "the braver you are, the more you will see"

9. This interview was conducted and transcribed by Trude Stapnes, who provided assistance to the seminar series Diala took part in.

5 Can stories inspire response-ability?

10. This quote appears and is illustrated in an animation video that Diala produced for the TRANSFORM project, entitled A Future for Syria. This video can be accessed on: https://vimeo.com/479767613.

11. Societal Transformation in Conflict Contexts is a four-year research project funded by the Research Council of Norway. From 2017 to 2021, a team of researchers, together with research assistants, artists, and civil society activists, explored the small but often heroic everyday acts of common people who attempt to challenge dehumanizing trends of exclusion and abuse in circumstances of violent conflict and civil war

in Syria, Somalia, and Myanmar. You can learn more through this online exhibition: https://transform.prio.org/transform/.

12. This quoted text does not appear in the latest version of the play but is in the English-language script of June 8, 2020.

13. See https://transform.prio.org/transform/ for an example.

14. Dekker, W. and B. van Raaij (2020). Dit zijn de invloedrijkste Nederlanders van 2020. [Online] De Volkskrant. Available at: www.volkskrant.nl/kijkverder/v/2020/de-volkskrant-top-200-van-invloedrijkste-nederlanders-2020~v410463/ [Accessed 3 March 2023].

15. See also Chimamanda Ngozi Adichie, TED talk "The danger of a single story", 2009, for a powerful rendering of the issue. Available at www.youtube.com/watch?v=D9Ihs241zeg.

Appendix: on data analysis

16. In the case of virtual interviews, it is easy to tape the conversation through the platform used. I have done this in most cases, although I was only interested in the audio and have not done any explicit visual analysis.

Assignment suggestions

1. Public narratives about refugees

In the introduction, we are told there is a dissonance between, on the one hand, human encounters and stories like those presented, and, on the other hand, the public narratives about refugees and others affected by war that are widespread in media, policy, everyday life, and academia.

- Identify key messages in recent media stories that are discounted in this book.
- Can you find counterfactuals—more nuanced stories about refugees and the human consequences of war?
- Discuss your findings.

2. A sense of responsibility

Watch and read the section "A Strong Sense of Responsibility as Driving Force" in the TRANSFORM virtual exhibition (see https://transform.prio.org/transform/). Drawing on this section and chapters 2 and 3 in this book, explore the many different motivational factors you can identify in people's narratives about why they fight for social justice issues.

3. A drop in the ocean?

Watch "A Future for Syria" (available in English or Arabic). You will see Diala's expression of being "a drop in the ocean" appear.

- Based on the animation and chapter 4 in this book, reflect on what the expression entails in light of transformative narratives and practices.
- What is your own understanding of your ability to "make a difference" in the world, and how does this narrative shape your action, do you think? Could you find an equally poetic way of describing your own understanding?

4. Gender and intersectionality

This book suggests that the roots of activism and people's sense of responsibility are shaped, experienced, and expressed according to their intersectional positioning. Can you identify five to ten examples that stood out for you?

5. Narrative approach—methods

Read chapter 1 and the section "Collecting Life Stories" in the TRANSFORM virtual exhibition. Carry out a life story interview, choosing whether to stick to verbal methods only or finding ways to include audiovisual material as well. Write a short reflection note about the process, and share your learning in class.

6. The transformative potential of storytelling

This book strongly argues for the transformative potential of storytelling. So does the section "The Transformative Potential of

Storytelling" in the TRANSFORM virtual exhibition. Split up in two groups and debate for and against the idea that storytelling can make a difference.

Appendix: on data analysis

All interviews were audiotaped or videotaped[16] and then transcribed, creating an extensive amount of data. A single interview session, transcribed, can easily yield a document of 13,000–15,000 words that must then be systematically analyzed. In addition to the interviews, I analyzed transcripts of audiotaped public events; digital materials, such as interviews, presentations, and other types of public appearances; and artistic and academic work by the research participants. In analyzing interviews, I focused on what was verbalized rather than on silences, tone of voice, or other forms of expression. However, the nonverbal aspects of the interviews did shape my full understanding of these women's stories, particularly their emotions in relation to specific past occurrences. I also include meaningful explicit silences and pauses in the transcription. I used a qualitative data analysis program to code the interview transcripts thematically, in line with sociologist Catherine Riessman's (2008) "thematic analysis". I developed themes on the basis of my reading of the transcriptions, my interview guide, and the larger research questions.

In addition to analyzing closely the coded thematical material for each interview participant, I followed each theme across interviews, which allowed me to make comparisons among the three women. I also did several careful readings of each interview, after which I wrote a short version of each life story based on the entirety of the material I had for each individual. Although I relied closely and systematically on the life story interviews, my own interpretations and interests, of course, influenced my analyses and the short life stories presented in the chapters. Narrative research always involves an ongoing process of interpretation; it is thus important to be as explicit as possible about how and when one is putting forward one's own interpretation. At this stage, I sought an additional interview from two of the participants either because I wanted to discuss my interpretations with them or felt I was missing vital information necessary to undertake a complete analysis of the story.

Drawing on Ricoeur, Moen (2006) highlights how multiple layers of interpretation are added when the conversation involving the telling of the life story is written down and thus becomes fixed as text. This process disconnects the narrative from the context of its telling and means that the life story can assume relevance and new meaning beyond that context. A researcher participates in creating new interpretive frames by connecting a particular story with others from other interviews and with relevant literature. As Moen points out, the interpretation does not end with the final publication, since audiences add new layers of interpretation. For Ricoeur (1991, p. 26, quoted in Squire, 2008), "the process of composition, of configuration, is not completed in the text but in the reader". Recognizing this is important. One of the key advantages of working with detailed, extensive life stories is that they afford the reader considerable space to gain insights and develop interpretations based on the lived experiences of others—as they are given meaning through one's own lived experience and perspectives on the world. Especially in cases where those others are unknown to us, this interpretative space can risk introducing misunderstandings; however, at the same time, it allows the reader to feel resonance and to draw on creative skills and imagination in seeking to comprehend other experiences.

References

Adam, Barbara. 2005. *Timescapes of modernity: The environment and invisible hazards*. Routledge.

Al-Sharmani, Mulki, and Cindy Horst. 2016. "Marginal actors? Diaspora Somalis negotiate their citizenship." In *Dislocations of Civic Cultural Borderlines*, 107–122. Springer.

Alcoff, Linda. 1988. "Cultural feminism versus post-structuralism: The identity crisis in feminist theory." *Signs: Journal of Women in Culture and Society* 13 (3): 405–436.

Andersen, Ditte, Signe Ravn, and Rachel Thomson. 2020. Narrative sense-making and prospective social action: methodological challenges and new directions. Taylor & Francis.

Andrews, Molly, Corinne Squire, and Maria Tamboukou. 2013. *Doing narrative research*. Sage.

Arendt, Hannah. 1958. *The human condition*. Chicago: University of Chicago Press.

Arendt, Hannah. 1960. "Freedom and politics: A lecture." *Chicago Review* 14 (1): 28–46.

Arendt, Hannah. 1968. *Men in dark times*. Houghton Mifflin Harcourt.

Arendt, Hannah. 1973. "The Origins of Totalitarianism [1951]." *San Diego and New York*.

Arendt, Hannah. 2017. "We refugees [1947]." In *International Refugee Law*, 3–12. Routledge.

Arsenijevic, Damir. 2010. *Forgotten future: the politics of poetry in Bosnia and Herzegovina*. Nomos Verlagsgesellschaft mbH & Co. KG.

Azoulay, Ariella. 2019. *Potential History*. Verso.

Bakhtin, M. M. 1986. *Speech genres & other late essays*, edited by Carl Emerson and Michael Holquist. Austin: University of Texas Press.Bamberg, M. 2006. "Stories: Big or small: Why do we care?" *Narrative inquiry* 16 (1): 139–147.

Bamberg, Michael. 2012. "Narrative analysis."

Bathmaker, Ann-Marie, and Penelope Harnett. 2010. *Exploring learning, identity and power through life history and narrative research*. Routledge.

Bauhn, Per. 2003. *The value of courage*. Lund, Sweden: Nordic Academic Press.

Bauhn, Per. 2017. *Normative Identity*. Rowman & Littlefield International.

Bauman, Zygmunt. 2000. *Liquid modernity*. Cambridge: Polity Press.

Beausoleil, Emily. 2015. "Embodying an ethics of response-ability." *Borderlands* 14 (2): 1–16.

Bell, Lee Anne. 2007. "Theoretical foundations for social justice education." In *Teaching for diversity and social justice*, 25–38. Routledge.

Benhabib, S. 1996. *The Reluctant Modernism of Hannah Arendt*. Thousand Oaks, CA: Sage.

Berman, Kim. 2017. *Finding voice: A visual arts approach to engaging social change*. University of Michigan Press.

Boggs, Carl. 1977. "Marxism, prefigurative communism, and the problem of workers' control." *Radical America* 11 (6): 99–122.

Braun, Robert. 2019. *Protectors of Pluralism: Religious minorities and the rescue of Jews in the low countries during the Holocaust.* Cambridge: Cambridge University Press.

Brown, Leslie Allison, and Susan Strega. 2005. *Research as resistance: Critical, indigenous and anti-oppressive approaches.* Canadian Scholars' Press.

Bruner, Jerome. 2003. "Self-making narratives." In *Autobiographical memory and the construction of a narrative self,* 225–242. Psychology Press.

Bulhan, Hussein A. 2015. "Stages of colonialism in Africa: From occupation of land to occupation of being." *Journal of Social and Political Psychology* 3 (1): 239–256.

Bunkers, Sandra Schmidt. 2014. "Witnessing." *Nursing science quarterly* 27 (3): 190–194.

Chabot, Sean, and Stellan Vinthagen. 2015. "Decolonizing Civil Resistance." *Mobilization: An International Quarterly* 20 (4): 517–532.

Christophersen, Sara. 2020. "Embodied Possibilities: A study of dance as artistic, everyday practice in Palestine."

Christophersen, Sara. 2022. "Embodied agency: creating room for maneuver through dance in Palestine." *Conflict and Society* 8 (1): 227–241.

Czarniawska, Barbara. 2004. *Narratives in social science research.* Sage.

Das, Veena. 2006. *Life and Words: Violence and the Descent into the Ordinary.* Univ of California Press.

Das, Veena, Arthur Kleinman, Margaret M Lock, Mamphela Ramphele, and Pamela Reynolds. 2001. *Remaking a world: Violence, social suffering, and recovery.* Univ of California Press.

Edkins, Jenny. 2003. "Humanitarianism, humanity, human." *Journal of Human Rights* 2 (2): 253–258.

Ewick, Patricia, and Susan Silbey. 2003. "Narrating social structure: Stories of resistance to legal authority." *American journal of sociology* 108 (6): 1328–1372.

Fanon, Frantz. 2008. *Concerning violence*: Penguin London.

Finkel, Evgeny. 2017. *Ordinary Jews*: Princeton University Press.

Fogelman, Eva. 2011. *Conscience and courage: Rescuers of Jews during the Holocaust*. Anchor.

Freire, Paulo. 2017/1970]. Pedagogy of the Oppressed (Penguin Modern Classics). Penguin Books UK.

Ghorashi, Halleh. 1994. "De Iraanse Revolutie. Van gemeenschappelijkheid tot verdeeldheid (The Iranian Revolution. From togetherness to dividedness)." MA, Anthropology, Vrije Universiteit of Amsterdam.

Ghorashi, Halleh. 2003. *Ways to survive, battles to win: Iranian women exiles in the Netherlands and United States*. New York: Nova Publishers.

Ghorashi, Halleh. 2008. "Giving silence a chance: The importance of life stories for research on refugees." *Journal of refugee studies* 21 (1): 117–132.

Ghorashi, H. 2016. "Wat als u een vluchteling was? (What if you were a refugee?)." *Tijdschrift voor Biografie*:4–11.

Ghorashi, H. 2017. The Changed Conditions of Critical Thinking. TEDx, Amsterdam University College. https://www.youtube.com/watch?v=OtU8vidBYF8

Ghorashi, H. 2017a. "A shifting quest for a sense of home." In *Seeking Home in a Strange Land: True stories of the changing meaning of home*, edited by S. Dijkstra, L. van Doorn and J. van Pelt, 135–154. Utrecht: Stili Novi.

Ghorashi, Halleh. 2017b. "Negotiating belonging beyond rootedness: Unsettling the sedentary bias in the Dutch culturalist discourse." *Ethnic and Racial Studies* 40 (14): 2426–2443.

Gilligan, Carol. 1993. *In a different voice: Psychological theory and women's development*. Cambridge, MA: Harvard University Press.

Gilligan, Carol. 1995. "Hearing the difference: Theorizing connection." *Hypatia* 10 (2): 120–127.

Glăveanu, Vlad Petre. 2017. "Art and social change: The role of creativity and wonder." In *Street art of resistance*, 19–37. Springer.

Goldfarb, Jeffrey C. 2005. "Why theater? Sociological reflections on art and freedom, and the politics of small things." *International Journal of Politics, Culture, and Society* 19 (1–2): 53–67.

Goldfarb, Jeffrey C. 2006. *The politics of small things: The power of the powerless in dark times*. Chicago: University of Chicago Press.

Goodson, Ivor, Ari Antikainen, Pat Sikes, and Molly Andrews. 2016. *The Routledge international handbook on narrative and life history*. Taylor & Francis.

Grabska, Katarzyna, and Cindy Horst. 2022. "Introduction: Art, Violent Conflict, and Displacement." *Conflict and Society* 8 (1): 172–191.

Groves, Tamar. 2012. "Everyday struggles against Franco's authoritarian legacy: pedagogical social movements and democracy in Spain." *Journal of Social History* 46 (2): 305–334.

Haraway, Donna. 1988. "Situated knowledges: The science question in feminism and the privilege of partial perspective." *Feminist studies* 14 (3): 575–599.

Harding, Sandra. 1987. *Feminism and methodology: Social science issues*. Indiana University Press.

Held, Virginia. 2006. *The ethics of care: Personal, political, and global*. Oxford University Press on Demand.

Horst, Cindy. 2006a. "Buufis amongst Somalis in Dadaab: The transnational and historical logics behind resettlement dreams." *Journal of Refugee Studies* 19 (2): 143–157.

Horst, Cindy. 2006b. *Transnational nomads: How Somalis cope with refugee life in the Dadaab camps of Kenya.* Vol. 19. Berghahn Books.

Horst, Cindy. 2007. "The Somali diaspora in Minneapolis: expectations and realities." *From Mogadishu to Dixon: the Somali diaspora in a global context.*275–294.

Horst, Cindy. 2008a. "A monopoly on assistance: International aid to refugee camps and the neglected role of the Somali diaspora." *Africa Spectrum* 43 (1): 121–131.

Horst, Cindy. 2008b. "The transnational political engagements of refugees: Remittance sending practices amongst Somalis in Norway: Analysis." *Conflict, Security & Development* 8 (3): 317–339.

Horst, Cindy. 2018. "Making a difference in Mogadishu? Experiences of multi-sited embeddedness among diaspora youth." *Journal of Ethnic and Migration Studies* 44 (8): 1341–1356.

Horst, Cindy. 2019. "Refugees, peacebuilding, and the anthropology of the good." In Refugees' Roles in Resolving Displacement and Building Peace: Beyond Beneficiaries, edited by M. Bradley, J. Milner and B. Peruniak, 39–54. Washington: Georgetown University Press.

Horst, Cindy. 2020. "Collective hope in "dark times." Refugee political agency influencing migration trajectories." In *Renewing the migration debate. Building disciplinary and geographical bridges to explain global migration*, edited by Simona Vezzoli and Hein de Haas, 66–71. Amsterdam: International Migration Institute.

Horst, Cindy. 2022. "Questioning Artists: Contributing Societal Critique and Alternative Visions in Dark Times." *Conflict and Society* 8 (1): 212–226.

Horst, Cindy, and Odin Lysaker. 2021. "Miracles in Dark Times: Hannah Arendt and Refugees as 'Vanguard.'" *Journal of Refugee Studies* 34 (1): 67–84.

Horst, Cindy, and Anab Ibrahim Nur. 2016. "Governing mobility through humanitarianism in Somalia: Compromising protection for the sake of return." *Development and Change* 47 (3): 542–562.

Horst, Cindy, and T Sagmo. 2015. "Humanitarianism and Return: Compromising Protection?" *PRIO Policy Brief (03 2015). Oslo: Peace Research Institute Oslo.*

Jackson, Michael. 2002. *The politics of storytelling: Violence, transgression, and intersubjectivity.* Vol. 3: Museum Tusculanum Press.

Jackson, Michael . 2016. *The work of art: rethinking the elementary forms of religious life.* Columbia University Press.

Jarstad, Anna K, and Kristine Höglund. 2015. "Local violence and politics in KwaZulu-Natal: perceptions of agency in a post-conflict society." *Third World Quarterly* 36 (5): 967–984.

Kleinman, Arthur. 2000. "The violences of everyday life." *Violence and subjectivity* 226:241.

Kleinman, Arthur. 2007. *What really matters: Living a moral life amidst uncertainty and danger.* Oxford University Press.

Kleinman, Arthur, and Joan Kleinman. 1996. "The appeal of experience; the dismay of images: Cultural appropriations of suffering in our times." *Daedalus* 125 (1): 1–23.

Korac, Maja. 2006. "Gender, conflict and peace-building: Lessons from the conflict in the former Yugoslavia." Women's Studies International Forum.

Korac, Maja. 2018. "Feminists against sexual violence in war: The question of perpetrators and victims revisited." *Social Sciences* 7 (10): 182.

Lakoff, G. 1987. *Women, Fire, and Dangerous Things: What Categories Reveal About the Mind..* Chicago: The University of Chicago Press.

Leach, Darcy K. 2013. "Prefigurative politics." *The Wiley-Blackwell encyclopedia of social and political movements*:1004–1006.

Letseka, Moeketsi. 2012. "In defence of Ubuntu." *Studies in philosophy and education* 31 (1): 47–60.

Lev-Wiesel, Rachel, Hadass Goldblatt, Zvi Eisikovits, and Hanna Admi. 2009. "Growth in the shadow of war: The case of social workers and nurses working in a shared war reality." *British Journal of Social Work* 39 (6): 1154–1174.

Lieblich, Amia, Rivka Tuval-Mashiach, and Tamar Zilber. 1998. *Narrative research: Reading, analysis, and interpretation*. Vol. 47. Sage.

Locke, Leslie Ann. 2017. "Finding my critical voice for social justice and passing it on: An essay." *International Journal of Qualitative Studies in Education* 30 (1): 83–96.

Maggio, Rodolfo. 2014. "The anthropology of storytelling and the storytelling of anthropology." *Journal of comparative Research in Anthropology and Sociology* 5 (02): 89–106.

Manresa, Gemma Argüello, and Vlad Glăveanu. 2017. "Poetry in and for society: Poetic messages, creativity, and social change." In *Poetry And Imagined Worlds*, 43–62. Springer.

Maynes, Mary Jo, Jennifer L Pierce, and Barbara Laslett. 2008. *Telling stories: The use of personal narratives in the social sciences and history*. New York: Cornell University Press.

McAdams, Dan P. 2008. "Personal narratives and the life story." *Handbook of personality: Theory and research* 3: 242–262.

McLeod, Julie, and Rachel Thomson. 2009. *Researching social change: Qualitative approaches*: Sage publications.

Moen, Torill. 2006. "Reflections on the narrative research approach." *International Journal of Qualitative Methods* 5 (4): 56–69.

Monroe, Kristen Renwick. 2008. "Cracking the code of genocide: The moral psychology of rescuers, bystanders, and Nazis during the Holocaust." *Political Psychology* 29 (5): 699–736.

Murithi, Tim. 2007. "A local response to the global human rights standard: The ubuntu perspective on human dignity." *Globalisation, Societies and Education* 5 (3): 277–286.

Naef, Rahel. 2006. "Bearing witness: a moral way of engaging in the nurse–person relationship." *Nursing Philosophy* 7 (3): 146–156.

Pinnegar, Stefinee, and J Gary Daynes. 2007. "Locating narrative inquiry historically." *Handbook of narrative inquiry: Mapping a methodology*: 3–34.

Polkinghorne, Donald E. 2007. "Validity issues in narrative research." *Qualitative inquiry* 13 (4): 471–486.

Polletta, Francesca. 2006. *It was like a fever: Storytelling in protest and politics*.

Chicago: University of Chicago Press.

Polletta, Francesca. 2008. "Culture and movements." *The Annals of the American Academy of Political and Social Science* 619 (1): 78–96.

Polletta, Francesca, Pang Ching Bobby Chen, Beth Gharrity Gardner, and Alice Motes. 2011. "The sociology of storytelling." *Annual review of sociology* 37: 109–130.

Ricoeur, P. (1991) 'Life in quest of narrative', in D. Wood (ed) *On Paul Ricoeur: Narrative and Interpretation*. London: Routledge.Riessman, Catherine Kohler. 2008. *Narrative methods for the human sciences*. Sage.

Robbins, J. 2013. "Beyond the suffering subject: toward an anthropology of the good." *Journal of the Royal Anthropological Institute* 19 (3): 447–462.

Robinson, Fiona. 2018. "A feminist practical ethics of care." In *The Oxford Handbook of International Political Theory*.

Said, Edward. 1991. "Identity, authority, and freedom: The potentate and the traveler." *Transition* 54 4–18.

Sapiie, Stephanie. 2016. "Intellectual Identity and Student Dissent in Indonesia in the 1970s." *Dissent! Refracted B*:117.

Scheper-Hughes, Nancy. 2008. "A talent for life: Reflections on human vulnerability and resilience." *Ethnos* 73 (1): 25–56.

Schrijvers, Joke. 1997. "Internal refugees in Sri Lanka: the interplay of ethnicity and gender." *The European Journal of Development Research* 9 (2): 62–82.

Schrijvers, Joke. 1999. "Fighters, victims and survivors: constructions of ethnicity, gender and refugeeness among Tamils in Sri Lanka." *Journal of Refugee Studies* 12 (3): 307–333.

Scott, James C. 1989. "Everyday forms of resistance." *The Copenhagen journal of Asian studies* 4: 33–33.

Scott, James C. 1990. *Domination and the arts of resistance: Hidden transcripts*. Yale university press.

Selvik, Kjetil. 2021. "Education Activism in the Syrian Civil War: Resisting by Persisting." *Comparative Education Review* 65 (3): 399–418.

Selvik, Kjetil, and Tamar Groves. 2023. "'The generation that will inherit Syria': education as citizen aid and political opportunity." *Third World Quarterly*:1–16.

Semelin, Jacques. 1993. Unarmed against Hitler: civilian resistance in Europe, 1939-1943. Praeger Pub Text.

Smith, Linda Tuhiwai. 2013. *Decolonizing methodologies: Research and indigenous peoples*. Zed Books Ltd.

Sémelin, Jacques, Claire Andrieu, and Sarah Gensburger. 2011. Resisting Genocide: The Multiple Forms of Rescue. Columbia University Press.

Smythe, William E, and Maureen J Murray. 2000. "Owning the story: Ethical considerations in narrative research." *Ethics & behavior* 10 (4): 311–336.

Sørensen, Majken Jul. 2017. "Laughing on the way to social change: humor and nonviolent action theory." *Peace & Change* 42 (1): 128–156.

Spanos, William V. 2012. *Exiles in the city: Hannah Arendt and Edward W. Said in counterpoint*: The Ohio State University Press.

Squire, Corinne. 2008. "Experience-centred and culturally-oriented approaches to narrative." *Doing narrative research* 1: 41–63.

Squire, Corinne, Molly Andrews, Mark Davis, Cigdem Esin, Barbara Harrison, Lars-Christer Hydén, and Margareta Hydén. 2014. *What is narrative research?*: Bloomsbury Publishing.

Stapnes, Trude. 2018. "The protest was our last and only weapon»: A qualitative study of how individuals in Myanmar understand their motives for participating in protest." MA Thesis, Oslo: University of Oslo.

Stapnes, Trude, Erik Carlquist, and Cindy Horst. 2020. "Responsibility to protest: An interpretative phenomenological analysis of motives for protest participation in Myanmar." *Peace and Conflict: Journal of Peace Psychology* 28 (1): 101–110.

Tec, N. 2013. Resistance: Jews and Christians who defied the Nazi terror. Oxford: Oxford University Press.

Tellander, Ebba. 2022. "The wind that blows before the rain: Resistance against oppression in northern Somalia in the 1980s." PhD, Social Sciences, International Institute for Social Studies, Erasmus University Rotterdam.

Valentino, Nicholas A, Ted Brader, Eric W Groenendyk, Krysha Gregorowicz, and Vincent L Hutchings. 2011. "Election night's alright for fighting: The role of emotions in political participation." *The Journal of Politics* 73 (1): 156–170.

van de Sande, Mathijs. 2017. "Prefiguration(s). Philosophical reconstruction of a repertoire of political change." PhD thesis. Nijmegen: Radboud University.

Walker, Margaret Urban. 2007. *Moral understandings: A feminist study in ethics*: Oxford: Oxford University Press.

Waterston, Alisse. 2020. *Light in dark times: the human search for meaning*: University of Toronto Press.

Willcocks, Michael J. 2016. "Agent or Client: Who Instigated the White Revolution of the Shah and the People in Iran, 1963?" PhD, School of Arts, Languages and Culture, The University of Manchester.

Young, Iris Marion. 1989. "Polity and group difference: A critique of the ideal of universal citizenship." *Ethics* 99 (2): 250–274.

Zinn, Howard. 2009. "The optimism of uncertainty." *Amass* 13 (4): 12–14.

References from data:

Brisly, Diala. Virtual interview. Conducted by Trude Stapnes, 15 April 2019a.

Brisly, Diala. "Art, peace and conflict. Artistic activism in Syria". Conversation with Cindy Horst and Kjetil Selvik. CCC seminar. Oslo, 26 April 2019b.

Brisly, Diala. "A future for Syria". Animation produced for Positive Negatives and PRIO. Research by Kjetil Selvik and script written by John Servante, 2020.

Brisly, Diala. Virtual interview. Conducted by Cindy Horst, 15 February 2021a.

Brisly, Diala. Virtual interview. Conducted by Cindy Horst, 28 July 2021b.

Brisly, Diala. Email communication to the author. 28 July 2021c.

Ghorashi, Halleh. "The Changed Conditions of Critical Thinking." TEDx Amsterdam University College, 12 April 2017c.

Ghorashi, Halleh. Virtual interview. Conducted by Cindy Horst, 17 April 2020.

Ghorashi, Halleh. Email communication to the author. 22 May 2021.

Hashemi, Monirah. *Sitahara* script, 2014.

Hashemi, Monirah. Virtual interview. Conducted by Trude Stapnes, 10 May 2019a.

Hashemi, Monirah. "Art, peace and conflict. Activism through theatre in Afghanistan". Conversation with Cindy Horst and Kristian Berg Harpviken. CCC seminar. Oslo, 4 December 2019b.

Hashemi, Monirah. Excerpt from *Sitahara* performed by Monirah Hashemi, PRIO, Oslo, 4 December 2019c.

Hashemi, Monirah. Email communication to the author. 1 March 2020a.

Hashemi, Monirah. *Who lights the stars* script. 8 June 2020b

Hashemi, Monirah. Virtual interview. Conducted by Cindy Horst, 9 April 2021a.

Hashemi, Monirah. Virtual interview. Conducted by Cindy Horst, 12 August 2021b.

Hashemi, Monirah. *Who lights the stars* script. 7 April 2021c.

Literature References:

Benhabib, Seyla "The Reluctant Modernism of Hannah Arendt". Thousand Oaks, CA: Sage, 1996.

Crenshaw, Kimberlé. "Mapping the margins: Identity politics, intersectionality, and violence against women." *Stanford Law Review* 43.6: 1241-1299, 1991.

Kearney, Darla (ed). "Positionality and intersectionality." In: *Universal Design for Learning (UDL) for Inclusion, Diversity, Equity, and Accessibility (IDEA)*. https://ecampusontario.pressbooks.pub/universaldesign/chapter/positionality-intersectionality/, 2022.

Ricoeur, Paul. "Life in quest of narrative." In: D. Wood (ed) *On Paul Ricoeur: Narrative and Interpretation*. London: Routledge, 1991.

Robbins, Joel. "Beyond the suffering subject: toward an anthropology of the good." *Journal of the Royal Anthropological Institute* 19 (3):447-462, 2013.

Tec, Nechama. *Resistance: Jews and Christians who defied the Nazi terror*: Oxford University Press, 2013.

Index

www.ingramcontent.com/pod-product-compliance
Lightning Source LLC
Chambersburg PA
CBHW070710280326
41926CB00089B/3446